# Valor

# Valor

## The American Odyssey of Roy Dominguez

*Rogelio "Roy" Dominguez*

AS TOLD TO *James B. Lane*

FOREWORD BY *Evan Bayh*

INDIANA UNIVERSITY PRESS *Bloomington & Indianapolis*

*This book is a publication of*

INDIANA UNIVERSITY PRESS
601 North Morton Street
Bloomington, Indiana 47404-3797 USA

iupress.indiana.edu

*Telephone orders* 800-842-6796
*Fax orders* 812-855-7931



♾ The paper used in this publication meets the minimum requirements of the American National Standard for Information Sciences–Permanence of Paper for Printed Library Materials, ANSI Z39.48–1992.

*Manufactured in the United States of America*

*Library of Congress Cataloging-in-Publication Data*

Dominguez, Roy.
Valor : the American odyssey of Roy Dominguez / Rogelio "Roy" Dominguez as told to James B. Lane ; foreword by Evan Bayh.
p. cm.
ISBN 978-0-253-00232-7 (cl : alk. paper) – ISBN 978-0-253-00595-3 (eb) 1. Dominguez, Roy, [date] 2. Guillain-Barré syndrome – Patients – Indiana – Biography. 3. Lawyers – Indiana – Biography. 4. Indiana – Officials and employees – Biography. I. Title.
RC416.D66 2012
616.85'6 – dc23

2011047320

1 2 3 4 5 17 16 15 14 13 12

*To my forebears, who fought hard to make a better life*
*on this continent for their families.*

*To my parents, for their courage and sacrifice on behalf of their children.*

*To my siblings, for their help and guidance.*

*To my beloved wife, Betty, daughters, Veronica and Maria, son-in-law,*
*Jason, and grandson, Dominic, who make my life fulfilled.*

*And a special thanks to Professor James B. Lane,*
*whose assistance was invaluable.*

# Contents

EVAN BAYH

# Foreword

I FIRST MET ROY DOMINGUEZ IN THE MID-1980S WHEN I WAS deciding whether or not to run for the office of Indiana secretary of state. He seemed to be a bright, articulate young man with an interest in good government whose encouragement I much appreciated. I got to know him during that campaign and when I ran successfully for governor in 1988. Even though he had been stricken with Guillain-Barré syndrome, a potentially debilitating muscular disorder that limited his mobility, he did not allow that to prevent him from having an active, vigorous life. Admiring his tenacity and devotion to public service, I appointed him chairman of the Worker's Compensation Board, the first Hispanic to head an Indiana state agency. His charge: to overhaul the rules and regulations of a board that had ceased to serve properly those in need of its services. With skill and patience he forged a consensus that modernized worker's compensation and made the agency responsive to those to whom it ministered. After Roy returned to northwest Indiana, I followed his political career with interest.

Reading *Valor,* Roy Dominguez's absorbing life story, reinforced my admiration for him and his parents, whom I was honored to meet when he was sworn into office in 1989. It is a fascinating story that not only will serve as an inspiration to Hispanics and others from working-class backgrounds but is a truly American odyssey of one who seized upon the country's unique opportunities and made the most of them. I recommend *Valor* to young people who aspire to a life of public service.

The center of everyday life was the family-household and the proximate community. It was here that past values and present realities were reconciled, examined on an intelligible scale, and mediated.

JOHN BODNAR, *The Transplanted*

The problems of the world cannot possibly be solved by skeptics or cynics, whose horizons are limited by the obvious realities. We need men [and women] who can dream of things that never were.

PRESIDENT JOHN F. KENNEDY, in Dublin, Ireland,
June 28, 1963, addressing the Irish Parliament

# Preface

*In Spanish the word* valor *means not only courage but also values and worth. Summers, when my Texas relatives arrived in Indiana to pick crops, I'd sometimes go with them into the fields. Looking back, the experience seems spiritual, almost sacred, connecting me with my roots and teaching me to appreciate not only the hardships and sacrifices of those who came before me but also their love, devotion, and practical wisdom. One day my maternal grandfather turned to me and predicted that his way of life was ending and that in the future young people would need a good education in order to provide for their families. It was a lesson I never forgot. During more than half his working life, he was in constant pain and experienced asthmatic difficulties while doing manual labor, but he always gave an honest day's work. His valor was an inspiration to me.*

In selecting a title for this autobiography, I sought to convey a quality of spirit that paid tribute to the sacrifices of my forebears and that might provide a moral compass for those moved by my life story. In Spanish the word *valor* is usually said with pride and emphasis, but I do not mean it in an egotistical sense. Rather I wish to honor those such as my parents whose strong heart and generous spirit made possible my own odyssey from Texas to Gary, Indiana.

On Friday, April 24, 2009, I spoke at Valparaiso University's Multicultural Center at the invitation of the minority law students. I had received a juris doctor (J.D.) degree from that institution's law school, so the day was full of memories for me. I told the students a little about myself and how fortunate and honored I was to be an alumnus of our law school. Recently the center had been defaced with racial epithets and vandalized by arsonists. The theme of my speech was, "Don't let racially insensitive people make you fearful of pursuing your dream." Earlier that day, I had met with lawyers representing labor organizations around the state, exploring their reaction to a possible bid on my part to pursue a candidacy for governor of Indiana in 2012. I was pleased by their encouragement since unions are major supporters of the Democratic Party in terms of day-to-day support and campaign financial contributions. So, driving back from Indianapolis on I-65 on the day of the speech, I was feeling tired but enthusiastic.

I made mention to the students of the sacrifices others had made on behalf of civil rights for women and minorities and the heroes who fought during two world wars. I mentioned the hard times millions faced during the Great Depression and explained my parents' struggles on behalf of their children. I told them about my ambitions to become a state trooper, a law school graduate, attorney, and sheriff. At each turn there were those who doubted I'd ever reach my goal. Then I said I was going to let them in on a little secret – that my next hope and dream was to be governor of the State of Indiana. Suddenly the audience of three hundred students broke out in applause, which was very humbling and inspiring.

It so happened that a *Post-Tribune* contributing columnist, Jim Wolf, was present, as well as Mike Puente from National Public Radio. I told them afterward that I was not ready to announce my candidacy but was traveling around the state listening to others and exploring the possibility. Nonetheless, the story appeared on page one of the *Post-Tribune* and on National Public Radio and was picked up by the AP wire service. I started getting telephone calls and e-mails from all over the state encouraging me to run for governor. It was amazing and encouraging.

When talking to the Valparaiso law students, I thought about those persons who had given me guidance along the way – my family first and foremost, and then other mentors such as Indiana Senator Evan Bayh, First District Congressman Adam Benjamin Jr., Indiana University Northwest counselor Elsa Rivera, Lake County chief of police Gary Martin, longtime adviser John Key, teachers, professors, and many others. I can never repay them, but I can continue to give hope to others as they would want me to do.

I was inspired to write this book by my family, past and present, and for those yet to be born, as well as to those who gave their lives for our country either in the military or as public servants so that we may enjoy the fruits of American liberty. The United States has been and will be the beacon of light for the world. We should never forget those patriots who fought to preserve our freedom, especially those who made the ultimate sacrifice and left behind loved ones who had to continue life without the touch of their dearly beloved. Let us go forth with life's passion, with animosity toward none and always mindful that we are "One Nation under God."

# Valor

God offers to everyone his choice between truth and repose.
Take which you please – you can never have both.

RALPH WALDO EMERSON

We [Hispanics] are of a different variety simply because,
unlike previous immigrants, most of us didn't come
to America; instead America came to us.

ILAN STAVANS, *The Hispanic Condition*

ONE

# Roots

*My parents met in 1947 while both were working at a vegetable packing plant in Mercedes, Texas. My mother was a couple years older and more extroverted than Dad. She called him a "ranchero," a reference to those who stayed on the farm and didn't go out on the town. His buddies, who were worldlier, had to coax him out of a truck to go mingle with her. One thing led to another, and they got paired up. Although she had other admirers, she liked the fact that he had eyes for her only.*

## INTRODUCTION

My dad's family members were farmers; my mom's were migrant workers. From them I learned to do my best and work hard for my dreams. They taught me the importance of family, getting an education, and other lessons in life as I worked beside them in the agricultural fields. They molded me into what I am and remain with me in spirit.

I like to think that I am a lot like my parents in terms of character and personality. Dad was a gentleman who told me, "Nobody likes a grouch." Mom was feisty and vocal in expressing her opinions. Responding strategically to those who would bully or disrespect them, both refused to be pushed around. Both made tremendous sacrifices on behalf of family and had high expectations for their children. As a child and into adulthood I found them always there for me to lean upon and learn from. Their giving me a source of inspiration has earned them my everlasting gratitude. All I've accomplished I owe to them and family members past and present.

I hope my memoir illustrates that we all have challenges in life and that nothing comes without obstacles along the way. In fact, overcoming obstacles is part of what makes life meaningful and worthwhile. Additionally, I will assert my patriotism for the United States and my reasons for encouraging others to be valued participatory citizens. At public forums I am often asked to explain my thoughts and family values in two or three minutes. In summary, I would say that I appreciate the opportunities our country has offered and I am motivated by my passion and desire to honor the sacrifices made by my parents for their children. Mom and Dad left the comfort of their family home in Texas and came to Gary, Indiana, so we could have opportunities to pursue our own dreams and find happiness and life's inspiration. My autobiography hopefully will also convey the belief, instilled in me by my parents, that holding public office is meaningless if the public servant is not helping others. As my dad said many times, "Remember son, it's always about the people." My mom echoed these sentiments by words and deeds. I have made their advice my guiding principle in community service.

My parents' generation has been designated as the "greatest" by author Tom Brokaw and many others because of their sacrifices during World War II in the defeat of Adolf Hitler and the Axis Powers. My dad was part of that crusade, and my mom was part of the home front that contributed to the war effort. In my opinion, they deserved the accolade "greatest generation" for their decision to move north, like so many of their Hispanic compatriots, so their children might enjoy a better life. For giving me opportunities to continue their legacy I salute them. To a very large degree I stand on the shoulders of giants, as scientist Isaac Newton famously said in giving credit to those scientists who came before him.

I was born on March 16, 1954, in the city of Mercedes, Texas, located just north of the Rio Grande River in Hidalgo County. Mom said that had I come into this world a day later, on St. Patrick's Day, she would have named me Patricio, after the fifth-century patron saint of Ireland. Since we don't have any other family members named Rogelio, I asked how she came up with my name. There was a Mexican singer by that name whose music she really enjoyed. It had a slightly exotic ring to it, and at school and on the playground I was nicknamed Roy.

As far as birth order, I was number five out of eight children. I have three older brothers and an elder sister. After me came another brother and two sisters. Though unique in some aspects, my story is typical of the struggles Mexican Americans of my generation underwent and the opportunities available to us because of sacrifices made by others from past generations.

I haven't traced my ancestors back to their Old World roots like author Alex Haley did in his classic book, but I have learned from family folklore that Dominguez family ancestors have been in Texas for over three hundred years, beginning with a distant relative, Spanish Captain Juan José Hinojosa, obtaining a land grant when the territory was part of Spain. His descendents continued to grow crops, including fruits, vegetables, and nuts, on the arable acres along the river and pasture cattle on grasslands north of the ranch when it was part of Mexico, then within the Texas Republic, and finally annexed into the United States. So, you see, my folks were citizens of numerous countries and never moved an inch.

The name of the Dominguez family farm was Rosario, meaning "Rosary" in English. Subdivided from the original Toluca Ranch, which stretched seventeen miles north from the Rio Grande River, it was located in the town of Relampago, Texas, which literally means "lightning." Indeed, violent storms periodically ravaged the sleepy hamlet. The word "Toluca" is of Aztec derivation and is the name of one of their gods. In the nineteenth century friendly groups of Coahuiltecan Indians visited the ranch from time to time to carry on trade. An old church built by distant relative Florencio Saenz and a cemetery where family members worshipped and were buried still remain. Both are listed as Texas landmarks in historic registries. Dominguez family members were Roman Catholics, and their patron saint was St. Therese, known as the "Little Flower of Jesus." My great-great-grandfather, Yndalecio Dominguez (1813–1902), one of the first commissioners of Hidalgo County, is buried there. According to *The Handbook of Texas Online,* Hidalgo County "was formed in 1852 and named for Miguel Hidalgo y Castilla, who gave the 'cry for Mexican independence' from Spanish rule." Perhaps there is some validity to the belief that love for politics is passed on from generation to generation in our customs because Yndalecio was the first of many family members to take time away from farming and other obligations to become involved in public service. In recent years I have relatives, in fact, who were public officials, and a judge in Hidalgo County, Texas, John F. Dominguez (1931–2010).

After my great-grandfather died, Yndalecio's sons split up the estate and went their separate ways. Grandfather Abelardo Dominguez (1894–1970) moved from the farm into the town of Mercedes, originally named Diaz in honor of Mexican president Porfirio Diaz but then renamed Mercedes in honor of the president's wife of that name. The city was incorporated in 1909 and had a population, according to the 1910 census, of 1,209 (at present the population of Mercedes is approximately 14,000). Abelardo, a tall, well-built man, constructed the house in town from lumber he obtained from structures on the Rosario farm. He ultimately found work with the Mercedes water department.

## JESUS "JESSE" DOMINGUEZ

My dad, Jesus Abelardo Dominguez, was born on February 6, 1927. His father had married a woman named Maria Treviño who lived in the town of San Juan in the Mexican state of Tampalipas just south of the Rio Grande River, which is the territorial border between the United States and Mexico. In the 1920s it was no big deal traveling back and forth across the river – there weren't any customs officials to worry about like today. So when grandma Maria was ready to give birth, she'd return to the Treviño farm in San Juan, Mexico, to be with her family for the delivery and recovery. Therefore, on my father's birth certificate, it records that Jesus Abelardo Dominguez was born in San Juan, Mexico. He was a United States citizen, however, by virtue of his forebears being U.S. citizens.

Shortly after Jesus was born, his mother Maria became ill with pneumonia, and she passed away when my dad was just three months old. He and brothers José and Felix and sister Adelaida, or Adela (1922–1972), were still with the Treviño family at the time, and my maternal great-grandfather, Juan Treviño, as told by my father, threatened to kill Abelardo Dominguez if he tried to come retrieve the four of them. He probably did this less out of selfishness than out of grief and love for his deceased daughter and because he did not know Abelardo well enough at the time to trust him with his grandchildren. He may have figured, these are my daughter's children, so go find another woman and start another family. That was plainly not acceptable to Abelardo, so he literally had to kidnap his own children in order to get them back. He hired some friends to help him accomplish the task, and in the middle of the night they arrived at the Treviño ranch. They gathered the four children and crossed the Rio Grande River back to the Dominguez ranch on Texas soil. The plan went off successfully, and nobody was injured.

My dad and his siblings were brought from the Treviño ranch to the Dominguez farm in Relampago, Texas, where they remained until the family moved to the nearby town of Mercedes. Later the families reconciled, and my dad and his siblings regularly visited their grandpa Juan in Mexico. Juan would pick them up in a horse-drawn wagon and take them to the farm in Mexico, where they'd have a good time at work and play. My dad cherished memories of those occasions.

Before Abelardo brought home the children, his sister Virginia (1886–1971) agreed to help care for my dad and his older sister, Adela, along with brothers José and Felix. She broke off an engagement and never married. Abelardo never remarried either. My dad's aunt, Virginia, became his worldly mom (later my siblings and I called this petite and very Spanish-looking woman Grandma). Dad's two brothers were considerably older and ran with rough crowds.

Felix was a tough, hard-driven, independent fellow. One evening, my dad recalls, he was awakened by the screams of his aunt Virginia. There was Felix holding his stomach, and blood was all over his clothes. Felix had a slash across his stomach, and his intestines were literally protruding out. Felix had his hand over his stomach as if to keep the intestines from falling out. He had gotten into a street fight, and someone had stabbed and slashed him, causing the horrific injury. Abelardo was already awake and took him to the hospital. Felix survived to fight another day.

During the late 1930s, José one day when seventeen or eighteen years old left the house and was never heard from again. Nobody knew if he had been waylaid or killed or had just left on his own – unlikely given his disposition. My grandfather subsequently spent endless hours unsuccessfully traveling to Mexico, California, and parts of Texas in search of him, up to his death in 1969 at the age of eighty-three.

Abelardo saw his role as working to provide for the family and left child-rearing duties to Virginia. Jesse's sister, Adela, also looked out for his well-being. She made sure that the teachers at school didn't discriminate against him. When she felt they did, out of ignorance probably rather than blatant prejudice, she felt duty-bound to go do battle for him. As my dad would tell me, Adela would remind him that family members were in Texas before the immigrant Americanos. Therefore they had the right to demand to be treated equally and not as second-class citizens. In fact, he recalled an incident when a teacher was belittling him and giving him a hard time. He told Adela what had occurred, and she went to confront the teacher and remind her that they were American citizens, too. Adela demanded that they should be treated fairly and not as conquered citizens. My dad said that after that, the teacher never gave him any more difficulties.

My dad completed school up to ninth grade. During this era, Tejanos (Texans of Mexican descent) were not encouraged to continue their education, but rather they were expected to go to work at an early age. When he was a teenager, he worked for his uncle Hector Dominguez, a successful businessman who sold clothing and other items and had good people skills.

Jesse had a favorite cousin, David Dominguez (1926–1951), who was two months older, and they were as close as brothers, exploring new places, thinking up new adventures, discovering girls. Both got drafted into the army near the end of World War II and were sent for infantry training at Fort Sam Houston, Texas. My father served in postwar Germany as a truck driver. One of his duties was to pick up former Nazi SS officers and bring them to Nuremberg to stand trial for war crimes. On January 4, 1946, he received an honorable discharge at Fort McClellan, Alabama. All in all, it was a great adventure, and Jesse was forever proud of having served his country.

As much as change was in the air, some things remained the same. The cultural discrimination against Tejanos had not changed even though many Mexican Americans served in the military with distinction during World War II and were proud to call themselves veterans.

After the war, for example, there weren't many good-paying jobs in southern Texas for Mexican Americans. Jesus was a truck driver by profession. In fact, there were two different pay scales for freight haulers, with Tejanos on the low end. The rationale was that since Caucasian truck drivers resided in more expensive neighborhoods, they needed higher wages than Tejanos living in barrios. Unfortunately, there were no federal civil rights laws nor recognized unions to provide security or protection against discriminatory treatment at work. During the post-war years the pay scale was low and work seasonal and erratic. Dad for a time worked as a migrant laborer and because of his light complexion was called *güero,* meaning "pale" or "fair-skinned." It was not an insult but rather an endearing nickname.

After the war Dad's cousin David decided to join the army reserves. It only required attendance one weekend a month of his time and paid soldiers a stipend that supplemented one's job income. He tried to get my dad to join, too, but Jesse refused, saying, "No, I already served my country." When the Korean War erupted, David got called back to active duty in November of 1950. Jesse said that he and David both cried when David received his orders. Dad saw him off and never set eyes on his closest cousin again. In fact, Jesse considered David his worldly brother since his real brothers were so much older and had moved out of the house in pursuit of their own life ventures by the time Jesse became a young adolescent. José was never found nor did he return home, and Felix moved to California and later settled in Seattle, Washington.

On March 2, 1951, David was on patrol attacking enemy forces in the vicinity of Koilli, South Korea, when his unit came under counterattack and was forced to retreat. Before he and a companion, Corporal Van W. Winters, an African American from Los Angeles, could link up with their unit, North Koreans killed them. For two years, he was officially listed as missing in action, and in 1953 his badly decomposed body was finally found in a shallow grave at war's end. Authorities identified the remains as Sergeant First Class David Dominguez because of two religious medallions his mother, Francisca Rodriguez Dominguez (1887–1959), had given him – one of St. Christopher and the other "Our Lady of Sorrows." It took until July 18, 1955, before the body was released to the family and laid to rest with full military honors in the Rosario Ranch Cemetery.

My dad, a sentimental fellow, rarely talked about cousin David. It was so painful to think about what might have been. Should Dad have been there to watch out for him or maybe persuade him not to join the reserves? Certainly not, but the thought sometimes reoccurred in Jesse's mind. Jesse died in 2006 and hopefully has been reunited with David in heaven, as well as with his mother whom he never knew and other family members. I must say my dad for the rest of his life never forgot the day David left to report for duty. The discussion about David always brought on a surge of emotional pain and watery eyes.

## INOCENSIA MATA DOMINGUEZ

My mother, Inocensia Mata, born July 28, 1925, came from a poor but close-knit migrant family. The name Mata in Spanish means "plant." At first glance that may seem an uncommon last name, but "Plant" is not an uncommon English name. (Led Zeppelin's lead singer was named Robert Plant, for example.) For agricultural people, planting is a metaphor for sustaining life. If one plants a garden, for example, one is providing necessities for the nourishment of loved ones.

During the Mexican Revolution Inocensia's parents settled in Mercedes with their respective families, who knew one another and had been recruited by American agents working for Texas landowners. At the time Mercedes was just a little stopover. There wasn't much there at all. Her father, Hinijio Mata (1902–2001), was originally from Santilla, Mexico. Her mother, Vicenta Castillo (1905–1996), was from the village of Ricé, located just outside Monterrey, Mexico. Hinijio was eighteen at the time and Vicenta fifteen. They subsequently got married at Our Lady of Mercy Church. The marriage lasted till their deaths. In fact, on their seventy-fifth anniversary, they received a letter of recognition from President Ronald Reagan. In the late 1920s they moved into a one-room wooden house in Weslaco, a newly incorporated small neighboring town. They were migrant laborers, and love of family was central to their existence since that was the only life they knew. They were very religious Roman Catholics, and they prayed to the Virgin of Guadalupe, patron saint of Mexico and of the Americas.

Family members worked in local produce-packing factories and also were seasonal cotton pickers in areas as far away as Rotan, Texas. When children reached their teens, they would also work in the fields to boost the family finances. Grandpa Hinijio and his brothers Juan and Noberto would ride to the destinations in Great-Grandpa Juan's truck. Over the years the trucks took on nicknames such as "El Charro Negro" (The Black Cowboy), "Tu Solo Tu" (Only You), and "El Rebelde" (The Rebel).

Migrant workers toiled from sunup to sundown and were subject to discrimination and exploitation. They made very little money from their labor, and their children also had to work to make ends meet. Even though family members, when old enough, worked in the agricultural fields, this part of life was cherished to the extent that family members were working together and thereby providing for a more close-knit and loving family unit. When federal laws banned child labor, farm workers were exempted from the legislation due to the lobbying influence of landowners. Often victimized by crime and discrimination, migrant families tended to stick together and be ultra-protective of children, traits instilled in Inocensia at a young age. While on the road, for instance, they wouldn't frequent restaurants but preferred to eat meals at parks or rest stops rather than to put up with insults and discriminatory treatment.

Back home, the Mata family didn't have a wooden floor or stove till the 1940s, much less indoor plumbing. That amenity had to wait till the 1960s. The women cooked outside on bricks and logs, and during inclement weather they made an indoor campfire under a makeshift steel roof. Cleanliness was very important in a culture where neighbors judged women according to the tidiness of their spouses, children, and homes. Inocensia was the second oldest of fourteen, so among her duties were cleaning the house and caring for younger siblings. Mom became a second mother to them.

Inocensia's father, Hinijio, who never spoke English, was a strict disciplinarian and very protective. His word was law. As a youth she tried to join the church choir, but her dad wouldn't let her continue with it. Though less authoritarian, in many ways Inocensia took after him more than her mother. Like her mother, however, safeguarding the family and religious teaching were very important to Inocensia. Though normally acquiescent to her husband's wishes, Vicenta made her opinion known on important family social matters.

Despite having lived sheltered from the dominant society as a daughter and young bride, my mother was assertive and not intimidated by authority figures. She didn't back down if someone crossed her. Quite the contrary. She had some kick-ass fire and brimstone in her if someone set her off. It may have come from having been the second oldest and taking on responsibilities at a young age while her mother subsequently had a total of fourteen children, all born at home with the assistance of midwives. Two sons died young, Pilar before his second birthday after accidentally swallowing detergent and Enrique just after his birth. Inocensia only went to school up to the third grade. My mother recalls that in first grade children of Mexican ancestry were segregated and required to attend school at a local church. Then in the second and third grades she attended public schools, but Mexican American children were separated from the white children within the classroom. In fact, the teachers kept the two groups apart all during school hours and did not permit them to socialize.

As a child, Inocensia was taught that practical skills mattered, and she learned to manage money. Because her father spoke no English and neither parent went to school, at times she had to be the family protector and stand up for brothers and sisters. By the time she got to us, she was a pro at child rearing, financial issues, and social matters.

Inocensia was tall for her background and generation – around five feet, eight inches, in height. As a young lady, she was quite thin, which made her appear to be even taller. Well formed and sturdy as she physically matured, Inocensia was always conscious of her strong presence. One's religious well-being and physical appearance were very important to her. She had pitch-black hair and dark brown skin with more Indian features than my dad, who was light complexioned and full of freckles. As my dad approached his thirties his curly black hair streaked with grey. If opposites attract, this was true of my mother and father.

Inocensia's old-fashioned father didn't want her to date, much less marry, so Jesse couldn't pick her up at the house and had to keep his distance at fiestas, dances, and other social functions when Hinijio was present. It fell to Vicenta to remind her husband that they once dated and to ease his overprotective, restrictive attitudes. She recognized that her daughter's suitor wasn't a ladies' man out on the prowl but loving, polite, respectful, and uninterested in playing the field. On such family matters eventually Hinijio relented to Vicenta's advice. My parents had been dating about a year when in the summer of 1948, Jesse proposed one evening on the way to see a movie. When she announced to her parents her intentions to marry, Hinijio refused to give his blessing despite Vicenta's pleas. Finally he relented and gave his consent.

My mom's family was more close-knit than my dad's. He used to say that he enjoyed hers more than his own. Holiday picnics were common, and aunts and uncles would take us to the local swimming pool. At Easter, an even bigger holiday than Christmas because the weather was usually perfect (at Christmas time it was often rainy, windy, and chilly), we'd have a family reunion and potluck picnic at Sunrise Hill Park in Mercedes. Bands would be playing Mexican music, and the mood was always festive.

## MARRIAGE

On July 4, 1948, a judge married Jesse and Inocensia at the Mata domicile at 214 North Palmas Street in Weslaco, where Hinijio and Vicenta lived the rest of their lives. Hinijio lived to the age of ninety-nine and Vicenta to the age of ninety-four. Jesse's sister, Adela, and her husband, José Zavala, attended the wedding, but Abelardo was with son Felix on the West Coast, too far away to make the trip. Two days later the couple had a church wedding at Our Lady of Mercy in Mercedes, a small ceremony attended by their *padrinos* (i.e., godparents) and a few other loved ones. They started out married life living with Virginia in Mercedes, and after a while she moved in with Adela and her husband. Shortly thereafter, Virginia moved back with Mom and Dad at their house on 248 North Indiana Street. Since my dad was the youngest of his family, his father, Abelardo, gave him the house he had built for his family decades before.

Jesus Jr., whom we called Jesse, was born in 1949. About two years later, my worldly grandmother Virginia noticed that Jesse Jr. was not able to walk correctly and urged my parents to take him to the doctor for a physical examination. After the doctor performed a spinal tap, it was diagnosed that he had contracted polio. He was quarantined in the hospital for two years. Mom and Dad would walk from bus stop to bus stop until they reached the hospital in McAllen, Texas, about twenty-five miles from home. There was no direct bus route to the hospital, a cab was too expensive, and they were too poor to own a car. The most noticeable outward symptom of tissue degeneration was in Jesse Jr.'s left leg muscles, which caused him to walk with a limp. In the early 1950s he eventually became a poster child for the March of Dimes, an organization that was a great help to my parents.

Maria Virginia, the second oldest, was named after my dad's deceased mom and his aunt who reared him. While my parents were working in the cotton fields of Rotan, Texas, they had their third child. Eloy, the third born, was given as a middle name my mother's maiden name, Mata, which is very typical in Mexican tradition, only in Mexico it becomes the child's last name whereas in the United States it was his middle name. Eloy was a name commonly used by my dad's family. He was two months premature, weighed not more than a couple pounds, and was not expected to survive. Mom and Eloy were released from the hospital early because they were without insurance or money to pay for Eloy's hospitalization. The family, hoping and praying for the best, made a homemade incubator for him. They used a crate box, put a light bulb inside, and covered him with a blanket. Upon release from the hospital Eloy was immediately given a Catholic baptism because the doctors told my parents that they didn't think he would survive. Mom knit little hats to keep his head warm and gave him milk through an eyedropper. He literally fit in the palm of her hand, she later recalled. With loving family care Eloy lived to the age of forty-eight.

The most doted over, Eloy became the favored son and ultimately the tallest at six feet, four inches. We were happy with Eloy's being presumed to be the favored son because of his wonderful demeanor and survival at childbirth. A fourth child, Armando (Mando), was born on December 17, 1952, and then I came along fifteen months later, followed by Hector on February 6, 1956 (who like Eloy was given the middle name Mata), Maria Yolanda (called Yoli) on June 16, 1959 – that's seven children in ten years – and then my sister Rosario (Rosie) on February 22, 1964. Only Hector and Rosie were born in Gary, Indiana. Hector was named for Dad's favorite uncle, the haberdasher. Although Hector was a Trojan prince in Greek mythology, I discovered, there were many Dominguez ancestors with that name buried in the family cemetery.

## INLAND STEEL

In 1951 my dad and some buddies from Mercedes heard that Inland Steel Company in the Indiana Harbor district of East Chicago, Indiana, was hiring truck drivers. The lure to the North was for good-paying jobs because locally such opportunities were nonexistent if you were Hispanic. Discrimination wasn't the sole reason why Jesse decided to try his luck up north, but it was a fact that Hispanics were the lowest-paid workers and the first laid off in hard times. He and five of his friends drove to northwest Indiana's Calumet Region, and he got hired at Inland Steel Company. The plan was to stick it out a year, save money for the family, and then return to Texas. For the time being Jesse lived in a boardinghouse located within the shadow of the mill and within the city of East Chicago, Indiana. It was a lonely existence, and he decided to ask Inocensia to move their family to nearby Gary, Indiana.

At Inland Steel the pay was significantly more than he'd have been making in Texas and the conditions were decent, which he attributed to the militant presence of Local 1010. Joe Germano was union district director during the 1950s and 1960s and quite forceful and pugnacious in protecting members against arbitrary practices. My dad quickly became an active union man and Germano supporter. He and other Hispanics would attend meetings together and urge union compatriots to seek leadership positions. Eventually they had their own faction and would join coalitions with other ethnic groups to put together successful union slates. My dad was proud of his steelworkers union membership.

For nearly all people there is a thing that is more important than money. It is a thing called dignity, or self-respect, or honor.

*EL MALCRIADO* EDITORIAL,
from Stan Steiner, La Raza

The Calumet Region was one of the world's leading industrial districts, a center for the steel industry, oil refining, and various allied industries. The population was diverse, attracting large numbers of immigrants [who] created community landmarks that remain scattered throughout the Calumet Region.

*A Virtual Museum for the Calumet Region Online*

TWO

# Growing Up

*After school let out for the summer, my mom would take us boys out to work the fields in the surrounding area from our home in Mercedes, Texas. My daughters and friends can't quite imagine that I picked cotton, but it was part of my early childhood. My brothers and I fondly recall working alongside our mom and took pride in the fact that we were collectively providing for our family. As it turned out, we were also developing strong work ethics.*

## MOVING BACK AND FORTH

During the first eight years of my life we kept moving back and forth between southern Texas and northwest Indiana. In 1955 for a time we lived in Cudahy, a subdivision within Gary's city limits. It was on the far west side, near Cline Avenue and Route 20, straddling the border between Gary and East Chicago. Pretty much a Latino barrio, at least on our block, Cudahy eventually disappeared to make way for highway construction and industrial businesses. In other words, the domiciles of people judged to be expendable were sacrificed to make way for "progress."

After Cudahy, we moved to Sixteenth Avenue and Johnson Street in the Tolleston district of Gary. During this time the sixth child, my brother Hector, was born. My dad's paternal uncle, a businessman, was also named Hector, and my dad spoke of him often. We had many new friends, most notably Mr. and Mrs. Silverio Arambula and their children. They all remained lifelong friends of the family.

In the late 1950s brothers Jesse Jr. and Armando became afflicted with asthma, and my parents upon doctor's advice believed they would fare better health-wise in a warm climate than living in a polluted industrial environment that wreaked havoc on the lungs of susceptible children. When we moved back to our previous home in Mercedes, Texas, in 1958, shortly before the long steel strike, I was just four years old. Upon our relocation, Dad went back to work and reside in Indiana. The rest of us stayed in Mercedes for four years. It would take him three days by automobile to travel back to be with us. But he'd make the trip whenever possible and felt sadness about missing family milestones. He was very sentimental about such things, and our family separation was difficult for all of us.

As lonely as life in East Chicago was for him, Dad made this necessary sacrifice because he knew employment was difficult to attain in Mercedes and that by working at Inland Steel he could provide us with a better standard of living. He knew that as we grew older, he would bring us to Indiana so we could be living together as a family unit. For me, it is unimaginable the emotional pain and sacrifice my parents sustained while we were apart; that was indeed "valor."

## TEXAS CHILDHOOD

In Mercedes, Texas, I attended Our Lady of Mercy Church and lived across from North Elementary School (later named John F. Kennedy Elementary School) in a wood frame house with a porch and fenced-in yard. Coincidentally, in view of where we would later live, the address was 248 North Indiana Street. Back then it was a gravel road with trenches for water alongside the street. My mother kept a close watch to see that nothing happened to her children, a trait that probably suited us well when we moved to an unfamiliar environment up north. She preferred we stay inside the fence because she wanted us safe, but we found ways to venture out when Mom wasn't looking and experience the thrill of being on our own.

Down the road from our house was a canal where we would go fishing, using a tree branch with a string. On its end we'd place a hook made from a bobby pin. For bait we used tortilla dough. The fish we caught were small, so inevitably we threw them back in the water. One day as Mando, Hector, and I were walking alongside the canal bank, the dirt gave out from under where Mando was walking. The current began to pull Mando into the canal, and none of us knew how to swim. With a terrified cry, Mando yelled for help. I was standing nearest to him, grabbed his hand, and pulled him out of the water. It was a close call, and we never again ventured so near to the canal banks.

At the time, we believed the legendary child snatcher La Llorona ("The Crier") might have been after Mando. In Spanish folklore a woman supposedly had drowned her children and then spent an eternity looking for them. Parents used the story to keep their kids away from dangerous bodies of water, warning that La Llorona might be out there and grab them. Needless to say, we didn't tell Mom about Mando's mishap for fear of being restricted to the house. It was our secret. Later, during family reunions I would brag incessantly about having come to Mando's rescue.

Our house in Texas didn't have central heat or air conditioning – no one's did then. Dad could afford indoor plumbing, however, and we had propane-powered heat registers for the winter months. He hired workers to make other extensive improvements and additions, including a porch, which became an important part of everyday life due to the many months of sweltering heat.

Like most houses in our neighborhood, ours sat on concrete blocks rather than a foundation. Below was a two- or three-foot space where Hector sometimes hid when in trouble with Mom. His dog would generally keep him company there. Sometimes Mom sent one of us after him, but we wouldn't go under there. It was dark and probably a breeding ground for spiders and red ants, whose bite left painful welts. Scorpions were so plentiful that if we had left playthings in the yard, we'd search for scorpions before picking them up.

Typically, for breakfast we had oatmeal with cinnamon and sometimes bacon, biscuits, and eggs flavored with spicy sauce. Instead of toast, we had tortillas, usually made from flour but sometimes corn. We all loved Mom's migas, corn tortillas with eggs and spices and cheese sometimes added. Lunch usually consisted of tacos filled with beans or potatoes, eggs, and chorizo (sausage). Mom always had Kool-Aid on hand for us. Soda pop was more of a luxury. Mom put Kool-Aid in some of the ice trays for a treat after we finished our meal. One popular dinner meal included menudo (soup) made with tripe; another was bits of potatoes and meat, such as steak or ground beef. Molé, brown gravy and chicken, was also popular. Like with tortillas, each household had its own recipe for molé. The main staples at lunch and dinner were rice and beans – the latter was rich in protein and both stuck to your ribs, so to speak, so you wouldn't be hungry. I still can't get enough rice, beans, and tortillas.

On a usual summer day we'd have breakfast, do our house chores, and then go outside to play in our fenced-in yard or across the street at the school playground, which had a swing and exercise bars (we called them monkey bars). Mom would call us in for lunch and have us take an early afternoon nap in the shade of the porch so we wouldn't get sunstroke in the heat of the day. During the summer months temperatures outside reached 110 to 120 degrees. The air was pungent but unpolluted. Even now on hot, humid days I fondly reminisce about my Texas childhood and its wonderful memories, when, as the saying goes, "Life was a lot simpler then."

Often we boys liked to run around in shorts but without a shirt or shoes. All except Eloy, that is. He was always neat and clean. Sometimes we played marbles, jacks, or hopscotch, drawing square boxes into the dried dirt and using small rocks to toss in the proper square. Later Mom bought a swing set for us in our backyard. Such thoughts of those family times bring tender smiles. When my older sister, Maria, played with us, she ruled. We did what she said. My younger sister Yoli, just a baby, stayed close to Mom, and sister Maria also helped take care of her.

As far back as I can remember, in the living room we had a small black-and-white console TV. My first recollection is rushing home in anticipation of watching *Bonanza,* which debuted in 1959. Everyone in the neighborhood loved the Cartwright brothers Hoss and Little Joe. That year the local stocks show – the Texas equivalent of a county fair – brought in members of the *Bonanza* cast as special guests. In a photo we five Dominguez boys are dressed neat and proper (Mom truly believed cleanliness was next to godliness) in cowboy hats, flannel shirts, and blue jeans, and in Hector's case, fringed chaps. Like Indiana rural fairs, the stock shows emphasized farm animals and agricultural contests but included carnival rides, games, and special festivities.

When my mom was in the hospital to give birth to Yolanda, her younger brother Saul and his wife, Josephine, stayed with us. Other helpful relatives lived nearby. Dad's aunt Manuela resided next door. Mom's younger sister Maria (nicknamed Mére) chipped in while Mom was recuperating. I vividly recall the family jubilation and neighborhood commotion when she brought Yolanda home from the hospital.

On trips to Indiana to see my dad, Mom usually took Hector with her, as well as baby Yolanda. Those of us in school would stay with her parents, or her brother Saul and his wife would stay at our house and watch over us. Mom would never have entertained the notion to go by airplane, so she'd catch the Greyhound bus in Weslaco. In fact, the bus stop is now a historic site in Weslaco, Texas. They'd board a train in Dallas and take it to Chicago. The first time Hector arrived at the Chicago train terminal, he saw a policeman with a man in handcuffs. Because he didn't see our dad that often, at first he feared that he had been arrested.

In the summer when Dad came home, we'd go to the beach at Padre Island in Corpus Christi. It was about a forty-five-minute drive from Mercedes. Frolicking in the Gulf of Mexico, I had my first taste of salt water. It was an eye-opener – or eye-closer because of the sting of the salt. Another favorite outing with Dad was to the local beach of Tampaquas in Mercedes.

## SCHOOL

In Mercedes kids in kindergarten and first grade went to an old wooden structure in our neighborhood that had served for a time as a typical one-room schoolhouse. If deemed to have proper command of English and the ABCs, you then entered second grade. Otherwise, those with limited English were put in what was labeled "First High." From an early age, Mom taught us the value of education, and none of us was relegated to "First High." In fact, the older siblings taught school lessons to the younger brothers and later to our younger sisters.

North Elementary School was an L-shaped brick structure, plus black portables were on hand nearby to handle the student overflow. Teachers were virtually all Caucasians. Perhaps because the name Rogelio was difficult to pronounce, many times they would just pass me by when going down the roster and then say, if I brought it to their attention, "I knew that was you." Or they would simply call me Roy. In fact, they tended to refer to all my classmates with Spanish names by English equivalents. For instance, Abelardo became Abel, Jorge became George, Jesus became Jesse, Maria became Mary, Juana became Jane, and so on.

On school grounds you were forbidden from speaking Spanish. If on the playground you inadvertently blurted out an expression in Spanish, you'd be reported and either spanked or sent to the principal for swats. In fact, children were encouraged to squeal to the teachers if they heard others speaking Spanish on school grounds. You could be suspended if the behavior was repeated too often. I remembered being paddled. The infraction wasn't something done out of defiance – the Spanish expression just slipped out and, after all, was part of my culture.

During that era there was no appreciation on the part of school officials for being bilingual or for Mexican American culture. Most teachers were very stern and demanded that students Anglicize. History lessons taught that the Mexicans Santa Anna and Pancho Villa were bad people – *banditos* – while the Texans at the Alamo were patriotic heroes. As a child you weren't aware of the segregation and ethnocentric bias, but looking back, you can see more clearly the lack of respect the teachers and society had for us and our Mexican cultural heritage.

Unlike our teachers, who treated Mexican Americans almost as a conquered people, the priests at Our Lady of Mercy spoke both Spanish and English and generally were respectful of our culture. It might have been due to Latin being akin to Spanish and because they believed God created different cultures for a reason. Church services and catechism were taught in both languages.

## WORK

Despite the sweltering heat we always worked summers in the cotton fields. For us younger guys, our bag may have held thirty pounds of cotton, whereas adults dragged ones holding up to a hundred pounds or more. We'd wear hats to protect us from the sun since we were of light complexion and could burn easily. It was honest labor and something we could take pride in; my mom was adamant about this work ethic. And it truly was a valuable experience. We were happy being with her and making money for the family. Sometimes after we picked "clean" cotton (without the husk) Mom would allow us to jump in it without fear of our hurting ourselves since it was so soft. What a thrill that was.

We'd take our sacks to get weighed, and my mom would keep track of how many pounds were in each bag. She'd have it figured down to the penny, so the landowner would not be able to take financial advantage of us. We didn't keep any money for ourselves; it all went into the family pool. I'm extremely proud that I picked cotton that contributed in this way to the family resources. As my mom would instill in all of us, "An honest day's work for an honest day's pay."

A typical workday began with Mom preparing breakfast and outfitting us in blue jeans and long-sleeve shirts. Thereafter, a large pickup truck with wooden side panels would stop by our house, and we would join other workers to go off and pick cotton. We were happy to be going off to the fields, where we developed strong work values.

In the early 1960s another opportunity for extra family income was selling a daily local paper called *The Monitor* – first Jesse and Eloy, then Eloy and Mando, then Mando and I. It was passed down until we moved back to Indiana in October of 1962. We walked from our house to the other end of town selling *The Monitor* for five cents an issue. We started after school and returned home after we sold them all, which usually took about two hours. Midway through the route was the home of my maternal Aunt Maria (nicknamed Mére), who looked out for us and always had milk and cookies for us. She had a wonderful smile and personality and, like brother Eloy, was a presumed family favorite.

For every paper sold, three cents went back to the newspaper company and the family got to keep the other two pennies. Every day, we then gave Mom all the money. She gave us an allowance for us to save or buy goodies at the corner store down the block.

My parents taught me that many people can do a good job, but an honorable person must do the best job he or she can do and see it through to its conclusion. For my dad and mom it was like a self-imposed honor code, and I have conducted myself in that manner. God knows, there are many ways to scam the system. For instance, when we were picking cotton, some workers would put chunks of dried mud balls into their burlap sacks so that they'd weigh more. Each worker was paid a certain salary based upon an amount of dollars per pound of picked cotton. Once the sack was weighed, one was required to dump it into a cotton trailer under the scrutiny of a landowner's agent, so cheaters had to first find a way to get rid of the mud balls. When caught, they were never allowed to work with the group again, and it was a stain on their family. Our family would never have done such a thing and feared the shame of such dishonor.

I remember that my mom would tell us to be honest regardless of the actions of others. She would say, "I don't care what others are doing, I care what you do, and you will guide yourselves by my rules, including an honest day's pay for an honest day's work." Her demand that we conduct ourselves with integrity served me well, especially later in life when friends got in trouble in school or in their professional life.

My dad was a gentleman who would never have thought of abusing my mom, but some of Mom's friends and their children encountered family abuse, especially after their husbands had been drinking alcohol. Mom would come to their aid and let the men know in no uncertain terms that their behavior was patently unacceptable. One time, she literally went and picked up one of her friends and her children and moved them into our house. While I was playing in the yard, the husband came to pick them up with an attitude as if they were his property. Mom refused to let him in the house, and when he tried to bully her, she chased him out of the yard with a water hose and, of course, a few choice words. I watched the drama unfold with amazement. A day or two later, he tried a different tactic, telling my mom he was sorry and wouldn't abuse his family again. He thought he was convincing, but although she listened attentively, Inocensia still refused to let him take his family home. She told him that the kids were afraid of him and that he should come back and she'd let him know if and when they were ready to leave with him. That set off another argument, and again my mom chased him away. By the third visit and with pleas of forgiveness, she was satisfied that he appeared to have repented.

I don't recall any further incidents of violence in that family. Neither do I recall my mother's brothers abusing their spouses, probably because of her lecturing them about it. On several occasions my mom would tell me that her dad never permitted such family abuse and revered her mother.

If my dad would hear of one of his buddies hitting a woman, he'd tell them emphatically not to engage in such nonsense and would avoid further association with them. There are many important facets of police work, but one thing I'm especially mindful of, because of my mother and father's example, is the need to work for the prevention of domestic violence. Quite apart from the physical safety of family members, domestic abuse has a devastating lifetime psychological damage on everyone, especially the children. On a personal note, in 2007 the Indiana Coalition against Domestic Violence selected me to receive Indiana's Police Officer of the Year award, an honor and a tribute to Mom and Dad.

## FROM TEXAS TO HOME LIFE IN GARY, INDIANA

In October of 1962 my family came to Indiana to stay – although we'd still go back to visit relatives in Texas from time to time. My mom's brother Saul drove us to Indiana in a blue Chevy truck with wooden side rails, a rear gate, and a canvas top. My dad was already working and living in Gary, Indiana. He had preplanned our reunification and rented a two-bedroom home at 1050 Durbin Street in Gary. We placed our family belongings in the back of the truck. Mom, Yoli, and Hector rode in the front cab with Uncle Saul. The rest of us rode in the back tucked between the furniture and other belongings. Once in a while, we'd pull the canvas flap up and peer outside. I recall stopping at gas stations, grocery stores, and roadside parks to stretch, rest, and eat taco sandwiches that Mom had prepared in advance. The journey took three days, and Uncle Saul and Mom kept watch for our safety from thugs and thieves. They were aware of the racial divide that existed during that era. After driving through Texas, Arkansas, Missouri, and Illinois, we arrived safely in northwest Indiana, overjoyed at being reunited with Dad and all living together as a family once again.

We sobbed when we left Mercedes, Texas, because we were leaving relatives and friends. It took valor to leave our comfort area and move north to a strange environment, and all of us missed our extended family. At night I would sometimes catch my mother crying due to the heartfelt loneliness of missing her family. The telephone wasn't as accessible as it is today. Even if you had a phone, long-distance calls were very expensive.

Although Dad went back to Texas for the funerals of his parents, he shed tears of grief that he had not been with them at the time of their deaths and lamented that he hadn't stayed in Texas to care for them. Other family members helped with their care, but seeing him so upset emblazoned in my mind the great sacrifice he and Mom made so that his family would have a better life and opportunity to capture the American dream. Although conditions in Texas had improved, societal discrimination still existed. Even in Indiana such difficulties existed, but not to such an extent. This life experience has provided me with a keen insight into and a passion for honoring my parents' sacrifices. In fact, I believe this indelible sentiment lies at the core of my passion for family and my drive to be a patriotic citizen, an integrity-based public servant, and motivates me to lead an inspired life. To this day, this formative experience inspires me to assist my loved ones in realizing their individual and collective hopes and dreams. This inspiration extends to my community and everyone willing to challenge themselves in the pursuit of spiritual happiness.

In 1963 Dad's brother Felix visited us one day in Gary, Indiana. Dad had not seen him since Felix had left home twenty-six years before, when Dad was about ten years old. After leaving Mercedes, Texas, Uncle Felix had worked as a migrant worker in California and subsequently moved to Seattle, where there were huge asparagus farms. He married a lady from there. They had three sons, Oscar, Richard, and Albert, and a daughter, Rosario. On occasion Felix's wife would write to Mom and send pictures of their children. Having divorced his wife shortly before passing through Gary, Felix never saw his family again. In fact, that visit is the only time I ever saw him. He looked very much like my dad and their father Abelardo. The resemblance to Dad was so strong that younger sister Yoli sat on Felix's lap until she saw Dad walk in the door. The only noticeable difference was that Dad combed his hair back while Felix had a flat top.

I can't imagine how difficult it must have been for Felix's children after he abandoned them. Not having his love, encouragement, and support during their formative years must have been agonizing and heartbreaking. My dad would never have thought of doing such a thing and never condoned the fact that Felix left his family.

In the summer of 2001 I decided that it was long overdue to visit our relatives, Uncle Felix's children, in Seattle, Washington. I simply dialed information, found cousin Oscar's phone number, and called him. We spoke for hours, and I asked him if Dad and I could visit them. He immediately said yes. A couple months later we flew to meet our long-lost relatives. Dad was seventy-four years old. Felix's children were in their thirties and forties. Dad had always wondered about them and often expressed the opinion that Felix was so wrong for abandoning his children.

My dad worried that they might be angry with him because of Uncle Felix and would have understood if they harbored some resentment, but they assured us that was not the case and lovingly welcomed us. It was such a joy for us and for them to have some contact with the Dominguez side of the family. Dad was able to explain to Rosario, who is called by her nickname "Letty," that she was named for the ancestral farm. They were very loving, and I knew our visit was heartwarming for one and all. My dad answered Oscar and Rosario's questions about their family's heritage and cherished our visit with them. He was a sentimental fellow, and I am pleased that before he died he had the opportunity to touch his extended family's heart as much as they touched his and mine.

As for Uncle Felix, after his brief visit in 1963, neither his children nor we ever heard from him again. Like his brother José, only God knows his whereabouts or gravesite.

## 1050 DURBIN STREET

Thus, upon our move to Gary, we crowded into a two-bedroom ranch house at 1050 Durbin Street that Dad rented from a friend. There was not even a garage or fenced yard. It was in the Ivanhoe neighborhood of Brunswick, which was a blue-collar section of Gary. We boys were in one bedroom, our parents slept in the other with baby Yolanda, and Maria had a sofa bed in the living room. In the summer my maternal grandparents, aunts, uncles, and other relatives often visited us on their way to pick crops in Michigan, Ohio, Illinois (near Blue Island), Hebron, and elsewhere in Indiana. Being migrant workers, they generally came north from Texas in May and stayed until October. It was a time of jubilation and reconnecting with our Texas roots.

I started at Ivanhoe School in the third grade, a couple months after school started, so it was a difficult transition for all of us. We arrived just as the weather turned cold. It was not "the season to be jolly," as the song "Deck the Halls" goes.

Hector and I were walking to school one day in the winter with Armando, who was in the fourth grade, and he said, "I hate this snow. When I get older, I'm leaving this place." (And he did right after graduating from high school.) Even though there were plenty of other Mexican American students from Texas at Ivanhoe, I shied away from participating in class much because I didn't know anybody and spoke limited English with an accent as compared to my classmates.

During our first winter in this new environment of Indiana, Mom gave us boys money to see the film *How the West Was Won,* starring Hollywood mainstays Jimmy Stewart, Debbie Reynolds, Gary's own Karl Malden, Carroll Baker, Lee J. Cobb, Henry Fonda, Gregory Peck, John Wayne, and many others. The story of a family over four generations during the years of western expansion, it became one of my all-time favorites. What stuck with me, more than the many adventures the family encountered, were the sacrifices family members made for their loved ones. I can relate this film to my own family's adventures here in the United States and the meaning of family love, life's opportunity, and love of this country.

Another movie the five of us attended was Walt Disney's 1957 movie *Old Yeller* about a boy and a stray dog in post–Civil War Texas, starring Fess Parker, Dorothy McGuire, Chuck Connors, and Tommy Kirk. When the dog contracted rabies and it came to the part when young Travis (Tommy Kirk) was forced to shoot his beloved pet, we all stared at each other to see who would cry. Of course, Hector, the dog lover, was bawling his eyes out, and we all shed some tears. The family was so poor, the children had never seen a dollar bill except worthless Confederate currency, and the father (Fess Parker) had to leave home, just as our dad had, to earn money for the family by joining a cattle drive.

Back in school, things were better in fourth grade at Ivanhoe, thanks to my teacher, Mr. Frank Coman. A natural instructor, he'd encourage everyone to speak out. "Come on, Roy," he'd coax. He was a role model for me, easing my adjustment to an unfamiliar environment and encouraging my personality to develop. He was a great role model, and it was a pleasure to be in his class. He persuaded me to go out for intramural basketball, saying, "You're tall. You have to play."

Mr. Coman was young, single, well dressed, and quite dapper. That must have been why, I realized later, the young lady teachers often found excuses to come by to see him. Years later, I ran into Mr. Coman when campaigning for sheriff, and he said he had followed my career with interest and insisted I call him Frank. To this day he and his wife, Mary, attend some of my political functions.

On November 22, 1963, when President John F. Kennedy was assassinated, I was in the midst of a fourth-grade art class. Mr. Coman gathered the class together, sat us down at our desks, and made us listen to the radio piped through the school's intercom about the tragic developments in Dallas. He led us in prayer for the president, and then we were sent home. Before that day, I hardly knew what were the duties of a president, least of all his importance in the world. The traumatic event opened my eyes to the significance of politics and how much difference a great leader could make.

When I got home in mid-afternoon the day President Kennedy died, the lights were out, the curtains were drawn, and my mom was watching our small black-and-white television and sitting on the living room sofa crying. She and Dad had been big Kennedy supporters in 1960. "Viva Kennedy" had been the rally cry in Latino neighborhoods. He had sought the help of Hispanics, and for that they were grateful. Now that valiant man, their hero, was dead. For the next few days Mom cried as she watched on TV details of the assassination and funeral. All of us were mindful to be considerate of Mom's grieving for the Kennedy family.

My mom was six months pregnant at the time. In February 1964, when she came home from the hospital with sister Rosario (Rosie), it was a joyful occasion. I recall family and friends coming over to the house to see beautiful baby Rosie and everyone taking turns holding and carrying her.

## 726 HAMLIN STREET

In the summer of 1965 Dad and Mom found a slightly larger three-bedroom house at 726 Hamlin Street, which was also in the Brunswick area but north of the Eighth Avenue railroad tracks. At the time we were the only Hispanics on the block, surrounded mostly by Southern whites. By the time we moved to Glen Park a few years later in the summer of 1970, we were still the only Hispanics on the block but had African American neighbors. We didn't understand the "white flight" mindset of those who did not want to live in an integrated neighborhood; but because gangs and drugs made our schools and neighborhood unsafe, we subsequently moved.

In fifth and sixth grade I attended Brunswick Elementary. Like at Ivanhoe it took a year or so to make the adjustment. My no-nonsense sixth-grade homeroom teacher, Mr. Richard Spradley, who also taught math and science, was helpful in that regard. A disciplinarian, he made you study whether you wanted to or not. He was a great teacher and role model. Like my fourth-grade teacher, Frank Coman, he would later attend some of my political functions and insists that I call him Richard. I tell audiences that Richard Spradley gave me my first job in law enforcement – as a safety patrol boy. My corner to monitor was at Seventh and Tompkins, right in front of the school, and my job was to help kids safely cross the street. Perhaps being tall for my age, around six feet – and my enthusiasm – got me on the squad.

On safety patrol I wore a reddish-orange belt that went across the shoulder and around the waist. You had to be on duty early mornings and after school without fail or you were taken off your beat. There were no safety patrol girls, but Brunswick had a woman principal, Ruth Deverick, appointed by Superintendent Gordon McAndrew. That impressed me. Given my mother's example, sex discrimination seemed nonsensical. At the time I had not heard of Verna Hoke, Lew Wallace's pioneer postwar principal at a time when Glen Park was an all-white blue-collar community.

On Hamlin Street the girls had a bedroom and we five boys shared another. Jesse and Eloy had bunk beds, and the other three of us slept in a single full-size bed. So we grew up close, which led to frequent altercations that could cause Mom to send us to our room and order us to go to sleep. On those occasions sister Maria became my protector. If Mom was looking to discipline us, Maria would pull me into her room. For some reason Mom wouldn't go in there to fetch me. So I was safe, and we sighed with relief. Mom respected Maria's space, which was important to anyone growing up in tight quarters.

Maria and I had a real bond. When she'd have friends over, I was drafted into being their dancing partner. On a portable 45-RPM record player they'd play songs by the Beatles, Motown groups, Jerry Lewis and the Playboys, Nancy Sinatra, and, of course, "La Bamba." Preparing for the sock hops, they'd pull me into the bedroom and I'd stand there and sway to the music while they practiced the dances of the day – the mashed potato, monster mash, watusi, the jerk, and others. What great fun, and what great memories.

Maria was queen of the house. When my parents were gone, she was in charge. Sometimes on those occasions we'd move everything out of the living room. Maria would get in the middle and try to hit us boys with the buckle end of a belt as we ran around, jumping from sofa to sofa. It was pretty cool. It certainly got the adrenalin flowing. Nobody ever got hurt. Maria sometimes made us coffee crumble cake in a rectangular pan from a recipe she learned from Mom. She also made buñuelos by frying tortilla dough and then putting sugar or cinnamon on them. When we went to the county fair and saw "elephant ears," we recognized them as buñuelos.

The five of us boys could be very energetic, breaking furniture or dishes or fighting – not out of malice, just carelessness. If we didn't listen to my mom, she might resort to throwing a shoe at us or swat us with a belt. We'd put handkerchiefs in our back pockets when she'd go to spank us, so she'd have my dad play the role of heavy disciplinarian when he got home. It was not an assignment he relished. A reluctant disciplinarian, he bowed to his wife's wishes by taking us into a room and taking off his belt.

Keep in mind, during Mom's upbringing her father's actions were the law for the family. Thus, to her thinking it would be easier for her and an important lesson for us because Dad had spoken. She did not relish the role of disciplinarian but believed such early tutelage was necessary to put her children on the proper path for later in life in terms of school, family values, and being productive citizens. You know, she was right, as we all turned out as they wished – good citizens who put family first. Her lessons would make a lasting impression on all of us. She instilled in us that hard work, honesty, people skills, and "stretching the dollar" were ingredients to success, along with prayers and being mindful of your surroundings to avoid being victimized by others. Mom taught us to chart our own course in life and to make things happen with a purpose.

Dad was a believer in the divine but not a regular churchgoer. Organized religion was more important to my mom. My dad and his family prayed to St. Therese of the Flowers while my mom and her family prayed to Our Lady of Guadalupe. Both families were strong Roman Catholics. I'm sure my mom would have sent us to Catholic school had there been enough money. In Gary we were members of Holy Rosary Church on Seventh and Clark, and she demanded that we boys attend Mass every Sunday, no matter if it was in the dead of winter. That meant walking for about a mile and a half and often having to brave the elements. Again, brother Armando absolutely hated walking in the wintertime. Dad, working or coming off a double shift, wasn't available to take us, and my mom didn't drive, at least when I was younger.

We'd arrive at Holy Rosary Church in the dead of winter with our faces all red from the wind off Lake Michigan. Inside we encountered, from our perspective as youngsters, what appeared to be these giant Italian church ushers – the Rendina brothers, whose family owned a nearby funeral home. One of them would say in a gruff, intimidating voice, "Hey, you boys, sit here and be quiet." They were scary physical specimens. Now when I run into them, I tease them about how scary and gigantic they seemed to me as a child. The Rendina Funeral Home is still in business in Merrillville. The brothers are great guys and highly revered and respected in our community. After church we'd pool our resources and buy candy at Grant's, located nearby at Tri-City Plaza. A bowling alley was in the strip mall as well.

My sister didn't have to attend Mass at Holy Rosary if the weather was bad, but we were mandated. Eventually my mom decided she could drive us. She never had driving lessons or a license, but she'd go bumping along with one foot on the gas pedal and the other on the brake. Thus, when she drove us, I was happy but scared at the same time. By 1962, while living in Texas, I had made my confirmation and first communion but was still more hellion than choirboy.

Mom didn't work outside the house since my dad was able to assume the role of provider. In fact, their generation's upbringing and way of life included the separate, traditional roles of provider and housewife. To do otherwise would have been unthinkable for both of them. Until Dad gained enough seniority to go on straight days, he drove a truck at Inland Steel for sixteen hours every other day – a double shift and then an equal amount of time off. He loved us dearly, as we did him, although we wished he didn't have to work so hard. It was a different era from today in terms of spending time with the children.

When he had time off from work, however, my dad enjoyed doing fun things. On Sundays, weather permitting, we went to Gary's Miller Beach. Mom would call up friends, and we'd all meet on a hill near the lagoon and south of the parking lot. We'd get there early to secure our spot. Dad did the grilling. It was Mom's day to relax, and we were to leave her alone. After we ate and the food settled, we'd swim in the lake. Dad would go with us and keep an eye on us. I recall leaping on his back and using him as a springboard to jump into the water. The outing was like a mini-vacation.

Mom took care that Dad looked his best – otherwise it would reflect badly on her. She was in charge of the house – and us kids – and instilled values and passions in the belief that it was what she had to do in order for us to have an opportunity to realize the American Dream. Sometimes she would make us boys iron clothes, clean house, and cook for ourselves. Back then it was almost unheard-of for males to do these things. Her reasoning was that it would make us self-reliant when we reached adulthood. She spoke to us in Spanish because she didn't want us to forget our native language and heritage, but she insisted that we speak English to her as well because she knew it was critical to succeeding in this country. She pushed us to make good grades and be conscious of how we talked to people.

Mom had an uncanny ability of being able to size up people from their expressions and body movements. These traits kept us safe in a neighborhood where there were many unsavory people. She'd warn us to stay away from certain people, and her forebodings were usually accurate. Mom was adamant about not letting others push us around. She'd keep an eye on us when we were outside and would yell at us if we didn't defend ourselves from bullies. She taught us that sometimes it was necessary to take a stand, and we learned that value well.

Analytically, Mom's nonverbal communication skills were more than simple intuition. She'd react to someone in a certain way because she claimed to know what the person was thinking. More often than not, she was right. She was the ultimate preemptive striker, out of fear of being taken advantage of and thus victimized. She handled financial matters and was very conscious of saving for a rainy day and doing everything possible, whatever the effort needed, to fend off failure. Her philosophy was, you saved money first and then you spent it when necessary. In her mind there was always some emergency bound to happen that one needed to prepare for. She paid attention to details and was very observant. I've tried to emulate those skills. As my dad would say, "Ma knows how to stretch a dollar."

Mom loved to sing. She'd often break into song while washing, ironing, or doing other household work. She also sang along to Mexican songs she played on her 45-RPM record player. At parties friends or family members would say, "Chencha [her nickname], sing us a song." In Mexican American circles Dad's nickname was Chuy.

Mom was a very practical and independent lady. While she instilled in us the distaste for not succeeding, my dad had a different perspective on life. He believed we would achieve our dreams if we took care of business. If we learned what we needed to go forward and worked for what we wanted, good things would follow from that. He was more of an optimist, while she knew firsthand the necessity of acquiring survival skills. We were never without life's necessities and plenty of love.

## YOUNGER SIBLINGS

My three younger siblings grew up under somewhat different conditions than my four older ones, who have vivid memories of south Texas. I was the one in the middle, which I think has helped make me more diplomatic and understanding than I otherwise might have been – although it might also be because I took after my dad. We had a great childhood. We never knew we were poor. We were delighted when we got treats and weren't envious of those better off than us. Mom and Dad always taught us to take care of our own business and not to worry about what others possessed. Also, they encouraged us to set goals and then achieve them through good old hard work. Depending on our personalities and needs, our parents reacted to each of us differently, always in a loving way but with sensitivity to our unique personalities.

Hector would tell you, I'm sure, that it can be tough being the youngest of five boys. Things always ended up in his lap – he got blamed for everything and sometimes deservedly so. When something got broken, Hector became the prime suspect. As his big brother, I was expected to look after him. We were about eighteen months apart and very close. He was feisty, artistic, fair-skinned like Dad's side of the family, and endowed with a multitude of freckles.

As a kid, Hector walked around with rocks in his pockets. If anybody picked on him or got him mad, he'd throw rocks at them and then run. He was not shy to say the least. He took no guff from anyone. We'd ride bikes together and get into minor mischief. I was blessed to have Hector as a younger brother.

Yolanda and Rosie were darlings, cute as buttons. We'd watch cartoons and play games like jacks, hopscotch, cricket, and checkers. On their birthdays or special occasions I'd treat them to candy or snow cones. I'd keep an eye on them to make sure nobody bothered them. Dad was very partial toward them. We boys knew he loved us – no question about that – but he was not one to say it. And the girls were his favorites. We didn't think anything about it, much less complain. Smart, personable, and great fun, my two younger sisters were self-starters like Mom and lead wonderful, family-centered lives.

Work was a natural thing. We grew up hearing, "Some day you're gonna be in the mill." I never thought about going to college. I was expected to get out of high school and go to work.

REMINISCENCES OF JESSE VILLALPANDO,
*Steel Shavings* 19 ("Steelworkers Tales")

Brunswick's community life [was] centered around Edison School, Holy Rosary Catholic Church and School, and the thriving Tri-City Shopping Center, located at Fifth Avenue and Clark Road.

ROBERT CATLIN, ed., Gary, Indiana,
Comprehensive Plan for 2000

THREE

# Teen Years

*My introduction to politics came in 1966 when I was twelve. Mom said, "You're coming with me to pass out flyers for Joe Arredondo." He was a candidate for state representative. We started at Seventh Avenue near Burr, and she said, "OK, we'll walk down Seventh, you on one side and me on the other, and then canvass the side streets." She handed me brochures and said, "Knock on the door or ring the doorbell and wait for a person to answer. If nobody comes, leave the literature by the door. If a kid comes to the door, ask for the parents. Look them in the eye, hand them the brochure, and say, 'Vote for Joe Arredondo for State Representative.'"*

## EARNING A TRIP TO NIAGARA FALLS

From an early age I found ways to find work and earn spending money. I would cut neighbors' lawns with my trusty gas-powered mower and kept an eye on people's homes when they departed on vacation, watering their lawns and gardens and collecting their mail, for example. Many neighbors were blue-collar families from the South who made annual visits back to Kentucky, Tennessee, or Alabama.

While we lived on Durbin Street, I assisted paperboy Gary Hanson in delivering *Gary Post-Tribune* newspapers on our block for fifteen cents a day. Gary, a few years older, was a great mentor and friend. Rather than throw the newspaper bundle on the doorstep, he insisted that we knock on the door and hand the customer the newspaper. In return many customers gave us a handsome tip on collection day. He later joined the United States Marines and fought in the Vietnam War. After we moved to Hamlin Street I asked paperboy Teddy Phillips if he needed any help and got paid a quarter a day for doing our block. Back then twenty-five cents went a long way. The *Gary Post-Tribune* was an afternoon paper in those days. Teddy had such a huge route he eventually transferred half of it to me – which led to the first great adventure and challenge of my life. Like Gary, Teddy was a trusted friend.

In March of 1967 the *Gary Post-Tribune* held a contest to determine which paperboys could sign up the most new subscribers. The prize for the top two in each district was an all-expenses-paid week's trip to Expo 67, the World's Fair in Montreal, Canada, along with a visit to historic Niagara Falls. I diligently canvassed the homes along my route and signed up enough new subscribers to be considered among the finalists. During the four-month-long contest the newspaper routinely posted our tallies in order to motivate delivery boys into working even harder to acquire new readers.

By the final week I was ranked third or fourth and had pretty much exhausted my area. Then I made my first business decision: I would use my earned paper route money and reinvest it back into my paper distribution area. Strategically, I decided to go back to those who hadn't subscribed with an offer to pay for their subscription for a month. That way the customer had a free, one-month trial subscription, I got credit for a new subscriber, and the *Gary Post-Tribune* had someone who might continue with the newspaper after the month was over. All in all, it was a win-win situation. Back then the newspaper cost $1.20 every two weeks, a small price, I thought, for an opportunity to visit Canada. I moved up to number two in the Tolleston district, as mine was called, and was on my way to securing one of the two district slots.

Looking back, I'm not sure about thirteen-year-olds going off on their own for a week, but we had adult chaperones, mainly district managers whose underlings signed up the most new subscribers. My parents dropped me off at the *Post-Tribune* building at Eleventh and Broadway, and with my suitcase I boarded a huge bus.

The *Gary Post-Tribune* paid for breakfast and dinner each day, and we stayed in nice motels. The company paid our admission ticket into the International Exposition, plus we received a stipend each day to cover lunch and other expenses. They'd drop us off at a certain spot and say, "Be back here by six." We'd go off in small groups and explore the sights on our own. The theme of the World's Fair was "Man and His World," and the U.S. pavilion was most impressive, featuring a geodesic dome called the Biosphere designed by visionary architect Buckminster Fuller.

In the amusement park my group spotted an entourage of beautiful ladies who were actresses or celebrities followed by reporters and cameramen. A spokesman approached us and asked whether we'd like to ride on the Ferris wheel with the ladies. Would we indeed! "Oh, sure!" we answered. The ladies asked where we were from and when we replied, "Gary, Indiana," they started singing the "Gary, Indiana, Gary, Indiana" song from *The Music Man* while we were riding the Ferris wheel being filmed by a television camera crew. We were all starstruck and went head over heels to be with such female luminaries.

Other Canadian trip highlights included a visit to Battlefields Park near the St. Lawrence River, where we saw a reenactment of the famous 1759 battle on the Plains of Abraham between the French and the English. Both commanding generals, James Wolfe and Marquis de Montcalm, died during the fighting. The next stop was Niagara Falls, which, of course, was incredible. I had never seen such a sight. Viewed from the Canadian side, Horseshoe Falls was spectacular. Another first was a visit to a wax museum.

All in all, the *Post-Tribune* contest gave me a sense of competition and ideas about how to succeed, plus the venture broadened my curiosity about the world outside Texas and northwest Indiana and gave me the desire to meet new people and expand my life experiences.

Thereafter, every two weeks paperboys dropped off what was owed to the newspaper at the *Post-Tribune* building at Eleventh and Broadway in Gary. What you collected over and above that amount was your profit. In other words, any shortfall was your responsibility. Usually four or five of us went together and after the drop-off we'd walk along Broadway from Eleventh to Fourth, where we'd catch the bus back to Brunswick.

Gary's best days as a regional commercial hub were over, but downtown was still bustling on Saturdays. As thirteen-year-olds, we'd go window-shopping and girl-watching and would check out the Palace

Theatre posters that advertised current and upcoming movies. We'd stop at Grant's Department Store near Sixth Avenue and spend some of our profits on hamburgers and milkshakes. Their dining area had the traditional high round seats that spun around and a long counter top that probably accommodated fifteen to twenty customers. We had a great time horsing around and being just "boys."

## ODD JOBS AND NEIGHBORHOOD CHARACTERS

In 1969, at the age of fifteen, I started working weekends as an usher at Gary's State Theatre for eighty-five cents an hour. Employees had to be sixteen, so I changed my baptismal certificate and turned the "4" in 1954 into a "3," so I could go to work. The manager, a Greek lady named Tula Kalleris, probably in her forties, hired me. I thought she had fallen for my ruse but learned the truth decades later. It was my first real paid position of service and responsibility. Dressed in an Andy Frain uniform featuring a black bow tie, red sport jacket, and white cardboard vest collar, I went up and down the aisles with a flashlight, helping people to their seats if necessary and trying to preserve order when people were talking, laughing, or putting their feet on the seats in front of them. One fringe benefit was that I got to see James Bond movies and Clint Eastwood spaghetti westerns many times over and vividly recall the scary *Rosemary's Baby* with Mia Farrow.

In 2003, some thirty-four years later, I was reintroduced to Tula at a Christmas party at the house of her nephew, attorney Mike Pannos. She told me that she remembered hiring me and knew all along that I had forged the certificate but gave me the job because I seemed to want it so badly. I was astonished that she remembered me after all these years, let alone had known that I had altered my baptismal certificate in order to go to work. I thanked her and told her that I was fortunate and honored to renew our acquaintance. At the time I had just been elected sheriff, and she told me that she had followed my career with interest. She died the following year, and I provided her funeral procession a police escort, one of the discretionary powers afforded sheriffs.

After I really turned sixteen, I started working at the Lure Hamburger Stand on Fifth Avenue in Brunswick. Brother Eloy was already employed there and well respected, so when they had an opening, he asked Carl, the manager, if I could apply. He said, "Why, sure," and I got the job thanks to my big brother.

On days off I spent hours hanging out at Damian Paz's house, and on weekend evenings at Danny Menchaca's garage a band would usually be playing or guys jamming to Motown sounds, Beatles music, or Latin rock made popular by Santana. Neighborhood friends Albert and George Roldan were talented musicians who actually earned money by playing gigs. Our family was friends with the De St. Jeans, the Salazars, the Berkmans, the Duques, and many others, so the camaraderie crossed ethnic lines. If we got into mischief, it was usually innocent enough – staying out late, others purchasing some Ripple wine or Schlitz Malt Liquor (called "The Bull" because of its logo) from a local grocer or tavern owner. We weren't big drinkers but drank because it was thought to be cool.

Quite a few childhood buddies from Brunswick became lifelong friends. Among people from the old neighborhood it's like a fraternal bond that extends to this day. Many of my friends became quite successful later in life, but there were occasional tragedies. For instance, freight trains passed by our neighborhood, and some guys liked to jump on them near Eighth and Colfax and ride them to Cline Avenue, then jump off and catch another train to get back home. It was not my thing, and I didn't participate, but many of my friends did.

One such neighborhood friend, John Haybron, lived right across the alley from us. His parents appeared to be nonexistent, so he did whatever he wanted. Infatuated with guns, he'd take a shotgun with him on the train and shoot at pigeons. One day during the winter of 1967 while he was riding the train, a railroad detective started chasing him and, as John said, without thinking he turned and shot the man, killing him.

The entire neighborhood was shocked by the death of the railroad detective, and the police came and arrested John. He was around thirteen years old and got sent to Boys School until age eighteen. After his release he was frequently in trouble with the law and sent to prison. Eventually he was arrested for robbing the Clark Station at Twenty-Fifth and Burr Street in the Black Oak section of Gary. Even though he only got a few dollars, the armed robbery was his third felony, guaranteeing virtually a life sentence if convicted. As a result of this last felony, he was found guilty as a habitual criminal, and his prison term was enhanced by about thirty additional years.

Ten years later, by the time of John Haybron's last incarceration early in 1977, I was an Indiana state trooper. One day after arresting someone and taking him to the Lake County Jail, I asked one of the county officers if I could talk to John. It was like a scene from a movie, and I vividly remember it to this day. There he was behind bars, and there I was in my state police uniform. Though we were glad to see each other, it was a sad reunion. He was happy for me that I had done so well and regretful that his life had taken such a bad turn. "You know, Roy," he said, "I never meant to kill that railroad detective."

That one fateful event altered John's entire life. That's the last time I saw or heard of him. I've told his story of sorrow to my daughters and others, and I'm sure John wouldn't mind being part of my object lesson. It's important for youngsters to know about succumbing to peer pressure, whether it be drugs, alcohol, guns, or some prank that might go afoul, and how all these things could have a lifetime effect upon many lives. I would use this example about John to describe to young people the lost life of the murdered railroad detective and the subsequent pain inflicted upon his surviving family members, who had to continue their lives without his love and guidance. Rightfully so, that senseless act also cost John his freedom and future prospects. The lesson: parents, like mine, must keep a watchful eye on their children and teach them life's guiding principles.

## MIGRANT WORK

When my mom's grandparents and other family members came up to the North from Texas, I would work summers in the fields with them. Eloy, Armando, and Hector did, too. My brother Jesse seldom went along because of the fear that the sun and pesticides might bring his polio out of remission. It was our way of visiting with them as well as a source of earning money. I treasure those experiences. They would come north in May at the start of the farming season and stay till the end of October. Usually they went to Ohio or southern Michigan. Once they went to

Traverse City to pick cherries but found northern Michigan to be too cold. The farm owners always took decent care of them, they recalled, in part to ensure that they'd return the following year.

In the summer of 1967, between seventh and eighth grade, I traveled with my relatives to Genoa, Ohio, located near the city of Sandusky. In the field my grandfather would have me work rows near him so he could teach me how to select the proper produce. It wasn't just a matter of picking the cucumbers, green beans, or tomatoes – you had to select the ones that were large enough and ripe. He'd say that we were being paid to do a job and that it was a matter of pride to do it right.

My grandfather and other migrants measured people's values by how hard they worked and how dedicated they were to family. They looked down on those they believed to be lazy or scam artists. You were judged, for example, on whether you could get up by yourself at dawn, have breakfast, and be ready to put in a full day's work. My maternal grandfather also emphasized the value of education, predicting that his way of life was coming to an end due to mechanization. If I expected to provide for a family, he advised, I needed to stay in school and get an education in order to be ready for opportunities in the future for those willing to work. Already corn was pretty much harvested by machine, and so was cotton.

In Ohio I was shocked to realize how poorly migrant workers were treated. On the roadways police regularly stopped my grandfather and uncle to check the car registration and other papers. The cars or trucks were always driven by uncles or male cousins. As they proceeded with a humiliating interrogation, my uncle or grandfather would say, "Just be quiet! Don't say nothing." Fearful of being abused or arrested, they'd assume a submissive role, saying, "Yes sir" and "No sir" in a timid voice. Such nonsense!

At the ranch campsite on more than one occasion local male juveniles threw rocks at the camp dwellings. The different households, I remember, would gather everyone inside their respective small two- or three-room cottages, turn off the lights and music, and have everyone lie down on the floor or take shelter by hiding under a table or bed. That has always left an impression upon me, the sense that all my folks could do was wait it out in disgust and hope nobody was hurt. If they tried to retaliate, police were standing by to intimidate them and protect the rock throwers.

That same summer of 1967, while I was working with my maternal grandparents my uncle Vicente, nineteen years of age, was drafted into the United States Army and sent to fight in Vietnam. Vicente was the youngest Mata family son and certainly revered. My grandparents cried and prayed for days on end for his safety. I was thirteen years of age and didn't fully comprehend the terror of the war.

Later, when my uncle returned from Vietnam, he was never the same happy-go-lucky person. Vicente's young adult life was stolen by the horrors of war. In fact, he suffered from what we now know as post-traumatic stress syndrome. At night he would run out of his house and crawl around as if he still was in the jungles of Vietnam. He suffered from psychological difficulties, but over time he was able to control the nightmares of the war. He didn't get professional psychological help because at the time post-traumatic stress was not a recognized illness, but his family helped him through his terror.

Uncle Vicente later married, had a family, and lived in Weslaco, Texas. At the age of forty-eight he died of cancer, which I believe could have been caused by his exposure to Agent Orange and other dangerous toxins while in Vietnam. Vicente, nicknamed "Chon," would not speak about his military experiences while in Vietnam but did say the airplanes sprayed Agent Orange defoliants while they were on patrol in the jungle.

In the summer of 1969 I stayed with maternal great-uncle Noberto and his family in Hebron, Indiana, in a migrant camp right off State Road 2 and U.S. 231. Gazing upon rows and rows of crops, we'd speculate whether they were half-day, full-day, or two-day rows. I had never heard of Hebron – or Valparaiso, for that matter, where we would go Saturday afternoons after the farm owners paid us and where I later attended law school, something I wouldn't have dreamed possible at the time.

My great-uncle had a large family just like my maternal grandfather, Hinijio, and also had strong religious values and work ethics. Noberto was easygoing, had a sly sense of humor, and loved to dance, which he continued to do in his nineties. From time to time he would in a brotherly manner jokingly mock my grandfather Hinijio for being so serious and straitlaced.

Cucumbers, the first vegetable we picked, were tough because the plant had stickers. Many of the briars would inevitably attach themselves to our hands, no matter what precautions we took. We'd load the produce into wooden bushel baskets that were about three feet high, and unlike with Texas cotton we'd be paid by the basket, not the pound. You'd stand between two rows with a container on each side. Next came green beans that grew on a knee-high plant, whereas a tomato plant (the next crop to be picked) grew horizontally. It was backbreaking work because you were bent over all day from dawn to dusk with only a break for lunch. It was exhausting. At the end of the day we ate supper, watched TV, slept, and then prepared for the next day.

I had to work hard to stay with the group. If you lagged too far behind, others would point out that you weren't suited for the work. The division of labor was very clear. The younger women went out to the fields, too, but the mothers with young children and the grandmothers stayed at the camp and performed household chores. My grandfather and uncles labored in the fields well into their seventies.

In migrant campsites the patriarchs were assigned private quarters for their families. The wooden buildings had no insulation, indoor plumbing, or air-conditioning. The stove was connected to a propane gas line. The beds were cots with mattresses on top of wire springs. There'd be a room where the guys slept and another for the ladies.

## POLITICS

During the mid-1960s, in addition to juggling all her household duties, my mom made time to serve as a precinct committeewoman at a time when very few women participated actively in politics, especially in the Latino community. Before elections it was common for Mom to support two or three candidates for different public offices. She would accept monetary contributions from them and then paid people to work on their behalf on election day to get the vote out, standing outside polling places, passing out literature, and providing similar services. Under no circumstances would she take campaign money or literature from someone she was not supporting. With some committee persons candidates did not get an enthusiastic commitment for their money, but my mom was very emphatic about whom she was supporting and gave more than her money's worth.

Mom's vast number of friends and practical tutelage would be of extreme benefit to me as I ventured into the world of politics. Although Mom was no-nonsense, she loved to meet and greet people and, like Will Rogers, never met a stranger.

Since then, I have enjoyed politics. I recall my parents saying that in this country we have an opportunity to effect change through the democratic process. Their central litmus test for candidates was whether they genuinely cared about poor people and the working class. As I continue my public service, I guide myself by their values and advice – that "it's about the people, their hopes and dreams for themselves and their children."

Dad served a term as president of Sociedad Mutualista de Mexico, a local Hispanic organization. I recall going to the club as a child. Dad was a real gentleman, soft-spoken and very classy. He didn't walk away from a fight, but he was not confrontational. He never pretended to be a tough guy but rather a good man with lots of friends. People liked to be around him. He enjoyed a good time and stayed positive. He'd say to us, "Nobody wants to be around a grouch." I've tried to emulate that attitude, too, and pass the advice on to my children. Because my dad had so many friends, it helped when I started out in politics, just as my mother's experience as a precinct committeewoman was valuable. His buddies would say, "You're Jesse's boy, and I like Jesse. You got my vote." Even though dad's name was Jesus, people called him Jesse. Here in the Unites States, as the saying goes, "it's tough to call someone Jesus other than the Lord."

My parents were also strong supporters of John Armenta, whom Mayor A. Martin Katz appointed to the Gary City Council after his predecessor, Paul F. Guist, resigned during a battle over a civil rights ordinance. The first Latino council member, Armenta subsequently won election in his own right. My parents got me involved in the Armenta campaign by going door to door passing out his campaign literature and attending rallies and bingo fund-raisers. His election was a source of jubilation in my family and in the Latino community.

My dad and two other community leaders, Abe Morales and Dr. Ramos, formed a Brunswick organization called the Latino Club. The purpose was to increase political awareness and participation. They rented a building on the southwest corner of Fifth and Burr across from Gary Edison High School. Joe Arredondo and John Armenta held numerous fund-raisers there. After Hispanics began moving elsewhere, the club dissolved itself.

My dad was quite proud of his union activities. Some of his buddies formed a bowling team to be a part of that facet of union life. My mom wasn't convinced that bowling was a legitimate union activity. They did have a disagreement over that, and she could be difficult, but he prevailed. Of course, he had to relent to Mom's other demands, mostly family time activities and, as my dad would say, "honey-do list."

My parents were active in many campaigns. For instance, at the house Mom hosted a coffee klatch for Frederick Work during his campaign for Gary city judge. Tall and blessed with a booming voice, he was intelligent, polite, and, given his six-foot-six height, surprisingly soft-spoken. My dad introduced him to members of the Mexican Mutualista Club at Eleventh and Washington (later the club moved to near Forty-fourth and Broadway). Attorney Fred Work won the election for Gary city judge.

Mom was a good campaigner, and many candidates would come to our house to seek her support. Some of these included Gary city clerk Betty Melinka, county treasurer Nick Angel, county official Les Pruitt, Gary city judge Charles Graddick, county prosecutor Ray Sufana, and county prosecutors Jack Crawford and Bernard Carter. Mom stayed actively involved with political campaigning until the 1990s. After that, she and Dad reserved their energies to my campaigns for sheriff.

Mayor A. Martin Katz was well liked in the Mexican community for appointing John Armenta to the city council and supporting a civil rights ordinance outlawing discriminatory practices. Nonetheless, there was a lot of support for Richard Gordon Hatcher's mayoral candidacy in 1967. My parents supported his candidacy. We were excited that he won and knew his election was history in the making. A lot of cheering went on, as well as, unfortunately, jeering in the nonminority community. Many whites viewed him as antagonistic and viewed his taking office as the beginning of the end for the city.

Our family members were big supporters of Adam Benjamin Jr. for state representative and later for state senate and Congress. Later in my life, Benjamin wrote character reference letters when I applied for the Indiana State Police and to Valparaiso University Law School. Congressman Benjamin was revered in the Latino community, and it was a great shock when he died suddenly at the early age of forty-eight. When I subsequently announced my candidacy for Lake County sheriff in 1994 and 2002, Benjamin's widow, Pat, supported my campaigns. She was a classy and gentle lady who gave me and our organization words of encouragement and political wisdom.

## HIGH SCHOOL

In 1968 at the age of forty-one my dad fulfilled a lifelong ambition and got his barber's license. When we had lived in Brunswick, he worked under the tutelage of two licensed barbers, Rey de La Rosa and Urbano Martinez, at the Northern Indiana Barber Shop on Fifth Avenue and Porter Street near Clark Road, so he already knew how to cut hair. He had worked on the practical part, but passing a written test was an obstacle. My brother Jesse and sister Maria used to read the barber's manual to him so he could memorize the things he needed to know, and it paid off. I still recollect his courage and tenacity in accomplishing his goal. For you see, the last time Dad had attended school was twenty-six years before at Mercedes High School in Texas. Dad completed school up to the ninth grade.

Brother Jesse and sister Maria graduated from Gary Edison in 1968, its final graduating class as a high school. Jesse had been held back in second grade because his English was deficient, so he and Maria went all through school together. Then with the completion of West Side High School for students in grades ten through twelve, Edison became a junior high. Armando started tenth grade at the brand-new school, and I was enrolled there a year later. In 1969 my older brother Eloy was a member of West Side High School's first graduating class. Though a modern facility, it was a rough environment, what with drugs and gangs and dropouts often mingling with students at lunchtime in the area in front of the building. My academics suffered because I skipped school a lot because of the unsafe atmosphere.

On the first school day West Side opened, a student was shot and killed inside the school gym lobby. There were many gangs, such as the

Tarrytown Rangers, Kangeroos, Latin Kings, Uptown Mystics, and Rican Brothers, to name a few. Some were formed in defense against being victimized by other gangs. Recruitment was intense and violent. If you were not in an organization, gang members would intimidate you and beat you up if you refused to join. Not only did Puerto Ricans belong to the Rican Brothers, but Mexicans and blacks did, too.

The pervasive gang violence was difficult for school officials and police to prevent. The principal, Quentin L. Smith, and educators did their best, but it was impossible to contain gang activities and bullying. Principal Smith, a Tuskegee Airman during World War II who was fondly referred to as "Q.P.," was a formidable yet caring man, but it was an enormous task to create a safe environment.

Many of us didn't go to school out of fear of gangs. Sadly, my academics suffered immensely. I really liked going to classes, but school was dangerous due to gangs and outsiders. I'm not proud of this, but I doubt if I went to a single full day of school during my sophomore year. I was far from alone in taking this position. It was probably worse for tenth graders. We would attend classes that we thought we could attend safely and then leave out of fear of gangs.

One evening I was walking the streets with a bunch of friends and a sharp white 1964 Chevy drove by, fully equipped with raised rear end and mag wheels. A couple of wise guys picked up rocks and threw them at the car. To our amazement some of them hit their target. As the Chevy screeched to a halt, everyone took off except me. I thought to myself, "I'm not running because I didn't do anything."

Two guys get out of the car, the driver, a high school senior, and his companion, an older guy named Joe who had served in Vietnam. As they approached me, they wanted to know who threw the rocks, but I said I didn't do it and refused to tell them any names. For some reason they left me alone for the time being.

At West Side High School a couple days later, Joe and some of his buddies spotted me during lunch hour and surrounded me, demanding that I reveal the names of those who threw the rocks if I didn't want to get beat up. A crowd formed, and people started yelling, "Fight! Fight!" I was just a skinny tenth grader and realized I was in big trouble but ready to fight.

Next thing I know, I look up and see my brother Mando and a couple of his buddies, including Willie Key, coming up behind Joe. Mando was pugnacious and had a tough guy reputation. When Joe spotted him, he looked back at me and said, "We'll talk later." I was relieved, but Mando wouldn't let him off the hook. He proceeded to tell him, "No, you won't." Without a word Joe and his buddies left and never bothered me again. Later when I saw the Jean Shepherd movie *A Christmas Story* I could relate to the character Ralphie in his confrontation with bully Scut Farcus, even if it was vicariously through Mando.

Armando and Willie Key were like brothers. A strong, free-spirited African American, Willie, as he said, grew up in a dysfunctional, abusive family. When he ran away from home, my mom didn't hesitate to let him live with us. There was a place for him at the table. It was seamless. He was one of us. The arrangement lasted several years. He was part of the family. When we went places, he came with us. He spoke Spanish phrases and learned the Mexican dances. He adopted a Mexican persona. He loved Mexican food and said, "When I grow up, I'm gonna marry me a Mexican woman." He and Hector fought all the time, just as the rest of us did (welcome to the family). He'd tell Armando and me, "Some day I'm gonna hurt him." He never did though because he and Hector were like brothers, too.

Sister Maria and her friend Donna Kula matched me up with my first steady girlfriend when I was a sophomore. Roseanne Sanchez was a year or two older and worked at the TriCity Plaza. After work I'd pick her up and walk her home, holding hands. It was puppy love. Roseanne's mother was friendly, but her dad rather old-school and intimidating. When we'd reach her porch, he would stand in the doorway and remain there staring at us until I left. I was not invited inside. Roseanne was thoroughly embarrassed and angry with him. She'd say to me, "Don't leave. Mom will take care of Dad." But there he remained.

After I moved to Glen Park, Roseanne and I drifted apart. She got married at a young age to Vincent Garza from East Chicago and had several children.

In tenth grade I joined the West Side swimming team and enjoyed it immensely. It was a way of connecting to school. Coach Lee Robinson was an excellent instructor and very motivating although the team was new and we did not win many meets. The school had a brand-new Olympic-size pool, and although I swam the other strokes, my specialty was freestyle at the distances of fifty and one hundred yards. We practiced at 5:30 or 6 AM and after school as well, and the pool was away from where outsiders hung out and caused trouble.

## GLEN PARK

In the summer of 1970 we moved to Gary's Junedale neighborhood of Glen Park. The address was 4767 Adams Street, which was in the Lew Wallace High School district. My parents keenly realized by then how difficult it was becoming for us at West Side because of the gangs. Mando would have preferred to finish his final year at West Side, but there was no transportation to get him there. Glen Park proved to be a lot safer than Brunswick, and in time we made plenty of friends there.

My junior year I was reintroduced to academics, but it took a while to make the adjustment. Classmates talked about going to college, but I figured I'd go into the mills like so many thousands of others before me. I hoped to make the Lew Wallace swim team, and at practice I did well, but the coach and most swimmers were rather standoffish. Even though I was faster than some on the varsity, I did not make the roster. Perhaps the coach saw me as an outsider and was more comfortable with swimmers he himself had developed. I certainly didn't feel welcome, so after a while I just moved on. Rather than make a fuss, I got a job bagging groceries at Thrifty Mart on Ridge Road and Tyler Street in Gary. Armando worked there, too. Previously I had done that at Jewel's Brunswick store.

My senior year at Lew Wallace I was able to spend mornings at the Gary Career Center and learned some practical things in their machine shop. My goal was to get into a machinist apprenticeship program after graduation.

In 1970 Willie moved with us to Glen Park. We were the only Hispanics on our all-white block. Unlike our neighbors in Brunswick, who were mostly from the South, many of our new neighbors were from Eastern Europe, with family names such as Stojsavljevich, Ostrowski, Gianapolus, Popovich, and Nahood, and first names such as Dusan, Christoff, Ontorfrio, Cvita, Boleslawa, and Jelena.

Some neighbors felt comfortable with us and others didn't, but they weren't openly hostile. Many of them subsequently moved to Merrillville after State Representative Chester Dobis and others provided the statutory changes that allowed for that town to incorporate. The fear had spread that Gary might annex that part of Ross Township known as Merrillville, resulting in an influx of blacks and Hispanics. Quite frankly, I believe Gary would have had a different history had that happened. For a time Merrillville was considered a white community and their police officers enforcers of that segregation. Things have gotten better since then. Thank God there were more good people than not.

At Lew Wallace some young blacks and whites were frequently fighting after school with sticks and bats. At that time Hispanic students couldn't understand and didn't appreciate the historical hostility. We were not oblivious to race relations, but resorting to violence did not seem appropriate. Sometimes we were drawn into it by either group who saw us as no different from the other. In fact, one main motive for forming Latino gangs was self-protection. For the most part, though, Hispanic students didn't care to participate in such confrontations.

## OLDER SIBLINGS

After high school Jesse went to St. Joseph College in Rensselaer and earned a teaching certificate, but while student teaching he decided he did not have the patience or the requisite temperament for the profession, and, besides, the pay was better in the mill. He subsequently worked at Inland Steel for thirty years.

Upon graduation Maria found a job as a clerk at Hudson's in downtown Gary, an upscale women's store. Maria was very stylish, so the store fit her perfectly. She took to Hudson's like a fish to water. I'd go in to safely escort her out when my dad picked her up after work because she didn't have a car. I was about fourteen years old at the time and proud of her. In the early 1970s after José Arredondo was elected county auditor, he offered Maria a job, and she leaped at the opportunity.

During high school Eloy had been meticulous about his grades and had his personal activities in order. He followed the rules, was neat in his appearance, had good manners and plenty of friends. While the rest of us couldn't keep a dime, he saved a substantial portion of his income from working at the Lure hamburger stand. After being part of West Side's first graduating class, Eloy bought himself a brand-new 1970 red Ford Mustang, for which he paid by cash in full – approximately $3,400.00. Tall, stocky, and very hairy, he reminded people of a big, lumbering bear and could grow a beard overnight, it seemed. I was proud of him, and it felt great to be his little brother.

Following a short stint at U.S. Steel's Sheet and Tin Mill, Eloy joined the U.S. Air Force. After going through basic training in San Antonio, he began working on C-130 cargo planes and became a jet mechanic, rising to the rank of master sergeant with his own crew under him. The crew was assigned to a particular C-130 plane and went wherever the plane went.

Armando gave me my first driving lessons, and thanks to him I passed the drivers exam. A month after graduating from Lew Wallace, Mando made good his vow to flee frigid northwest Indiana. Armando loved adventure and challenges. There was nothing he couldn't do. He had a warrior's heart. Like Eloy, he volunteered to go into the military, but the branch of the service he joined was the United States Marines. He became involved in radio communications. Much of his work was top secret, and he, too, was proud to have served our country.

Gary Martin, Jerry Ezell, and Roy Dominguez took upper division classes from me. Wherever you set the bar, they got over it. If you pushed them a bit, that was fine. They didn't whine and got it done. They had tenacity and stamina and were intelligent, highly motivated, and dead serious about improving their lives.

BARRY JOHNSTON, *Steel Shavings* 35
("Educating the Calumet Region")

Chief Andy Lazar made you realize that mistakes happened but that one should learn from them. He'd tell me that I should set my goal higher than being an I.U. Northwest officer. He emphasized getting an education and said that the pen was a more powerful weapon than a gun.

DONALD YOUNG, *Steel Shavings* 35
("Educating the Calumet Region")

FOUR

# Work and College

*One winter day my dad shocked me at the breakfast table by calling me a "dumb Mexican." He would never have uttered such an insulting remark to anybody else. Nor would he have tolerated anyone else saying that to any of us. He went on to say, "You think because you have a few nickels in your pocket that you're big stuff. What you ought to do is get an education and make something of yourself." Mom got mad and said, "Why are you talking to him that way?" He told her I was smart enough to go to college. He had never been so frank with me.*

## MILLWRIGHT APPRENTICE

Through the Gary Career Center, where I had gone for half-days during my senior year at Gary Lew Wallace High School, I found my first full-time job in June of 1972, at Ortman-Miller Machine Company, which manufactured hydraulic cylinders. It was located in north Hammond on Goslin Street near Calumet Avenue. I'd commonly be stopped by several long trains each way. It was a terrible commute. I enjoyed being an apprentice in the company's machine shop, but management didn't pay well. Therefore, I applied to be an apprentice machinist at Inland Steel, where my dad had worked for two decades. They didn't have any openings but promised to notify me when they did.

In August of 1972, a representative from Inland called, and I made an appointment to take the apprenticeship exam. Dad drove me to the personnel department and waited outside in his car. I passed the test, but the only opening available was for a millwright apprentice. I didn't even know the job duties of a millwright, but the job pay classification was pay grade 11 while for machine apprentice it was only pay grade 6. So I grabbed at the opportunity and took it. After all, it was the only one offered.

Dad couldn't believe my good fortune. He had been working twenty years and had a job pay classification of 10, and here I was an eighteen-year-old kid with a higher pay scale. I said, "Pa, what's a millwright?" I had no clue. He replied in a moment of humor, "Just take a sledgehammer to work. You'll be a sledgehammer mechanic." To this day I still laugh at his definition. He had a good sense of humor. A millwright was a mechanic in the mill, and he knew I had very little mechanical skills. Right then and there he told me, "You ought to go back to school because you're no mechanic." He was so right.

Since Dad and I were both working days at Inland's Plant 2, we'd get up at 4:30 AM and commute together after Mom lovingly made us breakfast and our lunches. He would drop me off and report to the truck and storage department. When he first got to Inland, he'd have to drive a truck to Chicago and back, but after he gained more seniority, he was able to stay inside the mill. He'd drive a fuel truck within the mill, and a helper would get out and fuel cranes, bulldozers, and other heavy machinery.

Fortunately for me, the company provided all the tools I needed. As an apprentice I was a helper and performed on-the-job training. Millwrights might say, "Do this, kid" or "Go to the shop for this." You'd do the heavy lifting or would be shown how to do something and then expected to do it. You ended up catching on. I was earning good money and eventually purchased a new car, but I gave my mom about a third of my net pay. She demanded that everyone contribute to the family treasury. I never thought anything about it. Nor did my siblings.

The morning my dad called me a "dumb Mexican" at the breakfast table, adding, "Why don't you go to college?" I thought, "He is in a bad mood." But he was letting me know that there was a lot more to life than my salary as a steelworker and following the young crowd scene with my buddies. Based on her life experiences, my mom felt that everything was fine. I had a good job, caused no trouble, and was a respectful and respectable young man. But with Dad, whose family background included business professionals and community leaders, it was different. Realizing

I had potential, he got my attention by jolting me with a combination of insult and advice.

For some months I mulled over what Dad said, and finally I took the plunge in the fall of 1973 to go to college, determined to, in his words, "make something of myself." Since that memorable morning, I have tried to live up to his injunction, knowing that what Dad meant included helping family and others foremost.

## TEXAS TRIP

In high school I used to send my maternal grandmother Vicenta flowers and postcards with notes in English that her friends would read to her. In 1973 after I earned enough money to buy a new car, Mom and I drove down to Texas. At age sixty-eight Vicenta was petite but fit; you'd never guess that she had given birth to fourteen children. We'd cross the border and haggle with sidewalk vendors in the Mexican town of Las Flores, located next to our ancestral town of Relampago.

One day we went to the Mexican city of Reynosa with Grandma Vicenta, Mom, and my aunts Maria and Oralia. At lunchtime my grandmother asked me whether I liked goat meat, and when I said yes, she took us to one of her favorite restaurants. Inside was an open pit where the meat was cooked. My grandmother told the owner we wanted baby goat, and he sent us outside to select our food. There in the backyard were a bunch of baby goats. "Pick out the one you want," she said. "Oh grandma, "I replied, "you pick it. I'm going back out front." I must admit, I was squeamish about picking out a live goat for lunch, but it was very tasty and a way of life in Mexico.

At the end of every visit her parting advice was, "Take care of yourself and take care of your family." Family always came first for her.

## IU NORTHWEST

Faced with the prospect of languishing in the mill for years to come, I decided that college was for me. My high school grades had been mediocre at best, and at Indiana University Northwest in Gary I took the SAT test and didn't do well. The admissions director told me that I ought to stay in the steel mills and forget about college. A friend suggested I go see Elsa Rivera, an IU Northwest counselor in Special Services, a program IU Northwest had instituted for students who were disadvantaged academically. She was a godsend and registered me into tutorials that prepared me for regular credit courses. By that time a light had gone on in my head regarding education. I realized that it was a necessary prerequisite to becoming a meaningful participant in society.

I am so thankful that Dad pushed me in this direction. As I truly believe, I stand on the shoulders of giants.

Learning what the admissions director had said to me, Elsa was infuriated. I thought she might find him and beat him up. She really cared. Her interest and passion started me thinking, "Maybe I'm not so bad after all. Maybe I can succeed in college." While it was tough at first, I got off academic probation after the first semester, and the work paid off as I later often made the college's Dean's List. That was quite an accomplishment given my academic deficiencies. I often tell audiences that, thanks to Elsa Rivera, IU Northwest and its professors gave me an opportunity to fulfill my dreams. For that I'll forever be grateful and work to make those who offered encouragement proud of their support of me.

At the time I started college at age nineteen, I had hopes of becoming a state trooper but couldn't apply until I turned twenty-one. Meanwhile, college courses would enable me to do better on the test. My only contacts with state police were the two occasions when I received speeding tickets on I-80, but the troopers seemed very professional. It seemed a desirable career worth pursuing.

Near the end of my freshman year Elsa Rivera showed me a brochure explaining the IU Police Cadet program being introduced at the Gary campus for the first time. A friend of mine, Ed Rysiewicz, and I applied. After being interviewed by Andrew Lazar, head of the Safety Division, we were, along with Sam Trapane and an African American woman named Roberta, the campus's first cadets. That summer of 1974 we attended a three-week training session at the Poplars Building in Bloomington and subsequently went back to IU for an eight-week session the following summer of 1975.

The program was a win-win situation for me as well as the university. Campus cadets worked part-time for minimum wages but were introduced to the law enforcement profession. Safety Division secretary Lorraine Ensweiler was pleasant as could be and very efficient. Coming from working the fields, a machine shop, and the steel mill, I had my first exposure to a professional office. I quickly felt at home there and met people who would become my lifelong friends.

The first year we were considered cadets with no police authority but were the eyes and ears for the other officers. We'd also work the radio room as dispatchers and go out in patrol vehicles with the police officers as observers. Lieutenant Andy Lazar, whose designation as chief came with enactment of a subsequent statute establishing the University Police Department, gave us what we called our "Father Flanagan" talk, so-named for Edward J. Flanagan, the driving force behind Boys Town as played by Spencer Tracy in the 1938 movie.

At the end of the day the job of campus cadets was to make the rounds and make certain all the doors were locked. Often Andy would decide to accompany one of us, and we'd say to ourselves fondly, "Here comes the Father Flanagan talk." Ed Rysiewicz later became chief of the Crown Point Police Department and remained a friend. We still remember those times with fond appreciation.

Lazar, a retired Gary police officer, used to call me Rog. If it was my turn he'd say, "OK, Rog, you're coming with me tonight." The themes were always the same: education, professionalism, and public service, or, put another way, living up to the police motto, "To serve and protect." He instilled in us that the essence of police work was dedication to serving the public while enforcing the law. He taught us the importance of having a calm, pleasant demeanor even in a crisis or when people were speaking to you disparagingly. He'd say to an irate student, professor, or campus visitor, "We can't work out your problem if you're angry." I have tried to pick up on that. It didn't hurt that he was one big guy. He may have been a gentle bear, but still nobody in his right mind wants to tangle with a bear, gentle or not. Andy Lazar was a great role model. It was an honor to receive his tutelage.

Another role model in that vein was Officer John Redmond, who was about five-foot-ten and a large fellow with a pleasant demeanor who made sure people were safe. He generally worked the evening shift in the patrol vehicle (which resembled an SUV) and wore a patrol uniform.

Brady Ratcliff, a retired army veteran, worked the day shift without a uniform. Instead he wore a blue blazer with the police insignia on the front pocket. Brady had much practical sense, and I learned a lot from him. He was more curt with those who crossed him than John or Andy. If someone was causing him grief, he'd say, "Now look here. I've already told you two or three times. I'm done explaining. I'm trying to be nice, but if you won't have it that way, then we can do it my way." With Andy or John, it would never have reached that point. Brady was stern when he had to be, another lesson I learned.

My second summer at Bloomington I roomed with Ed Rysiewicz and Paul Whitesell, who was enrolled at IU and had a house in Bloomington. Some thirty years later Governor Mitch Daniels appointed Whitesell as superintendent of the Indiana State Police, and to this day we remain great friends.

Heading the summer program was Irwin Owens, a retired FBI agent. His assistant, Jim Kennedy, was a great teacher and a person I wished to emulate professionally. Although in police work, Kennedy had a law degree, which impressed me and put the idea in my head of doing the same. He introduced himself not as a lawyer but as a police officer with a law degree. He also taught classes at Indiana University Law School. He told us that many police agencies, including the Indiana State Police, were establishing legal divisions, where attorneys were drafting operating procedures that were legally sound for police officers and then educating the officers on carrying them out in ways that would not jeopardize getting convictions against those apprehended. Occasionally local prosecutors would deputize them to help in the prosecution of a case. That sounded intriguing and something worth pursuing down the road.

While at Bloomington in the summer of 1975, we provided security at Assembly Hall during a Rolling Stones concert that coincided with Mick Jagger's thirtieth birthday. Beforehand, our superiors told us, "When the lights go down, don't bother anybody who's smoking marijuana. So many people will be smoking that we won't be able to take everyone out." I thought, "Whoa!" That was so foreign to me, but who was I to disobey orders. The band put on an amazing performance, and backstage afterward, I got to shake Mick Jagger's hand.

When I was at Bloomington, one evening I ran into Willie Key, our worldly brother, dancing and partying like in days of old. He had been in the service, and I had lost track of him, but we embraced like long-lost brothers. He eventually married a Mexican American woman and had three children. Unfortunately he had trouble finding steady employment and experienced marital difficulties. Shortly after encountering those setbacks, Willie took his own life. Many friends arranged for his funeral services and took up a collection for a memorial cemetery headstone. It was such a sad end to such a vibrant spirit and a great worldly brother. He is dearly missed.

In 1975, during the second cadet summer session, I became certified in the use of firearms. I qualified with a .38 Smith & Wesson revolver and also had training with a shotgun. Being physically fit, I had no trouble with the push-ups, sit-ups, rope climbing, and running. While at IU Northwest I had frequently jogged around the Gleason Park track and exercised routinely.

After the second summer session I had enough hours to qualify as a graduate of the IU Law Enforcement Academy. On the Northwest campus during my junior year, I wore a police uniform and carried a gun and a PR-24, similar to a baton but with a handle on the side. It replaced the former traditional baton, which could be quite lethal if you hit someone over the head. The PR-24's primary purpose was not to inflict serious injury but to subdue someone if necessary while making a legal arrest. I never had the need to brandish a weapon, however. The campus was a safe place. What difficulties we had were with outsiders coming onto the campus for dances, to cruise the parking lot, or whatever.

In the spring of 1976 I helped provide security when presidential candidate Jimmy Carter spoke at the campus theater. The former naval officer, peanut farmer, and Georgia governor had entered the Democratic primary and spoke of the need for federal cabinet-level departments of education and energy. On his request we assembled behind the stage after the speech because he wanted to thank us and shake our hands. I was impressed that he took the time to do that. I wished I had a camera with me because I was so impressed with then Governor Carter.

At age nineteen I met Gary police sergeant Gary Martin soon after I joined the cadet program. He was an administrator with the Gary Police Department and finishing up his master's program. Mingling with us at headquarters from time to time, he treated us with kindness and respect and was everybody's cheerleader. He'd praise me for going into police work, build up my confidence about applying to be a state trooper, and let me know what to expect. His view was that education was the wave of the future in police work, and we young folks would be the next generation's leaders.

Based in part on her past dealings with police as well as concern over my safety, my mom was not in favor of my becoming a state trooper. It hadn't been an issue while I was a cadet, but then she started thinking, "Is he really going to do this?" It's not that she didn't want me to follow my dreams. She just couldn't understand what the allure was about becoming a police officer. Though she made her feelings known, she ultimately supported my dreams.

## BETTY

Betty Olayta was attending IU Northwest while I was a cadet. Riding in a vehicle with the officer on patrol in the parking lot, I saw this cute little thing and took another pass by her. Later on Betty revealed that she knew I was eyeing her. I must say, it was love at first sight. First came the physical attraction and then the loving friendship.

We asked mutual friends about each other, and one said, "Betty is having a Valentine's party and wanted to know if you wished to come." I was a bit of a snot and replied that I'd consider it if she asked me herself. So she did, much to my relief. Ed Rysiewicz and I went to her parents' house on Forest Avenue in Miller together. Neither of us were big drinkers, but we fortified ourselves with more orange juice and vodka than was prudent. We were unfamiliar with her neighborhood, which seemed devoid of streetlights, and were lucky to find it.

At Betty's house I was sitting on a chair when Betty's dad, Ponciano Olayta, came over to meet me. I had been taught that it was common courtesy for a gentleman to stand up in situations like that and to respect your elders. I was the only one seated who stood up and proceeded to shake his hand. From that moment, he told me later, he knew that I was a good young man. He had been in the Philippine military during World War II, serving with U.S. Allied forces, and was a survivor of the Bataan March, which took place in 1942 and involved the forcible relocation of 75,000 prisoners of war to prison camps. Along the way over 25 percent of the prisoners died or were killed.

Ponciano was a planner for Gary MANPOWER under Mayor Richard Gordon Hatcher, Indiana's first African American mayor. Betty's dad had five martial arts black belts and was the most universal man I had ever met. He had written books on yoga and played a half-dozen instruments, from the violin to the drums, in a professional manner. With his shaved head he looked like actor Yul Brynner, who starred in *The King and I*.

I had first met Mayor Hatcher with my parents at Sociedad Mutualista Mexico. I met him again when Betty's dad hosted a home fund-raiser for him. He was very intelligent and humble. I've always enjoyed his company and advice.

Betty arrived in Gary from Manila during the winter of 1967, endured the legendary blizzard when everything came to a standstill for nearly a week, and graduated three years later from Horace Mann. She came from a family of educated people, including many military officers. Her uncle was a doctor and her maternal grandmother, Fortunata Mijares, one of the first Filipina nurses, helped bring others in her profession from her native country to the Calumet Region. Her mom, Rosalina, was a pharmacist at Methodist Hospital and a beautiful and charming lady. In the Philippines the family had four servants who took care of the cooking, cleaning, and other household chores. Married during World War II, Ponciano and Rosalina remained together sixty-one years, all their lives.

Betty's best friend at Horace Mann High School had been Cathy Balanoff, whose father, Jim Balanoff, was a union activist. The two were virtually inseparable. If Betty's mother would tell Cathy, "You better go home because your parents don't know where you are," she'd say, "Oh, they know I'm here." Cathy went on to marry Jim Robinson, who became a district director of the steelworkers union. In 2009 Jim Robinson and I brought our wives to a political function, and they were like long-lost sisters. Since graduating from high school in 1970, they had not seen or heard from each other for over thirty years. Jim joked that when they were dating, he usually picked up Cathy at Betty's house.

My parents preferred us to date Mexican Americans, so when I first brought Betty home, their reaction was, "Who is this?" It didn't take her long to win them over though, and Betty's family was accepting of me. Although very hospitable, Betty's mom, Rosalina, wanted Betty to marry a Filipino. Keep in mind that both mothers grew up during an era when multicultural marriages were the exception rather than the norm. Both gave their blessings, however, and we have been a loving family unit. Betty's sisters Evelyn, Louisa, and Tessie were classy ladies and also very receptive.

Betty was all of ninety-five pounds and about five-foot-two without her three-inch platform shoes. I tell the story in jest about her taking off those shoes and I thought she had fallen down.

After dating Betty for two years, I asked her to marry me. She was willing but said I'd have to obtain her parents' permission first, a Filipino tradition. So I did, successfully, and then we had dinner with my parents and received their blessing. We had an apartment in Merrillville all set up by the time of the wedding. On August 25, 1978, Judge Lorenzo Arredondo married us at my sister Maria's house in Gary, Indiana. It was a garden wedding, and members of both of our families attended. Counting guests there must have been seventy-five people in Maria's backyard at Forty-sixth and Harrison. We didn't have a best man and matron of honor. Instead Mr. and Mrs. Aviña – Alfred and Alice – were our godparents. They were contemporaries of my parents and the aunt and uncle of my friend Damian Paz, who, along with his mother and brother, lived with them as a teenager. I'd visit at their house, and they'd be mindful of how I was doing and advise me to stay out of trouble and study hard. I could ask them things that I might not want to bring up with my parents. After I met Betty, I introduced her to them, and they embraced her as they had me.

For our honeymoon Betty and I drove to Wisconsin Dells for a week. I'd never been there. We stayed in one of the resort's one-room Tahitian huts and had a great time canoeing, bike riding, shopping at Native American crafts shops, eating at restaurants, attending the water ski show and fireworks display, and just being with each other. We went on a boat trip and a Duck tour in a vintage World War II vehicle that operated both on land and in the water.

Up to this time Betty had never cooked. Servants had done kitchen chores in Manila, and she was the baby in the family with three older sisters. At first she smothered everything in soy sauce to mask if it was burnt or undercooked. I took her to my mom to teach her how to cook Mexican dishes; then her mom taught her how to cook some Filipino recipes. She learned both traditions so well I've been on a diet ever since to keep my weight in check.

## HECTOR

Younger brother Hector was so much fun to be with and such a daring spirit. I always admired his "go to" attitude, as if nothing were impossible for him. Although kind and personable, he didn't take any "guff" from anyone. He was artistically talented and a real animal lover. He and Dad both loved pets, even more than the rest of us. I think we always had a pet because of them. Mom loved pets, but not in the house.

Hector reminded my dad somewhat of his older brothers José and Felix. He wanted to make sure that what happened to them – getting in trouble, leaving home, being cut off from family – didn't happen to Hector. The two had a special bond that increased with age.

Hector married Karen Massengill, and they had one son, named Nicholas David. My sister Maria liked the name Nicholas, and David was Hector's choice of a middle name in honor of Dad's cousin David who was killed in the Korean War while serving in the army. Hector and Karen later divorced, and Hector was awarded custody of Nick by the court. Hector was very involved in Nick's school and upbringing. Thereafter he met his current companion, Cindy Kambesis. Hector and Cindy had two children, Madalyn and Andrew Vincent, the latter named in honor of our maternal uncle Vicente. All three children are smart, athletically inclined, and have wonderful personalities. Cindy is an attorney for the Indiana Family and Social Services Administration. Hector and Cindy follow the motto "Family First" and are very involved in their children's school and sports activities.

## YOUNGER SISTERS

There was a double standard to Mom's treatment of her sons and daughters, a vestige of the way she herself was raised. Even as she continued to serve meals to the sons, she'd expect the daughters to serve themselves by the time they were twelve or thirteen years of age. More significantly, they did dishes, cleaned their own clothes and rooms, and ironed. Boys took care of the outside work and some of the heavy cleaning – Mom wanted the windows washed regularly, for instance. We didn't do the inside chores, however, on a regular basis.

During the 1970s, with feminism coming to the forefront, Mom's expectations and tight rein became a source of difficulties, especially with Yolanda. The two were a lot alike. The discord got to be intense. They'd get into arguments and one thing led to another. Mom was a strict disciplinarian and could be unyielding. She never fully adjusted to the cultural evolutions of the seventies.

The mischief Yolanda got into was minor stuff, similar to what we boys did at that age. When she hung around with kids Mom didn't trust, it could turn into a fight to the point where both mother and daughter stopped listening to one another. Yolanda went to live with Armando and his wife and finished high school in Oklahoma City. Mom cried for days after Yolanda left. The separation left a void that weighed heavily on all of us. I know it was extremely difficult for Yoli and a comfort that she was in the care of Mando.

After Yolanda graduated from high school, she married a lanky fellow named Dewey Carriger, whose folks had been Sooners since the land rush. He was pleasant, a hard worker, and a family man. Yolanda felt bad being so far from us, and we dearly missed her as well. As she matured and raised a family herself, she has come to more of an understanding of Mom's perspective. Yoli's son, Christopher, and daughter, Averi, are bright, charming, and fun to be around.

Rosario, easygoing like Yolanda, had done well academically until she started at Lew Wallace, which had become a pretty rough place, not unlike West Side when I was her age. At sixteen, Rosie dropped out of school, married twenty-year-old boyfriend Tony Cuba, and gave birth to Andrea, who became the apple of the family's eye. Fun-loving twin boys soon followed. Marriage has its challenges, to be sure, but they stayed together thrity-three years.

As she matured, Rosie resembled our sister Maria in looks, sensitivity, and class. Daughter Andrea went on to make the National Honor Society, graduated from Indiana University with a degree in computer graphics, and teaches English to the children of Americans living in Libya. Artistic, a self-starter, and a world traveler, she is a jewel. Rosie's twin sons, Tony Jr. and Adam, are both doing well and work in northwest Indiana. With Rosie, as with all of us, family comes first, and she assures us her family is doing well.

An Indiana State Police Officer's primary responsibility
is to enforce the state criminal and traffic laws
and to render aid to persons in need.

"Trooper Job Description,"
Indiana State Police Handbook

You come here with a skull full of mush and
you leave thinking like a lawyer.

PROFESSOR KINGSFIELD
(John Houseman) in *The Paper Chase*

FIVE

# State Trooper and Law Student

*At the Indiana State Police Academy there was one cadet who had been making racially insulting remarks and shunning other minority students and me. The instructor paired us up in the ring. Several of my buddies knew that I had had boxing lessons and gathered around, chanting for me to knock him out. Within seconds I hit him so hard he started staggering, and the instructor immediately halted the fight. My vocal supporters were disappointed I didn't get more swings at him. Afterward, the cadet treated us with more respect.*

## INDIANA STATE POLICE ACADEMY

At the time I set my sights on becoming a state trooper there were no Hispanics on the force – or women, for that matter – and no more than a half-dozen African American troopers. That didn't deter me. I was determined to push through that barrier. Sometime around 1974 the Indiana chapter of the NAACP sued the Indiana State Police in federal court for discriminatory practices. About a year later the parties entered into a judicial consent decree. The agreement stated that half the slots for the next several police recruit academies had to be reserved for women, African Americans, Hispanics, and other minorities.

I took the state trooper exam in the fall of 1975 but was passed over when the first police class began under the consent decree that started in March of 1976. Then state senator Adam Benjamin, a family friend, wrote a reference letter and without my knowledge asked the program directors why I had not been chosen. They told him I had passed the recruiting background checks but they thought I was too young and not ready for the police academy rigors. "Why don't you just give him a chance?" he told them.

So, at Senator Benjamin's urging, the state police program directors accepted me into the second class, beginning July 4, 1976. Talk about opportunity, the country's bicentennial with celebrations going on, and I was starting my dream of becoming a state trooper – but with a great deal of anxiety about what lay ahead. It was a giant leap for me. I would suspend my schooling for a year and then hopefully go back and finish later.

At the academy, some instructors and fellow students who felt standards were being lowered as a result of demands for affirmative action made me feel that I and the other minorities and women were there only because of the lawsuit and not on merit. I was determined to prove them wrong and not to fail. At the end of the session, out of approximately sixty in the class, I was ranked in the top ten based on academics, physical fitness, and firearms testing. My experience with the IU cadet program was invaluable in familiarizing me with the profession and preparing me in the use of firearms and with police academics. You had to pass two written exams each in criminal law and traffic. We also had defensive driving tests.

At the State Police Academy we ran one or two miles daily; I was the second-fastest. One cadet left us all behind. Then there I came, followed by the rest of the group. As part of the physical fitness program, we also had boxing, with which I was already familiar. While at IU Northwest, I had heard about the Gary Boxing Club, located under Gilroy Stadium. When I asked African American boxing legend Bill Murphy, who ran the program, if I could participate, he replied, "Well, come on in." Just like that, no questions asked, no money requested. Coach Murphy expected us to come every day, be on time, and follow his regimen. Otherwise, he added, "don't come." You'd do strenuous exercise and get beat up. Murphy even got in the ring with guys even though in his fifties. What a physical specimen. Of course, in those days I thought someone his age was ancient. He was tremendous and prepared me well. And it was all free of charge. Coach Murphy didn't even ask for donations, although we all contributed when possible.

The day during academy physical training when I was in the boxing ring facing the cadet who had been making racially insulting remarks,

I didn't think about his attitude toward me and others and certainly didn't feel it my responsibility to punish anyone, no matter how insulting or indifferent he might have been. I was simply doing my best given the physical exercise. I hit him once and almost knocked him out. My fellow cadets wanted me to keep punching him, but I didn't. He had enough.

Being in the top ten in the class academically automatically made me a semifinalist for the coveted Donald Flint Award, designating the "Number One Cadet," an honor our classmates voted on. Our names were put on the chalkboard, and we left the room. Upon returning I learned that I was in the top three. One of the others was the son of a major on the state police force. The three of us left the room; I was told later that the lieutenant in charge of the academy pointed to the major's son and reminded the cadets of his father. Even so, my fellow cadets selected me by an overwhelming margin. I was very honored, especially because it helped put to rest the viewpoint that standards had been lowered. In fact, the previous class had named a woman the top cadet. When I received the plaque my name was reversed, as if Rogelio was my surname. They sent it back, and the second time the engravers downstate got it right.

On October 15, 1976, we graduated, and many state dignitaries attended, among them Indiana attorney general Theodore L. "Ted" Sendak of Crown Point, Indiana. As our names were called to receive our police badges, Mr. Sendak presented me with mine. He was a real gentleman, and it was an honor I'll never forget. Later my dad and mom pinned the badge onto my uniform. Betty, Yoli, Rosie, and Jesse also attended the graduation ceremony, which was held at Plainfield High School, just southwest of Indianapolis.

My parents held a graduation party in my honor at the old Sportsman's Club on Forty-second and Grant Street in Gary's Glen Park neighborhood. About three hundred people attended, including state senator Adam Benjamin. When he saw the plaque for the Donald Flint Award, he said, "I can't wait to tell the doubters on the state police that you graduated first in your class." Then he proceeded to tell me what they had first said about me, that I was too young for the rigors of police work. I was very pleased that Senator Benjamin was proud of his recommendation on my behalf. That has remained with me and reminds me to continue to do my best in emulation of those who lent their assistance on my behalf.

## PROBATIONARY OFFICER

Ordinarily probationary officers are not assigned to their home district, but by virtue of graduating first in my class I got to pick my post, and I selected Schererville. I was assigned to Zone One, which encompassed the northern tier of Lake County and included U.S. 30, I-65, 80/94, Ridge Road, and various unincorporated areas, including Black Oak until it was annexed to Gary.

A former marine, Trooper Glen Bovard, became my trainer during the three-month probationary period. He was very professional and courteous with people we confronted while on duty, but the saying "Once a marine, always a marine" proved true in his case. He was very much the drill instructor, but this was very beneficial, as he taught me how to protect myself and remain alert for threatening body language and other nonverbal indications of danger.

Some other trooper trainers hazed those under their care, but not Glen. In addition, nobody harassed me because Glen would have none of that. It just wasn't his method of operation. He wasn't going to allow others to haze me. He was a good guy with a dry sense of humor, but his primary job was to make sure I'd know how to stay alive and keep safe when on my own. It was a matter of life and death. He'd have unannounced inspections of my weapon and uniform, but that was all part of the training. Looking and being professional was all part of being a state trooper.

Glen was not a big writer of traffic tickets. He felt that anybody could give tickets but that our main job was protecting people, so we should concentrate on those driving recklessly. Some troopers ticketed those going just ten miles over the speed limit; for Glen the standard was more like twenty. The main issue was whether the driver was being reckless and endangering himself and others. So he was less interested in the number than the quality of arrests. That became my standard as well.

Glen also usually let off senior citizens with warnings and would tell me, with just the hint of a twinkle in his eyes, "Don't ever give a doctor or nurse a ticket because you never know if you'll be in an emergency room with them."

After a three-month probationary period, I was called up to face the captain, first sergeant, and sergeants who had examined Glen's reports on my progress. They questioned me on various procedural matters and asked me to express to them why I thought I was prepared to go out on my own. Then it was a matter of waiting for their verdict. If you passed, they'd tell you, "Go to Indianapolis and pick up your police car." That was your diploma, and I received the word to go to Indianapolis. All excited, I called Glen to thank him. He played it cool, but certainly must have been excited, too, and gratified that he had trained me well. It was a source of pride for him and an honor for me.

## STATE TROOPER

My first vehicle was a 1975 Chrysler Newport. It was literally about the size of a good-sized boat. It started slowly but had a powerful engine and could reach high speeds. As I recall, the speedometer went up to 140 or 150 miles per hour. It was the middle of winter, and with the roads often icy the defensive driving classes came in handy. Now that I was on my own, my initial feeling was, "What did I get myself into?" Any trooper who doesn't admit to a sense of anxiety when new at the job is just not recalling the moment accurately. But Glen had prepared me well and knew I was ready, so the nervousness passed quickly, replaced by growing confidence. I was finally doing what I had dreamed of for as long as I could remember, and I loved it.

For the next nine months a squad sergeant would evaluate you on the quality of your reports, your enthusiasm and willingness to work overtime when required, your interaction with other troopers, the public, and the prosecutor's office, and, of course, your professionalism. We didn't conduct investigations but filed the initial report, and we were involved in incidents involving auto theft, drugs, and domestic violence. We never had a quota regarding tickets or arrests, but we had to show some evidence of activity during the course of an eight-hour tour of duty. For me, overtime meant an opportunity to do more of what I loved.

My first big emergency occurred while I was driving east on I-80 near Clark Road. The CB (citizens band) radio started going nuts with frantic messages from truckers and other motorists about a low-flying plane. Suddenly, straight ahead of me was a low-flying object that I first thought was the Gary police helicopter, till I realized it was a small plane in obvious distress. I thought it was going to hit me, and I swerved off the highway. In the rearview mirror I saw that it crash-landed on the westbound side and flipped over into a ditch filled with icy water.

After I called in a report in a voice that the dispatcher later told me was very excited, my training kicked in and I assumed command of the plane crash scene. Traffic having stopped, I crossed the highway to the aircraft. People trapped inside were screaming and hanging upside down. Other police cars and an ambulance arrived, and with additional help from volunteers we bent the door open to get the passengers out.

The two couples in the plane were missionaries from Texas on their way to Fort Wayne. They had gotten caught in a snowstorm and ran out of fuel. They were taken to Methodist Hospital, but everyone emerged OK. About a month later someone told me my name was in the *Star* tabloid newspaper, which had done a story on the incident.

My first traffic accident fatality involved a vehicle going south on I-65 between Fifteenth Avenue and Interstate I-80. It was a sunny but very cold day. The driver must have fallen asleep or become inattentive because she crossed the median strip and struck a northbound vehicle. She was driving without a seat belt and fatally injured. She basically shattered the windshield and was crushed against the steering wheel. Her young child was thrown from the car and also died. Another child and the husband survived. It happened almost at the end of my day shift.

I was on I-65 and arrived within minutes of receiving the call. The scene was chaotic. I called for an ambulance and the coroner because it was obvious the driver was already dead, and the husband was screaming that his one child was missing. Meanwhile, the driver of the other car was in the last trimester of her pregnancy and trapped behind her steering wheel, screaming. Among the troopers arriving on the scene was Glen Bovard. He was like a big brother, making sure I had all the help I needed.

I later learned that the woman in the northbound car recovered from her injuries and delivered a healthy baby. Still, the death of the mother and child affected me with a sense of grief for them and their family. Such a loss and tragedy.

The first time I arrested a drunken driver, I took him to the Schererville state police post because I was not at that time a certified Breathalyzer operator. While waiting for an operator to arrive, I was trying to obtain the guy's driver's license and other information in order to complete my report. The arrestee was being uncooperative and nasty. He stood up and when I told him to sit down said, "You can't make me."

I had been trying to treat the inebriated man with respect, but a detective on duty, Richard Snipes, heard the interchange and walked over to us. Mean, burly, and over six feet, three inches, tall, Snipes snarled, "Didn't this trooper tell you to sit down?" The guy started to mouth off, and Snipes gave him a chop to the throat using the space between his thumb and index finger. As I looked on in amazement, the man slumped back in the chair. Hovering over him, Snipes muttered, "When this trooper tells you something, you better do it. Understand?" Snipes then turned to me and said, "He's all yours." I had no problems with him from then on.

One time during my rookie year I got a report that a fight was about to ensue between two rival motorcycle gangs. The first to arrive on the scene, I arrested one person for public intoxication and radioed for backup. When I called in the name and driver's license, seasoned police veterans realized that I had arrested one of the most notorious members of the Invaders. Lucky for me, the backup arrived quickly because the guy was considered an extremely dangerous person.

On one occasion, we raided an after-hours beer joint in Indiana Harbor known for hosting high-stakes card games. We arrested the owner and those who were gambling but let the other patrons go. One of these was an old acquaintance of mine who was quite embarrassed.

## SENIOR YEAR

After successfully completing my one-year police probation, I enrolled back at IU Northwest for my senior year. I juggled going to class with my hours on patrol. My superiors at the post treated the time off like a break, to be made up either before I came on duty or after my shift ended.

At this time communication professor Camille Schuster had a great deal of influence on developing my communication skills. I had been scared to death in my first speech class but soon I took a liking to it. Professor Schuster, who was new in her profession, really excited my interest in the art of delivery in its verbal and written forms. She made the art of communication relevant and exciting and taught me the importance of being able to express oneself cogently. I had several of her advanced classes, including individual readings where I'd meet with her one-on-one to discuss books and do special projects.

For one assignment Professor Schuster suggested that I organize a public forum. I proposed putting together a Traffic Fatality program. It was held at the IU Northwest Theater. Under her tutelage the conference was a great success. Among the guest speakers were Adam Benjamin Jr. (now a congressman, having defeated incumbent Ray J. Madden in 1976), a commissioner from the Indiana Department of Transportation, newly elected Sheriff José Arredondo, and newly elected Lake County prosecutor Jack Crawford, a former Hammond city judge and rising star who had defeated incumbent prosecutor Ray Sufana. High school driving instructors brought their classes, and local police departments participated. The *Post-Tribune* covered it extensively. Professor Schuster was impressed, and area officeholders and police administrators took notice.

Had I not already been a sociology major with only a half-dozen courses to complete in order to graduate, I might have been tempted to be a communication major. Sociology had appealed to me because it was the study of group dynamics and interaction. The sixties and seventies had been a time of social unrest, and I thought the course material would best benefit me in police work.

Professor Robert Lovely also was a big influence. He was an extremely caring, patient, and dynamic professor, and I wanted to take more advanced sociology courses with him. He'd explain a concept and say, "OK, did you get it?" If not, he explained it another way or would set up special Saturday morning sessions for those who needed additional help. Sometimes I'd attend them even if I understood the subject matter because he cared enough to hold them for his students.

Dr. Lovely and his colleague Barry Johnston were both recent PhD graduates from Notre Dame. Their styles couldn't have been more different. Barry was an excellent lecturer who knew his subject but would move on to the next topic whether the class comprehended the material or not. He held no special study sessions, and you had to come up to his level if you wanted a passing grade. I guess Professor Johnston felt his role was to challenge students intellectually and enhance their educational ability. He prepared his students well for the rigors of academic life as well as a tough and dynamic world. I must say I was fortunate to learn from him, and my grade was well earned.

Dr. Lovely taught statistics, two semesters of which was required for majors. Since I had never had calculus, I had to get special permission from him. (I hadn't had algebra, let alone calculus or trigonometry.) It was a tribute to Dr. Lovely that I got through it. I made a B the first semester and an A the second. Like Dr. Johnston, he didn't give high grades easily. You earned what grade you received. Because of Professors Lovely and Johnston, I elected to pursue sociology as my college major.

My final semester I took introduction to criminal justice with Gary Martin as an elective. By now he was teaching on a regular basis and was animated, funny, and excellent at drawing out students in discussion. Even though I already knew most of the material because of my police training, I loved the course. Betty took several classes from Gary, graduated in May of 1978 with a criminal justice degree, and got hired as a probation officer by Juvenile Court judge Darlene Mears. I graduated in May of 1979. Later, after I became sheriff and appointed Gary Martin the police chief of Lake County Sheriff's Department, he would ask audiences to guess who was the better student, the sheriff or his wife, Betty. Then he'd smile and say, "the one not elected sheriff." That was quintessential Gary. It embodied his sly wit.

My professors had great passion for helping students grow intellectually. If I can convey to people the importance of education through my personal story, it should give others hope. If you are able to touch even one heart, it is worth it.

## LAW SCHOOL

I was pretty naïve about law school, and nobody among my circle of family or friends had the legal education to offer guidance. Before taking the LSAT exam, for instance, I worked the evening shift, not realizing how long and difficult the test would be. Fortunately I did well enough to be admitted into Valparaiso University's Law School. It was a three-year program. I did not know that at several Chicago law schools four-year programs were available that might have fit better with my job. I knew that I was taking on a difficult task, but ever since I had learned about the state police legal division from IU police assistant director Jim Kennedy, acquiring the skills to be a part of it had been my goal.

## GUN SCANDAL

In previous police peer reviews, I had made clear to my superiors my ambition to join the state police legal division, but once I started going to law school, I encountered much animosity from various supervisors, who put roadblocks in my path. This was partly the result, I believe, of the shakeup that took place in the aftermath of what became known in the press as the State Police Gun Scandal, which pre-dated my arrival at the Schererville post. Thus, anyone associated with the post was guilty by association.

In the past, if a trooper had arrested an armed person who did not have a gun permit, justices of the peace would order the weapon confiscated and, commonly, let the arresting officer keep it. Under prodding from the press and Republicans, state police officials in Indianapolis, who tended to look down on the Calumet Region, launched an investigation of practices in District 13 but not other posts, even though similar practices existed statewide. Rather than propose, "this was the practice in the past but won't be any longer," bureaucrats downstate wanted legal action to be taken against these individual Lake County troopers.

To his credit, Lake County prosecutor Ray Sufana refused to prosecute officers who had kept confiscated guns until this policy was implemented throughout the state. As he pointed out, it was common knowledge that the supervisor of another post allegedly had his entire den walls decorated with confiscated weapons and nothing was being done to him. Besides, justices of the peace had sanctioned such practices.

Even though they were spared criminal charges, thanks to then prosecutor Sufana, many officers had their careers negatively affected. Some were demoted or denied promotion; others retired. Starting in 1978, the Schererville post closed, as did the Dunes post in Porter County, and a new post opened in Lowell. None of the new administrators came from the Schererville post, and they tended to disrespect officers who did not deserve such treatment. The divisions made for a tense work situation and caused dissension within the ranks.

So long as I was a rookie and then concentrating on finishing at IU Northwest, there was no problem. I just took orders and stayed clear of the police politics. All that changed when I became a first-year law student. The swords really came out. One source of hostility may have been that upon graduation from law school, one is automatically promoted to lieutenant and then captain. Many line sergeants had worked their entire careers and never been promoted to lieutenant. As I soon discovered, the intentional obstruction by many to derail someone else's promotion was intense.

My squad sergeant also had racial sensitivity issues. For purposes of harassment he'd call me in at two or three in the morning to nitpick my reports when the common practice was simply to send them back if they required revisions. Or he'd give me service calls near the end of my shift that should have gone to another trooper on duty, forcing me to see it through.

One time at the Lowell gas pumps an officer who I thought was my friend said I should quit law school because I was too dumb to be a lawyer. That really stung. I had some choice words for him. The insult just gave me more resolve. On the other hand, such officers as Jerome Ezell, Joe Kirk, and Paul Fotia were supportive and encouraging. Even so, in October of 1979, I came to the realization that the situation would have to change if I were to have a chance of succeeding in law school. I didn't have time to study, and it was harder and harder to make up the hours on patrol.

Desperately seeking a recourse that would enable me to remain a trooper yet stay in law school, I applied for straight midnights (from 11 to

7). The request was denied. Then I asked for an unpaid leave of absence until May, when the first (and hardest) school year would end, and was denied again. One night while I was working midnight shift, my squad sergeant, still harassing me, called around 3 AM and told me to report to the Lowell post. Upon my arrival, he asked if I would sign a statement promising to remain a trooper for three years if I were given a leave of absence. I told him to draw up the contract, and I would sign it. Then he took back the offer, claiming it would set a bad precedent. I am certain there never was an intent of such offer; it was just harassment.

I was so disgusted and furious I told the squad sergeant that the contract would not have been valid anyway since indentured servitude had been outlawed a long time ago. The sergeant was so angry with me that he took off his clip tie and unbuttoned his collar. I wouldn't have been surprised if he had taken a swing at me, but at least I had the final word and lived up to my parents' teaching not to permit others to disrespect me.

Now I had a decision to make. Exams were coming up, and I was woefully unprepared. Law school had a whole new jargon and required much reading in order to comprehend the relevant issues in the cases examined in class. My writing skills weren't the greatest either. When I turned in my first assignment, which was worth 20 points, I thought I had done well. When the instructor posted the scores for the 165 first-year students, they ranged from 3 to 19. I got a 3 and was devastated, but I worked harder and was even more determined to succeed.

## LEAVING THE STATE POLICE

Contemplating my options, I thought how my parents weren't quitters and what my grandfather had told me about getting an education. Betty was the first one I talked to about leaving the state police. For her it was a no-brainer. She told me to stay in school if that was my dream and that we'd make it by scrimping on her salary. My brothers and sisters offered moral and financial support. Still, resigning from the state police was terribly difficult. I loved being a trooper and had planned to have a lifetime career in its legal division. I was twenty-five years old but not ashamed to say I shed tears agonizing over the decision. In the end it came down to deciding that I couldn't go through life remaining a trooper and wondering "what if I had completed law school."

With a heavy heart I submitted a letter of resignation to the State Police, a career I had long coveted. As difficult as that was, it was time to explore new adventures in life. I never understood why my superiors were so negative about my pursuit of education. This decision was a huge personal gamble because of the law school's high first-year dropout rate. Getting through that first year was going to be rough, even with the extra time to devote to it. I had much catching up to do. I studied every day and every night and barely passed my first-semester exams. During the second semester my grades improved. I was determined to work hard to pass. In law school the only exams were given at the end of each semester, so whether one passed or failed came down to that single test.

In order to continue, one needed a seventieth percentile or better to pass, and professors were not generous with grades. An estimated one-third of the class would not be returning. Fortunately some classmates welcomed me into their study group. One was a bright fellow named Mark Bailey. I was in the law library searching for a book and feeling overwhelmed when Mark said to me out of the blue, "Do you want to work on the project together?" He didn't need my help and clearly was lending me a hand. From Decatur County, he had a southern Indiana drawl and wore cowboy boots. We became great friends before he transferred to IU Law School in Indianapolis.

Another member of the study group, Julia Jent, later became a Porter County Superior Court judge. Born in Germany, she was orphaned at age two after her father died and her mother abandoned her. Adopted by a serviceman, she grew up in Texas. After dropping out of high school, she joined the army and later moved to northwest Indiana. She received her GED from the Portage Adult Education program and graduated from IU Northwest. Her middle name was Margarete, and we called her Marge. She was a great classmate and remains a dear friend of mine.

Valparaiso Law School had an excellent faculty. Professor Charles Gromley, who taught property and trusts and estates, was revered by students and very approachable. During the period when I was deciding whether or not to stay in school, he walked me through the options and was encouraging. Professor Gromley was a quiet fellow, but once in the classroom, he lit up like he was on stage and was quite captivating. I have tried to emulate him when speaking to audiences, in terms of being informative and engaging.

Professor Paul Brietzke, who taught contracts, was tough and somewhat terrifying in the classroom, employing the Socratic method as he drilled students about cases we supposedly had studied. He taught in a style reminiscent of John Houseman as Professor Kingsfield in the 1973 movie *Paper Chase*. He even wore a bow tie. I'd sit in the back row and keep my head down to avoid his gaze. One day, looking straight at me, he went down his roster searching for Spanish surnames. First he called out "Mendoza," who was absent. Then he tried "Garcia," who thankfully was present. He probably passed over Rogelio Dominguez because the others were easier to pronounce, but had Garcia been absent I probably would have been next because there were just three students with Spanish surnames in the class. That was the closest I came to being called on by Professor Brietzke.

Professor Ivan Bodensteiner taught civil procedure, a tough subject to grasp and not as interesting as, say, torts or property, but he was a great professor and more easygoing in the classroom than those who had you stand up and be grilled. During my second year I signed up for Professor Rosalie Levinson's constitutional law class. She was so intelligent, excellent, and popular that our class selected her as our class adviser.

There were student groups representing African American, women, Jewish, and Christian law students, and others. I joined the International Law Society, which put together a forum on human rights. Thanks to the training from IU Northwest Professor Camille Schuster, I had a hand in organizing it.

I decided a Latino law student association might encourage more Latino college graduates to apply and then help mentor them and ease their adjustment to the rigors of law school. The only trouble was that there were only two Latino second-year law students, myself and Tonatzin Garcia, whose parents had been migrant workers before settling permanently in Michigan. (Mendoza, who had been called upon by Professor Brietzke, had not returned for the second year.)

With Marge Jent listening nearby, I said to Tonatzin Garcia, "Look, I'll be the president, you can be vice president, and Marge can be secretary-treasurer. People won't know that there's only three of us." Of German descent, Marge loved the idea and agreed to join. Interested in promoting diversity, the Law School dean was very supportive.

In the winter of 1981, for our annual presentation the Latino Law Students staged a debate between Ivan Bodensteiner and Lake County Superior Court judge James Letsinger. Bodensteiner had written an article that had attracted much publicity, criticizing the State of Indiana for not adequately funding the office of public defender compared to resources available to prosecutors. In his opinion, this tipped the scales against indigents who could not afford to hire their own attorney. Thus, innocent defendants got convicted due to inadequate funding and resources. Bodensteiner himself represented poor people, but he knew from experience that many were shortchanged in terms of the quality of legal representation.

Judge Letsinger was a conservative, no-nonsense guy who expected lawyers to be well prepared. Otherwise he literally dismissed them from his courtroom. Having known him from my days as a state trooper, I asked what he thought of Bodensteiner's article. He strongly disagreed with it. That was just what I was hoping to hear. I asked if he'd participate in our debate forum, and he replied, "Of course I'll do it, Roy." So we put up posters, contacted the media, and notified interested people. The response was overwhelming. Here we were, just three of us, and our presentation surpassed all of the other student organizations' presentations. And sparks flew, at least in one direction. Bodensteiner was methodical and scholarly, but Letsinger was quite confrontational at times. At one point, suggesting Bodensteiner lived in an ivory tower, he said, "You're in the classroom, and I'm in the courtroom." Bodensteiner answered him saying, "I do both."

In short, both forum participants were prepared and eloquently advocated their respective opinions and arguments. We law students were honored and at the conclusion gave them a vigorous round of applause. The press covered the forum, and it received a good deal of notoriety. The law school was pleased with how well it went and the media attention it brought to the university.

My second year of law school was rewarding because I had the time to read and prepare for class. I wasn't always tired, and thanks to the love and support from my wife, Betty, and Mom and Dad and the rest of the family, I was still in law school. I didn't work my second year, so I had more time to study and enjoy law school life. Then Betty became pregnant with our first child. I considered quitting law school and going to work to support my family, but Betty and others close to me insisted that I stay in school, and they helped financially.

Betty kept working as a probation officer. We didn't have extra money, but we survived. Of course, abortion was never a consideration or discussed as an option. Children are always a blessing, planned or unplanned. We had one car that Betty drove to work. I walked about a mile to law school. I ate at home and kept two dollars a day for coffee and snacks. I left for school at 8 AM and returned home for dinner with Betty. Then it was back to school until 10 or 11 PM.

In May of 1981, I finished my second year and started as a law clerk to a local attorney for the summer. Betty was five and a half months pregnant, and she and the baby were in good health. Then a month later Betty said to me that for the past few hours she had not felt the baby move or kick. I immediately drove her to the hospital, where her doctor met us. Betty was rushed in and tests were taken. Betty and I waited nervously in the ER until her doctor joined us. He informed us that the umbilical cord had severed from the baby, and she was not alive.

Words cannot express our grief and loss. Our baby girl, whom we named Sabrina Marie, was delivered stillborn. I had an opportunity to see her; she was beautiful and had more of Betty's Filipino features and shiny pitch-black straight hair. Betty's mom and dad came in from Clearwater, Florida, and her sister Evelyn as well, to help Betty recuperate physically and emotionally. They stayed with us for about a month and were godsends. My side of the family was equally supportive. Telling them of the loss was amongst the hardest things I ever did. To this day, Betty and I get a feeling of loss in our hearts when we think of our baby Sabrina.

During this time I felt really bad because I had no money for a proper burial for Sabrina. As fate would have it, my sister Maria knew the Rendina family – yes, those giant Italian church ushers back at Holy Rosary Church who ran a funeral home. When they heard what happened, they graciously offered their services free of charge, including funeral parlor, services, casket, limo – everything. My family and I will always cherish the Rendina family's generosity toward us. I had to pay $125 to Calumet Cemetery for a plot and valet services. I didn't have the money, so my sister Maria paid it. Yes, she still was our protector. I must say – family first.

After barely surviving my first year of law school, the grades steadily improved, and by the time I graduated I was ranked in the upper third of my graduating class. I decided to take the bar exam in February of my third year, even though most students wait until after graduation, so I would be better able to find a job ahead of those who waited until the summer. Typically more than 90 percent of those taking the exam pass, but in my group a third failed. Fortunately I was among the 66 percent who passed, thank God. For you see, upon graduation in May of 1982, I would be ahead of graduating law students who were waiting to take the bar exam in July and, if successful, would have to wait until October to be sworn in as new attorneys. This way I was in a better position to apply for employment. It went back to Mom and Dad's ethics of hard work and being prepared that have always been valued lessons. Upon learning of my successful bar exam, my state trooper friend Bob Rogers came over to the house with a bottle of cognac and we drank a toast in celebration. Betty and I were overwhelmed with jubilation.

With the law on your side, great things are possible.

Motto of the National Women's Law Center

Too many children find themselves in traumatic, unhealthy, and unsafe circumstances in which their lives are put at risk.

GOVERNOR JOSEPH E. KERNAN, September 2004, Indiana Child Welfare Policy Manual

SIX

# Advances and Setbacks

*In the spring of 1984 while campaigning to become the Democratic candidate for Congress in Indiana's First District, prosecutor Jack Crawford one evening after attending Hispanic, Greek, and Polish social functions jokingly said at the end of the day with his Irish twang, "Hey, Dominguez, are we going anywhere tomorrow where they speak English?" Like me, he loved the ethnic diversity of northwest Indiana.*

## PROSECUTOR'S OFFICE

After I passed the law board examination and was admitted to the Indiana "Roll of Attorneys" on June 4, 1982, I applied for work as a deputy prosecutor at the Lake County prosecutor's office. My primary goal was to get back into law enforcement and to gain valuable experience as a trial attorney.

In July of 1982 and prior to my interview with prosecutor Jack Crawford, I was sitting in his anteroom. Joanne Gerrard, whom I had met as a state trooper, had an appointment to see the prosecutor and asked what I was doing there. She was the prosecutor's county courts clerk/supervisor. Upon learning that I was applying for a job, she promised to put in a good reference for me. After she came out of Jack Crawford's office, she said, "I spoke up for you and hope you get the job. And, by the way," she added, "if the subject of baseball comes up, the prosecutor is a Chicago White Sox fan." Not realizing the practical importance of her advice, I said, "OK."

During the interview Jack Crawford and his chief deputy, Joe Curosh, asked me questions pertaining to law enforcement, my legal training, and my job expectations. As the interview was drawing to a close, Crawford said, "Dominguez, I just want to know one last thing, are you a Cubs or a Sox fan?" Remembering Joanne's advice, I replied, "Mr. Prosecutor, of course I'm a Sox fan." "You're hired," he exclaimed. Turning to Joe Curosh, whom I found out later was a Cubs fan, he said, "He starts Monday." In the days to come, recalling my parents' belief that an honorable person does his best and sees things through to the end, I made certain that he didn't regret the decision.

The entry position for incoming attorneys in the prosecutor's office was to handle minor cases in the county courts division, misdemeanors and Class D felonies – things like trespass, theft, public intoxication, driving under the influence – rather than serious violent offenses. It was a training ground for new lawyers, an opportunity to gain valuable legal experience.

In fact, Joanne Gerrard trained more new lawyers in the actual practice of law than any one person I know. Our legal supervisor, Bob Neumaier, had been a deputy prosecutor in Porter County and tended to the overall operation while Joanne organized most of the day-to-day details. Bob was an outstanding supervisor – knowledgeable and dedicated to helping us learn trial strategies and other practical instructions necessary to be a competent lawyer.

## IN COURT

My first bench trial was a DUI case in Judge Orville Anderson's court. I was nervous enough to begin with, but opposing me was renowned local attorney Nick Thiros, famous for defending members of the Family drug gang and Leonard Smith, indicted for shooting California Angels baseball star Lyman Bostock in 1978. Smith suspected his wife of infidelity and when he saw her in the back seat of a car with Bostock, he did not realize that they had met only twenty minutes before and had no intention of pursuing a sexual relationship. Smith claimed he had fired at his wife and that the bullet struck Bostock, in the right temple, by mistake. He died two hours later. Amazingly, in view of the evidence, Thiros convinced a jury to find his client not guilty by reason of insanity. Smith was released after being under psychiatric observation for twenty-one months. The Indiana legislature subsequently changed the insanity statute as a result of the case and created the charge of "guilty but mentally ill."

At our bench trial the courtroom was packed as Nick Thiros began attacking the reliability of Breathalyzer tests. One of his ways of intimidating opposing counsel, especially me, a young deputy prosecutor with no prior trial experience, was to scowl and lower his voice into almost a growl. If he could get an adversary to get rattled and stumble during his presentation, he could gain an edge on him that translated into a favorable verdict. Nick's client had prior DUIs, and another conviction would cause him to lose his driver's license for a number of years and possibly face prison time.

Due to my training as a state trooper and a licensed Breathalyzer operator, I was familiar with police operations as well as precedents that upheld their results as evidence in court. I had prepared the case diligently and subpoenaed witnesses who testified that the defendant was drunk shortly before a police officer had pulled him over. Judge Anderson ruled in our favor. The defendant was arrogant and just flouted his disregard for the law. Stuck with a bad client and bad facts, Nick didn't have much to work with. The judge found the defendant guilty of the charges. Securing a conviction was an enormous confidence booster and what a relief! After the case Nick became a dear friend. He was a true gentleman and one of the best legal counsels around in criminal cases. In December of 2010, Nick was suffering from cancer and wheelchair-bound. I had an occasion to see him and thanked him for his friendship and for being a role model for me. He died shortly thereafter.

My first jury trial was also a DUI, this time in Judge Steven Bielak's courtroom. The opposing attorney, public defender John Halcarz, was an exemplary, experienced adversary who did everything he could for his client, as every lawyer must do. I secured a conviction. Again, opposing counsel was stuck with a difficult client and bad facts. Even though there is a competitive animosity during trials, John was a gentleman who treated everyone with respect. Around the courthouse everyone fondly referred to him behind his back as "Hoss" after the favored son in the television series *Bonanza.* Given his build, demeanor, and endearing temperament, the nickname fit perfectly. John, who recently passed away, was highly respected and a great role model for many of us young lawyers.

The overwhelming majority of cases ended up being resolved by a plea bargain agreement. Our superiors handled that process but often based their decision on our recommendation. During the discovery process defense lawyers would size up the soundness of our case and seek a plea bargain agreement if fearful of losing in court. In marginal DUI cases and first offenses and where there had been no accident or injury, charges often were reduced to reckless driving, with the recommended sentence including a fine and mandatory attendance at an alcohol counseling program. With such a high volume of DUI arrests in Lake County, the system would have come to a standstill otherwise.

During this time a federal investigation dubbed Operation Bar Tap was under way that ultimately resulted in two judges going to jail along with a couple of their bailiffs and the county clerk on federal charges for making false statements to a grand jury. What had been happening, the U.S. attorney discovered, was that in certain cases where bribery was involved, records of DUI convictions were not forwarded to the Indiana Bureau of Motor Vehicles. As a result, guilty offenders were able to retain their licenses and be on the road, a potential menace given their proclivities toward alcohol consumption.

After about eighteen months I was transferred to the felony division. When vacancies occurred, Bob Neumaier would seek Joanne Gerrard's advice. The promotion was like going from triple-A to the major leagues. I was assigned to Superior Court judge James L. Clement's courtroom under the supervision of Jimmy Olszewski, a great teacher who gave his protégés leeway once they gained his confidence. He'd advise you what to look for in a case, how you might want to try it, what evidence to employ, when to introduce it, and so forth. It was a great opportunity to acquire invaluable legal skills.

The two public defenders assigned to Judge Clement's court, Lou Holcomb and Herb Shapps, were impressive lawyers with years of experience. They took their work seriously and had our respect. If they made an agreement you could count on them keeping it, something vitally important in situations where your word was your bond.

Once, Herb Shapps and I were sparring over a legal motion having to do with the admissibility of certain evidence. Being a seasoned veteran, Herb had a methodical manner, whereas I as a rookie was more emotional in my delivery. At one point Judge Clement asked us both to approach the bench, and we continued our legal argument. Herb said something that got my goat, and without realizing what I was doing, I started pounding my fist on the bench, saying, "No, he can't do that." Judge Clement calmly leaned over to me and in a stately manner said, "Settle down. I can hear you." In other words, gather your wits about you. Knowing he had gotten to me, Herb was smiling like the cat that had just swallowed the canary. Gentleman that he was, he patted me on the back and said, "You're learning."

Judge Clement taught me a valuable lesson about controlling one's emotions and maintaining a professional demeanor. This is especially important for prosecuting attorneys since criminals may go free if you don't control your spirit. You are not made of stone but don't want felons to be set free by virtue of your losing your composure. Sometimes apparent miscarriages of justice occur, but it is important for opposing attorneys to realize that they are a vital part of the process. First, someone in the prosecutor's office decides whether or not to take the case. Then comes the question of whether to work out a plea bargain or go to trial.

Anyone who believes he can second-guess a jury is doomed to failure. I had a murder case, for example, that at the last minute ended in a plea agreement. I was well prepared to do battle, and then others reached a compromise. Once you get a conviction, it is up to the judge to determine the sentence. The defense attorney will argue why there might be mitigating circumstances, and you may point out aggravating factors.

## JACK CRAWFORD AND POLITICS

One day out of the blue in the spring of 1984 Jack Crawford said, "Hey, Dominguez, do you like politics?" When I had been a state trooper, I was required to be nonpolitical, but, remembering my experiences with my parents and past campaigns on behalf of Fred Work for judge and Adam Benjamin Jr. for Congress, I replied, "Absolutely!" He asked if I wanted to accompany him on some of his campaign appearances, and

I said, "I'd love to. Thanks for the invite." He was running for Congress in what turned out to be the most exciting First District House race in many decades.

Amazingly, two years out of law school, and I am campaigning with one of the most powerful, brightest, highly charged, energetic politicians, a star of the Lake County Democrats. A graduate of Notre Dame and Indiana University Law School, where he had been law review editor, he was soft on the eyes, as some women would say, and had an intelligent, attractive, and wonderful wife, Ann, and two sons. From my mom I had learned what it was like to be one of the frontline troops. Now from Jack I gained valuable lessons on how an elected official applies himself on the campaign circuit and is always professional.

I saw how politics requires enormous energy, patience, dedication, and hard work. On the way to a special gathering, he'd say, "Roy, did you ever hear of this club?" Then he'd tell me some things about its mission, how long it had been in existence, or what particular thing they were celebrating that day. He'd be preparing and practicing for when he'd be asked to say a few words. "Always have a few paragraphs prepared in your mind," he'd say.

In other words, Jack gave me tips and taught by example. He'd know the leaders by name and recall little anecdotes about them, so they'd give him a warm introduction. Then the audience would conclude, "If our club leaders like Jack, then we do, too." If someone had a problem, he'd promise to look into it and make sure someone on his staff followed up on it the next day. At informal community events, such as a high school basketball game, even if he didn't speak and deliberately avoided being the center of attention, the message he was conveying was "I'm glad to be here with you and proud to be your prosecutor."

Jack taught me the importance of tolerance toward critics. Public officials need to respect people's emotions even when they believe those people are misguided or simply wrong. He reminded me of IU Northwest chief Andy Lazar, a real gentleman. He was masterful at deflating potentially confrontational situations. He'd listen to gripes, and often the other person would walk away feeling, "At least he respects my views." Politics is a combative field, especially in Lake County, and loyalties run deep. To someone supporting a rival, Jack would say, "That's fine" or "Maybe next time." He didn't travel with an entourage, so people could approach him. He'd say, "Just talk to me. And call me Jack." I learned from that. If you make people comfortable, they'll be more likely to tell you their likes and dislikes and offer advice.

Elected officials, Jack believed, needed to be accessible to people in all walks of life and all parts of the county or district they represented. He'd say, "OK, Roy, we were in Whiting and East Chicago yesterday, let's go to Gary and Lake Station today." And so on. That made him a better public servant because he'd learn his constituents' concerns, whether they were about juvenile problems, drugs, domestic violence, alcohol abuse, or whatever.

In short, Jack Crawford was an awesome mentor. From him I learned the importance of assembling an organization that brings together people of diverse talents, religious backgrounds, and racial and ethnic origins. He reinforced my respect for the value of public service and the importance of communication skills. He was a great orator without being a demagogue and could convey his ideas clearly both in public settings and to individuals. Public figures need to be careful with words and resist the temptation to exaggerate or make promises they cannot keep. Otherwise, unfortunate things may happen such as hurt feelings or a contempt for governmental officials.

## 1984 CONGRESSIONAL DEMOCRATIC PRIMARY

Jack was very confident in 1984, but his opponents had strong support bases. Incumbent Katie Hall had served in the Indiana General Assembly for eight years before being appointed the Democratic nominee following the sudden death of Congressman Adam Benjamin in September of 1982. Nobody worked harder on behalf of his constituents than Adam, and it was sad but ironic that his heart attack occurred at night when he was working at his office on behalf of his constituents. He was a dedicated family man. How fortunate the First District was to have Adam Benjamin serve them, and how tragic that his time on earth was so short.

The three party congressional district officials who made the selection of Benjamin's successor consisted of Gary mayor Richard Gordon

Hatcher, East Chicago mayor Robert Pastrick, and Mary Cartwright, who worked for Crawford. Both Pastrick and Crawford had hoped to be the candidate, as did the widow of Adam Benjamin, but Hatcher held out for Hall, who became the first African American woman member of Congress from Indiana. For the final tally Mayor Hatcher convinced Crawford to have his assistant Mary Cartwright cast her vote for Katie Hall. Hall solidified her support among African Americans by playing a major role in making Martin Luther King Day a national holiday.

Peter Visclosky entered the 1984 contest as the perceived long shot, seemingly without adequate money or a strong base, as the city of Hammond provided for Crawford (where he had been a city judge) and the city of Gary for Congresswoman Hall. Formerly a staffer for Benjamin, "Pete" mobilized support from the old Gary guard, Club SAR mainstays who had moved to Merrillville and other points south. His father had been interim mayor of Gary after popular mayor George Chacharis had gone to prison after a plea bargain that spared friends and relatives from prosecution. Of Slovak and Croatian descent, Visclosky had strong support amongst Eastern Europeans, who were indisposed to support "that Irishman Jack Crawford," as some would indelicately state it. Pete also could claim to be the natural successor to the hardworking Benjamin and was a dogged campaigner, setting out on foot and knocking on doors for hours on end.

Crawford's senior advisers urged him to concentrate his efforts in Hammond. The idea was, if he could garner a high plurality there, it would offset his opponents' advantages in Gary and Merrillville and among Slavic Europeans. I was in the room during these discussions but not a political strategist. Jack refused to write off Gary or the white ethnics and continued to campaign throughout the First District, including Porter and LaPorte counties, where he was not well known. He wanted to demonstrate that as a good public official he would represent all his constituents. That strategy had worked for him in the past, but perhaps this time he should have followed his advisers' advice of a more strategic vote campaign.

The race was close, and Jack probably could have beaten either opponent in a two-way race (Katie Hall had received only 56 percent of the vote in the 1982 general election against a weak Republican opponent), but he came in third, with less than 4,000 fewer votes than winner Visclosky. Losing was difficult for Jack, and some county politicians took great joy in his defeat because he was so high-powered and threatening to traditional power alliances. He genuinely wanted to be a congressman and gave it his best, but it wasn't in the cards. He never gave any thought to challenging Visclosky two years later. It took some time for political wounds to heal between Crawford and Hatcher, but the two men were professionals and maintained a mutual respect.

Visclosky's people were always friendly toward me, and I reciprocated, even though the campaign got heated. Some Crawford supporters wondered, "What's that about?" Just because you are campaigning for one person against another, that doesn't mean you're enemies. It doesn't have to get personal. Like my dad, I think being a gentleman is important.

Hispanics had voted for Jack in a big way. Katie Hall didn't attend Hispanic functions, and Visclosky stopped coming when he saw the handwriting on the wall. If it wasn't for Hispanics' strong support, Jack would have been out of the running, and he thanked me for helping mobilize those voters. In fact, when Jack ran for reelection as prosecutor, he asked me to be his campaign manager. I guess he felt I'd learned something about politics, and we became good friends.

So it went from, "Hey, Roy, do you like politics?" to "Hey, Roy, how about being my campaign manager?" I was honored, and we worked hard, getting Jack back on the campaign circuit. He thoroughly enjoyed being with people and repaired most of the wounds of the previous campaign. In the end he ran unopposed. He said, "Roy, you did a great job." I replied, "Jack, all I did was get you out there being Jack." He was a natural, a compelling figure who loved serving people and promoted good government.

## GUILLAIN-BARRÉ AND ITS IMPACT

In June of 1983, within a year after starting at the prosecutor's office, I became afflicted with an illness called Guillain-Barré, a neurological disorder that adversely affects the immune system. Antibodies that normally attack invading organisms instead turn on one's own nervous system. Like polio or multiple sclerosis, Guillain-Barré causes muscle deterioration and can lead to paralysis. Some believe it is caused by a virus or in reaction to shots such as vaccinations. It may remain in remission for years before striking without warning. The disease is rare but has afflicted such notables as actor Andy Griffith, former presidential daughter Luci Baines Johnson, and former Chicago Bears football lineman William "The Refrigerator" Perry.

Suddenly my muscles started betraying me. I had no idea what was wrong with me, but before long my limbs were affected so badly I could hardly walk more than a few hundred feet and couldn't even write my name or serve myself. It was a nightmare, and I could not have gotten through it without the love and help that Betty and my family provided.

My family doctor, Dr. Rodolfo Jao, a board-certified internal medicine specialist and longtime friend of Betty's family, recommended the Mayo Clinic, and I was there for about a month. They diagnosed the disease, put me on very heavy medication, and instituted a program of physical therapy that involved, among other things, walking on uneven ground and up and down stairs. They wanted me to put on stiff plastic braces that one wore underneath one's pants and socks. I balked because it reminded me too much of what my brother Jesse went through with polio. I did agree to a cane, however, which I continued to use for about five years.

I took mega-doses of prednisone for about three years and reduced amounts for two years more. At the beginning I took 180 milligrams of prednisone every other day, and later reduced dosages. The medication caused my weight to balloon and for me to become easily agitated when I'd fall down or not be able to do simple things like eat soup with a spoon. Those were the dark days because Betty and I were ready to start a family and I was embarking on my legal career when suddenly the future was uncertain, to say the least. Through it all, my employer, prosecutor Jack Crawford, was very compassionate. Betty and my family helped me through this difficult time of my life. My sister Maria, who knew I was very ill, cried for me and was equally very supportive.

I reflected on my illness and its possible consequences and challenges. At this point in my life I was twenty-nine years old, apparently in great physical condition, with a good job and ready to start a family, and then like a tornado I was crippled by this awful disease Guillain-Barré. I didn't even know how to pronounce this French-named illness. It was tough to understand why, but I didn't let it control me. Rather I decided early on to deal with the physical limitations and the effects of the medication. I felt that this was a challenge in life and resolved to live life to its fullest. That is still my motivating philosophy. I was determined then and now to lead an "inspired" life – not just for me but for my family, friends, and those I serve as a public servant.

For a period of time I wanted to get physically back to where I was before the symptoms struck. It was tough coming to grips with having subpar reflexes, not being able to go jogging, and having to be constantly aware of maintaining my limited balance due to muscle loss, but I lived through it and felt blessed to be alive. Obviously, a lot of family prayer and faith helped. I've always been an optimist and believe that positive people are the ones who achieve things in life and respond to challenges. Later, perhaps seeing my sister suffering so with leukemia made me cease feeling sorry for myself and look forward, not backward, blessed to be alive.

When I realized I had been challenging myself too much and had set my expectations too high, I started enjoying life again. The disease affects everyone differently, but with treatment I was able to regain 80 to 90 percent of my former physical abilities. The Guillain-Barré went into remission, but I remained mindful not to overextend myself. I still have a slight tremor in my hands and pain in my feet, due to the neuropathy and atrophy. Some days I might walk with a limp because the neuropathy is greater than usual. I accommodate myself in subtle ways not noticeable to those who aren't aware of my condition. I might lean against the wall or a chair. My immediate staff makes sure I'm comfortable without fanfare. I appreciate their kindness and am thankful for their compassion but don't want people to treat me as if I'm handicapped or disabled.

Surviving a serious disability will build character, but I wouldn't wish Guillain-Barré on anyone. I believe the experience taught me patience, compassion, and a sense of perspective in dealing calmly with potentially combative situations. It tested but did not destroy my faith in realizing my dreams of family and public service.

## DAUGHTER VERONICA

Betty and I tried to start a family after I finished law school, but she had some health problems that obstructed her ability to get pregnant. While at the Mayo Clinic, I asked whether the illness would affect my ability to procreate and if there was a chance the disease could be passed on to offspring. I was relieved to find that the answer in both cases was no. The first week in Minnesota I was an outpatient, and Betty stayed with me at a local hotel in Rochester, Minnesota. During that time, we figured out later, our daughter Veronica was conceived. So there was a silver lining to this ordeal, and the discovery that Betty was pregnant brought us joy at this very difficult time.

With the advent of the ultrasound we decided not to be informed of the gender of our baby. As the due date drew near, Betty's parents arrived from Florida. They were godsends and much appreciated. Betty told her doctor, Yung Roc Kim, that a Caesarian delivery might be best. He recommended natural childbirth, however, so Betty agreed. On June 29, 1984, Betty's water bag broke, and her parents took her to Methodist Hospital in Merrillville, where I met them. Dr. Kim examined her and predicted that the labor shouldn't take very long. He was sorely mistaken.

During the next twenty-two hours of labor Betty was in much pain and discomfort. Finally Dr. Kim told Betty, "I think we better do a C-section." Raising her voice in anger, Betty retorted, "That's what I said in the beginning." I thought luckily for Dr. Kim, he was a safe distance from Betty's grasp. Before leaving to inform Betty's parents, I conveniently told Dr. Kim, "I don't think you need me anymore. She's all yours. Take great care of Betty and the baby, doctor. I'll wait in the father's room."

Veronica came into this world around 1 PM on June 30, 1984. When aides wheeled her out to the father's waiting room in an incubator, I marveled at her pitch-black hair and big brown eyes, and how alert she seemed, as if she were looking all over the place. Later in the maternity ward, Betty's mother said to us, "Well, you make beautiful babies. Make more." We hoped to have another, but it probably was not something Betty wanted to hear at that moment.

While in the recovery room Betty said, "Let's name the baby Veronica." I had favored Celena but didn't argue with her. Needless to say,

I was at a severe disadvantage, so Betty prevailed. Our daughter's full name was Veronica Celena Olayta Dominguez. We thanked God for a healthy baby. Betty's parents stayed with us for about a month and were a great help. Betty's mother gave Veronica her first bath. Betty's sister Evelyn, who is very personable, helpful, and caring, came as well.

Betty took an unpaid leave from her job and stayed home for about eighteen months. The following Christmas, we visited Betty's folks in Florida, and Veronica was doted over. Dealing with Guillain-Barré in the ensuing years, I believe Veronica's presence helped me stay focused in doing my best to overcome the effects of the disease. It was one more motivation to pursue life and give it my best.

### *EL CHORRITOS*

In 1985 we visited my eighty-year-old grandmother Vicenta in Texas. She knew I was very ill and wanted to take me on a pilgrimage to a religious shrine near her hometown of Ricé and on the outskirts of Monterrey, Mexico, called the Virgin Mary of *El Chorritos,* meaning small waterfall. According to legend, the Spanish conquistadores were intending to slaughter the local Indians who refused to convert to Catholicism. The night before, the village Catholic priest entered a cave by the waterfall and prayed for a miracle. Miraculously, an apparition of the Virgin Mary appeared. The image was engraved on one of the stalagmites. Before dawn the next morning the padre warned the Spanish soldiers not to kill the natives because of the saintly appearance. This was sacred ground and their souls would be condemned to hell if they did so. Ever since, people with serious illnesses have visited the shrine in hopes of being cured.

Grandma Vicenta arranged for her younger brother, my great-uncle Natalio Castillo, a Mexican national, to take us by bus from McAllen, Texas, an American-Mexican border city, to the industrial city of Monterrey, Mexico, and then to the shrine in an outlying village. The bus ride took six hours, and from time to time farmers came aboard with chickens and goats. Sitting in the back, I felt miserable and looked very ill, with yellowish eyes and my face swollen round like the moon from the megadoses of medicine. After we transferred to another bus in Monterrey, the paved roads gradually narrowed as we ascended the mountain until it was just gravel and then a dirt walking path. The feeling was like going back in time two hundred years. The area had not been modernized, and Indians lived in grass huts. They had on native attire and lived as depicted in many movies. We did not bother them and heeded warnings not to photograph them.

At *El Chorritos* we knelt in front of the shrine, and my grandmother led us in prayer, lit candles, and took my cane and left it there after praying that I'd be restored to health. During the long ride my grandmother told me for the first time about her youth. Her mother had died shortly after she was born, and an aunt raised her. Her father was a traveling musician, a Don Juan with lovers and families in several localities, who had been a captain in Pancho Villa's army. One day when Vicenta was in her early teens, her dad took her and the aunt to Mercedes, Texas, to live with other relatives. Soon afterward, his philandering and gambling got him in trouble, and he was shot and killed in a Mexican cantina.

## OLDER SISTER MARIA VIRGINIA

In 1984 my sister Maria was diagnosed with leukemia, and she died eighteen months later at the age of thirty-six. That was very painful for our family, and it was a tremendous loss and emotionally difficult for all of us.

Maria was a beautiful person in both appearance and personality. She was like Adela, my dad's older sister, our family's role model, and like Mom, our leader and protector. Maria showed us class, dignity, and zeal for life and had many close friends who loved her. In fact, she and Mom were best of friends and had a great relationship. Indeed, when necessary, she looked out for Mom as well as the rest of us. In 1974 she married Carlos Mangual, and in 1981 their daughter Amanda was born. When she was diagnosed with leukemia, daughter Amanda was approximately two and a half years old. Maria underwent chemo treatment, and it was a dark period for our family as we became aware of this deadly disease and its symptoms.

Family and her many friends all cared for Maria during her battle with leukemia – especially her two close friends, Louisa Montemayor and Nana Navarro. They tended to Maria's needs in such a devoted manner that she considered them her worldly sisters. Maria fought the illness with all her might for the opportunity to live and see her daughter Amanda grow up. Now four-year-old Amanda knew her mom was sick and always asked, "Mommy, when are you coming home?" Crying, Maria would hold her and tell her how much she loved her.

For all of us, seeing Maria hospitalized from time to time was so difficult and caused a great deal of heartfelt sorrow. We all cried and prayed for her. She fought hard to live and would give an outward appearance of strength for us, but it was devastating to observe her health deteriorate.

About ten days before Maria died, I went to see her late at night at Methodist Hospital in Merrillville. As I approached the room, I could hear her screaming and yelling at the hospital staff that she had suffered long enough. The machines and pain had become unbearable. It had been eighteen months, and she knew she was going to die because she wasn't getting better. Her family, she said, had to understand that and let her go. As I entered the room, she was trying to get out of her bed, with her arms flailing and legs kicking. The hospital staff members were trying to hold her gently, some with tears in their eyes.

When Maria saw me enter the room, she immediately stopped crying and struggling and calmly turned and looked at me as if nothing was wrong. That was my sister Maria being strong for me, despite her despair of dying. She assured me she was going to make it, but we knew otherwise. I stayed with her all night, and we cried and cried. The hospital staff left us alone except to make routine checkups and to administer medicine.

After eighteen months of chemo and other invasive measures to battle the leukemia, Maria was exhausted, thin, and fragile, she had lost her hair, and her body was shutting down. The doctors cried silently, and Mom cried loudly asking why God had not taken care of Maria. Dad embraced her and did what he could to console her. Dad would recall the emotional difficulties of never having the loving touch of his mother, and now Amanda would have to experience the loss of a mother's love and touch.

Realizing the end was near, we informed family members in Oklahoma and Texas. Our uncle Pablo drove our maternal grandparents up to northwest Indiana from Weslaco, Texas. Our brother Eloy was in the

U.S. Air Force stationed in Germany, but with the help of the USO, he returned in time to see his sister alive. When these relatives came in to see her, Maria knew her life was coming to an end.

Maria died in November of 1986. The last few days she slipped into a coma, before passing away silently one afternoon. We were all by her bedside. The funeral arrangements were held at Rendina Funeral Home, and the church services were at St. Maria Goretti Church in Dyer. She was buried in Calumet Park Cemetery in Merrillville, Indiana. Our family's fairy-tale life came to a screeching halt. Of course, she had been "daddy's little girl," and Dad went into a deep depression until finally coming to terms with her loss and regaining the desire to live.

As we cared for one another, our greatest concern was Maria's daughter, Amanda. Maria had loved her so much – she was her pride and joy, and the two of them had been inseparable. They would have shared a lifetime of love, and the loss of those opportunities weighed heavy with all of us.

My sister's last request was that Amanda live either with us or Mom and Dad, who had moved into her house in Dyer during the final months. Amanda lived with them until her father remarried. From then on, he made it very difficult for us to see Amanda, and it was very traumatic for all of us. Fortunately, at the time an Indiana statute awarded grandparents certain visitation rights, and we were able to include Amanda in many family outings despite roadblocks put in our way. Amanda now has four kids, lives in Gary, and is in close touch, allowing me to play the role of doting uncle to her children. I'm very much the "fifth child" who looks out for everybody. In that regard I would like to think that I pattern myself after Ted Kennedy and the family role he played after his brothers died.

## DAUGHTER MARIA

Maria was born August 23, 1988, five days after Betty's birthday and two before our wedding anniversary. At first I wanted a son, but after my sister died in 1986, I prayed for a girl whom we would name Maria Virginia. Again we chose not to know the child's gender in advance, and I favored the name Diego if it was a boy. The only Diego I had heard of, other than the patron saint of San Diego, was Don Diego de la Vega, the secret identity of the fictional character Zorro (Spanish for "the fox").

This time Dr. Kim raised no objection when Betty insisted on a C-section delivery. April 23 was the last date he could perform the operation before he went on vacation. Maria was born in mid-afternoon and had even more black hair than Veronica and a darker brown complexion – like my mother and Betty. Her demeanor was calm, almost laid back. While we were making a fuss over her in the waiting room, she stared at us as if to demand, "Now settle down. Stop making all this noise." Again Betty's parents stayed with us, and her mom gave Maria her first bath. Veronica, excited over the new addition, immediately took over a big-sister role. She'd get her bottle and alert us when she was crying. As she matured, Maria favored my mom in looks and determination.

## HISPANIC CHAMBER OF COMMERCE

While with the prosecutor's office, I decided to get more involved in community activities. Family friend Francisco Maya had started a Hispanic Chamber of Commerce and convinced me that I didn't have to be a business owner to join. I could work for the aims of the organization, which included community development. Maya wrote a Spanish-language column for the *Post-Tribune* and years before had mentioned my being top cadet in the state police program. His younger brother Felipe was one of my mom's favorite dancing buddies at social functions. Maya had an office on Main Street in Indiana Harbor, so that's where we held our meetings. Afterward, we'd go to a nearby restaurant owned by Vincent Garza to socialize and have something to eat. My old teenage girlfriend Roseanne worked there, and had married Vincent Garza. I was pleased to resume our friendship. She was a wonderful lady.

One night near closing an armed robber entered the Garza restaurant and fired a bullet that struck and killed Roseanne. It was such a tragic way for such a beautiful person in the prime of life to die. She had tons of friends and a loving family. In 1994 I was at a function campaigning for sheriff when a young lady introduced herself to me as Roseanne Garza's daughter. We embraced, and I told her how special her mother had been and how much her friendship had meant to me.

## CHILD SUPPORT DEPUTY DIRECTOR

Between 1985 and 1989 I served as Jack Crawford's deputy director of the child support program. The division comprised approximately two dozen employees, including six lawyers. When I took over, the program was collecting approximately $3 million annually from parents who owed the custodial parents the child support that they were entitled to by law. We revamped the process, streamlined the paperwork, extended the hours, made services more accessible, and within three and a half years were collecting over $10 million annually.

During my tenure the General Assembly made the intentional nonpayment of child support a Class D felony. Congress, meanwhile, passed legislation allowing us to pursue people out of state (we went as far as California to pick up offenders) and to garnish tax refunds until back child support was paid. Furthermore, we also had the administrative power to place a lien on someone's house so they couldn't sell it until they fulfilled their financial responsibilities. We also had the power to report the person to businesses doing credit rating checks, which meant that they might not be able to get a personal loan. I strongly supported these policies because I saw it as a case of child abuse. Coming from my background, I knew how destructive it was for children to go without proper food, clothes, and personal necessities – or to have the embarrassment of not being able to pay the book rental in school.

We were among the first Indiana counties to file criminal charges against so-called deadbeat dads (although in a few cases women owed child support). I instituted a police roundup of people who had outstanding bench warrants for nonpayment of child support. Also for the first time, we issued criminal warrants on certain "deadbeat dads." We organized a special team of police officers throughout Lake County, and at approximately five o'clock one morning they went out and arrested numerous culprits. This police roundup was the first of its kind. In fact, Oprah Winfrey, who was just beginning her rise to fame in nearby Chicago, brought her television crew to the Gary county building and interviewed Jack Crawford live on her morning program.

When people didn't show up for civil hearings or ignored court decrees, we obtained bench warrants for their arrest. One way we rounded them up was to send out bogus notices to their last known address claiming that they had won a prize in a contest and that they should collect it at a certain time at the Merrillville Holiday Inn (now the Radisson). Men from all walks of life showed up, and we filed charges against ten or twelve individuals who we believed had the ability to pay and were intentionally not paying.

Because our program was such a great success, delinquent parents began voluntarily to pay their back child support rather than face arrest. We also publicized the names of those who were still wanted on warrants. This led to anonymous tips on people's whereabouts, and some who were fearful of arrest surrendered themselves.

If someone had a job, we tried to reach an agreement, because the whole idea was to obtain money for the children. If the person failed to live up to his obligations, we could have a judge revoke the agreement and then send the parent to jail. Then the judge would say, "Either agree to a wage assignment or stay in jail." Or the judge could issue a garnishment order. In either case the person's employer would send a portion of the paycheck to the clerk's office, from which it went to the custodial parent.

Sometimes fathers claimed that their spouses were just using the money to go out partying. In that case, we'd say, "OK, why don't you just agree to pay the rent?" Payments were very low, approximately twenty dollars a week, much less than the amount of the rent. Others simply refused to work if part of their earnings went to their estranged custodial parent. In those cases we'd ask the judge to apply what was called "an ability to earn." Each week the judge could demand to know where the person had applied for work and, with payments mounting up, warn that sooner or later he was going to have to pay it.

Jack Crawford thanked me and the staff for the things we had accomplished. I was pleased for the parents who were beginning to receive their back-owed child support and equally pleased that Jack was proud of what we had accomplished. I must say that without a great staff no supervisor can achieve success. It requires that a leader inspire and work as hard as other employees in order to earn their trust and respect. Valued public service stems from such teamwork.

Evan Bayh's tenure as governor was highlighted by: eight years without raising taxes; the largest single tax cut and budget surplus in state history; "welfare-to-work"–type social programs; increasing annual school funding; high academic standards and new college opportunities; the creation of over 350,000 new jobs; strengthened law enforcement; and improved environmental quality.

*SourceWatch.org*

Workers' compensation systems developed as a compromise between employers and employees. The fault-based common law system was abandoned for a system which provides a more expedient administrative remedy in place of civil litigation.

Guide to Indiana Worker's Compensation Handbook

SEVEN

# Evan Bayh and Statewide Office

*During the 1990s my dad, now retired from the mill, wanted to visit my brother, who was in the Air Force and stationed in Spain. When he applied for a passport, immigration officials examined his birth certificate, learned that he'd been born in Mexico, and told him that first he'd have to become a naturalized citizen. Having fought for this country, he wasn't about to go through that process since he was already an American citizen by virtue of his father. It even stated that he was a U.S. citizen on his army discharge papers. So he never received a passport from the government bureaucrat even though Congressman Pete Visclosky's staff tried to help and the county clerk gave him a document attesting that he was a citizen. He was a patriotic American but also proud of his Mexican heritage and wasn't going to beg for what was rightfully his. My father often stated that our ancestors were Americans long before most families came to this country.*

## EVAN BAYH

One day in 1985 Lake County prosecutor Jack Crawford asked if I wanted to meet Evan Bayh, who had decided to run for Indiana secretary of state. He predicted that the son of former senator Birch Bayh was going to be governor and some day run for president. That piqued my interest, so I said, "Let's go."

Five of us met with Evan Bayh at attorney Mike Pannos's office in Merrillville. Pannos was director of the Lake County Voter Registration Board, appointed by County Chairman Robert Pastrick. He had been a staff member for former congressman Ray J. Madden and prominent in the Young Democrats. Also present were attorney Ed Grimmer and bank executive Dave Bochnowski, owner and president of People's Bank in East Chicago, like Pannos with ties to Mayor Pastrick and Evan's father, former Senator Birch Bayh.

Evan was about thirty years old, a first-time candidate. Despite his being untested, I trusted Jack's judgment that Evan had the requisite political abilities. Observing him up close, I concluded that he clearly had the political acumen to run a statewide campaign. He was very intelligent and rather quiet, but he made everyone comfortable. It was a pleasant meeting and represented the beginning of what has become a lifelong esteemed friendship.

What many of us wondered was whether this seemingly untested young man was tough enough to have a chance. Bayh had already decided to run, and we discussed how we could best help him in Lake County. Still, at that time the Republican Party juggernaut looked unbeatable. Under Otis R. Bowen and Robert D. Orr they had held the governorship since 1973. In 1980 they had run Dan Quayle for Senate and defeated Evan's liberal father. With their wealthy backers, an army of patronage jobs (including Bureau of Motor Vehicles employees), and a fine-tuned organization, it was like rakes and shovels going against a well-armed arsenal.

Even so, we were ecstatic to have the opportunity to be part of Evan Bayh's campaign and to get in on the ground floor, so to speak. When he came to Lake County, we'd take him around to various events, advising him of the community groups he'd be speaking to. Sometimes, after Jack introduced him, Evan would say, "Boy, with that introduction I don't know why I need to say anything else now." Sensing that Bayh might be a formidable candidate, the Republicans countered by nominating Rob Bowen, the son of the revered former governor. Perhaps the ploy was a bit too cute for a majority of voters. Confounding the experts, Bayh was elected secretary of state in November 1986. As it turned out he had plenty of campaign savvy and proved to be a consummate campaigner.

Skeptics claimed that the only reason Evan Bayh won was because of his "Daddy," Birch Bayh. Of course, his dad helped in a big way, but on his own merits Evan earned what he achieved. In addition, growing up he had acquired values and learned practical lessons from his father and his mother, who had passed away due to breast cancer. Those who underestimated Evan Bayh, however, were proved wrong, as subsequent campaigns would show.

A year or so later, Jack called me to his office and informed me that Evan Bayh was planning to run for governor. He told me to hang on and got the secretary of state on the speakerphone. We told him we were excited about his gubernatorial candidacy and that he could count on our support. His chief opponent in the Democratic primary was House minority leader Frank O'Bannon, a seasoned politician who believed Bayh should accept running for lieutenant governor on a ticket headed by him. Jack believed Bayh had better name recognition and the experience of having won a statewide contest to his credit and urged both men to settle who should head the ticket without a bloody primary fight.

When Secretary of State Evan Bayh announced his candidacy for governor, it was at the family farm near Terre Haute, Indiana. He was carrying on a tradition started by his father, former senator Birch Bayh, who was masterful in adapting a down-home, "Aw, shucks" persona when the occasion called for it.

One afternoon both candidates were scheduled to appear at a Democratic rally at Wicker Park. Beforehand, the two candidates worked out an arrangement. Bayh would head the ticket and O'Bannon would accept the lieutenant governor's spot. We were delighted that there would be no primary fight and that we could save our resources for winning in the general election that November. The Republicans nominated Lieutenant Governor John M. Mutz and Marion County prosecutor Stephen Goldsmith, but Evan ran on a platform of fiscal responsibility and change. The 1988 campaign for governor was hard-fought, and in November the Bayh-O'Bannon Democratic ticket upset the favored Republicans with strong support from the people of Indiana. In January 1989, he was sworn in as Indiana's forty-sixth governor.

In March of 1989, two months after Evan Bayh was sworn in as governor, I was appointed chairman of the Indiana Worker's Compensation Board. Three months later, Jack Crawford became director of the new Indiana Lottery. Governor Bayh appointed Joseph Hogsett to finish out Bayh's term as secretary of state. A year later Hogsett ran to retain his office against Indianapolis Mayor William H. Hudnut, who considered the office as a springboard to running against Bayh for governor in 1992. Hudnut and the Republican Party wanted to win this election in the worst way. So it was a heated campaign with implications for the future.

I worked hard in Hogsett's campaign for secretary of state. When Hogsett came to Lake County, I sometimes drove him to social and political functions, introduced him to friendly audiences, and organized fund-raisers on his behalf. Like Evan Bayh, Joe Hogsett was young, intelligent, personable, and a hard campaigner. Some people compared his style to the late Senator Robert F. Kennedy. Great with people, he was warm and friendly, and the electorate responded favorably. Seeing him win was deeply satisfying since it derailed Hudnut's plan to oppose Governor Bayh's reelection bid.

## WORKER'S COMPENSATION BOARD

In February of 1989, two months after Governor Evan Bayh took office, his chief of staff, Bill Moreau, called, offering me the job of chairman of the Worker's Compensation Board. Betty and I had bought a home in Hobart, Indiana, on an acre of land and were not looking to move. By now Veronica was four and Maria six months old. I told Moreau I knew almost nothing about the statutory aspects of worker's compensation, a legal specialty I was unfamiliar with. He said he was confident that I could learn it and that the governor wanted people like me who would do the right thing by working people. The system needed to be revamped, so it was an enormous challenge. Flattered, I told him to give me time to think about it.

The previous chairman was part-time, but they wanted me to work full-time and move to Indianapolis. The salary would be $49,000, no more than what the previous chairman had been making. I was earning more than that in the prosecutor's office, and living in Marion County was going to be expensive. I recalled that on the campaign trail Bayh had promised to run a frugal administration, so $49,000 it would be.

After discussing the offer with Betty and my family, I decided to take the challenge and the opportunity to join the Bayh administration in hopes of taking my law career to a new level. It would also mean new friendships and experiences for Betty and the children, as well as for me. I remembered Dad's admonition to develop my talents. So I called Moreau back and said, "Count me in." "All right, you're on," he replied. During the transition Moreau was of great help and assisted us like we were members of his family.

Later I learned that Bayh had previously told Jack Crawford, "I'd like to bring Dominguez down here in Indianapolis with me." I believe I was selected because the governor knew I was a hard worker with integrity whom he could trust, coming from a labor background, and perhaps, given my own physical challenges, had sensitivity toward the needs of those injured on the job.

Crawford's good friend Joe Manley, business manager for the carpenter's union, also prodded the governor to make good on promises to do something for labor and to fix the worker's compensation system. Joe took me under his tutelage, as did attorney Sam Furlin, whom I knew through federal judge Rudy Lozano. Sam gave me an overview on the worker's compensation laws and how the board operated. I read books and studied hard, listening to audiotapes provided by the legal education division of the bar association. Preparing for my new job was similar to being back in law school because everything was new to me, the jargon, the acronyms, the procedures. It was a fascinating field covering everything from on-the-job injuries to diseases resulting from contact with asbestos, pesticides, and other chemicals that might cause cancer, asthma, or other debilitating illnesses.

For all practical purposes, the worker's compensation system was outdated and broken. The original laws had been enacted in 1925 and last revised meaningfully in 1929. In fact, Republicans used to tell employers, "Come to Indiana because the worker's compensation benefits are so low." Well, that was on the backs of injured workers. With Governor Bayh in office, it was time for meaningful reform.

Compensation benefits came in two ways, either through an insurance company or, in some cases, if a company was self-insured, through a pool of funds set up with the approval of the board. The insurance companies had to be approved by the Department of Insurance. The system was based upon the philosophy that if an employee is injured while in the performance of his or her duties and in the scope of the job, then rather than have lawsuits based on negligence, the system provides a no-fault resolution. Benefits included medical care (100 percent) and pharmaceutical care (100 percent) through the first two years. After that, a claimant needed to file additional claims. If unable to return to work, you received very low weekly benefits. With a permanent injury you got a certain amount depending if it was an arm, a leg, an eye, or whatever.

Occupational diseases had a two-year statute of limitations even though it often took much longer for symptoms to become apparent. These regulations pertaining to conditions that did not manifest themselves for at least two years were so complicated that there were times when we did not have any claims. There was a "second injury" fund, which assessed employers, that was intended for the replacement of prosthetic devices such as artificial limbs that might have worn out. Again, the Republicans, who had dominated state government for twenty years, had so emasculated that part of the statute that only a handful of applicants qualified.

While commuting to Indianapolis for several months while we looked for a house to purchase, I lived with friends – attorney Lacey Johnson, whom I had met at the state police academy, attorney Alan Mills, and community leader Joseph Smith. All three African American men and their wives treated me like family. They made a place for me at their home and dining table and welcomed me with loving grace. I'll never forget their generosity and love. We remain cherished friends and stay in contact from time to time.

Betty and I, not wishing to base our future decisions on being tied down with personal property, sold our house in Hobart in July of 1989. It was a tough thing to do, and needless to say, Betty shed tears over it. We had many fond memories of family gatherings, and my sister was there with us before she passed away. Having five bedrooms, a large garage, and an outdoor shed, we had accumulated a great deal of furniture; and now we were moving into a two-bedroom townhouse in an area called Greenbriar subdivision near Eighty-second and Ditch Road in Indianapolis. We moved in August of 1989 because my eldest daughter Veronica was ready to start kindergarten and we wanted to get settled in before that August.

When I started as chairman of the Worker's Compensation Board I was still very stiff physically from the effects of Guillain-Barré but didn't tell the staff of my condition because I didn't want people to feel sorry for me. On one occasion, I was in the governor's office with several department heads, and we headed outside to attend a community forum together along with Governor Bayh. It was raining hard, and walking from the east side of the statehouse to a parked office vehicle required going down many flights of stairs, something I was unable to do quickly or easily. Nor could I hold an umbrella because I needed to use the handrails.

Already in the office car, Governor Bayh noticed the trouble I was experiencing; he came out of the vehicle, grabbed the umbrella an aide was holding for him, came back up the stairs, and escorted me down the steps, holding the umbrella over my head while it rained on him. In order to negotiate the stairs I held onto his shoulder with one hand and a handrail with the other. Otherwise it would have been impossible. I thought to myself, how blessed am I, the governor getting rained upon so he could help and protect me and ensure that I didn't fall down the stairs. His thoughtfulness and compassion was something I would never forget and for me sealed a friendship beyond words.

Another time Betty and I had been invited to dinner at chief of staff Bill Moreau's house. Beforehand, unbeknownst to me, he went over the menu with Betty to see if it presented any problems for me. I have difficulty with teacups, so that evening everyone had a coffee mug. I have trouble slicing meat, so it was served already sliced. That was extremely kind and typical of the kindness of Bayh's inner circle. Bill and his wife, Ann, are very kind people, and we remain best of friends. Intelligent and charming, Ann is a classy lady. Having the opportunity to work closely with Bill, I found him to be a good listener and one of the brightest and most practical people I had ever met in public service. He could size up a particular situation and implement a detailed solution unlike anyone else I had ever met.

When Governor Bayh delivered his State of the State address in January of 1990, other department heads joked that I had a front row seat because I was the only Hispanic in his cabinet and he wanted me there to show diversity. We had a great camaraderie and teased each other a lot. As I joked to my colleagues, "Jealousy will get you nowhere." Unfortunately there were no handrails leading from the top entrance of the balcony to the front row. Realizing there was no way I could negotiate those steps, I asked then budget director Frank Sullivan, who was next to me, if I could put my hand on his shoulder. He said, "Well, sure, Roy." Every year thereafter Frank waited for me and we took our seats together. I appreciated his kindness. Sullivan is presently a justice on the Indiana Supreme Court. Of course I was proud that Governor Bayh believed in diversity, and I worked hard to earn his respect and confidence.

The fact that I was the first Hispanic to run an Indiana state agency received much publicity. The board consisted of seven members – all lawyers – three Republicans, three Democrats, and a chair, who serves at the pleasure of the governor. The board made its decisions based upon the facts and the law, not partisan politics. Its mission was to be the arbiter of benefits and oversee how the system was managed. The other board members were very knowledgeable in this field. Some had been on the board for more than twenty years and taught me the essence of the system. Having six experts to consult with and seek advice from was fantastic. Knowing how cumbersome the system had become, they were in agreement on the need to overhaul it. The benefits were minimal. The insurance companies were thoroughly taking advantage of injured workers. Former chairman John Shanks, a Republican, was very helpful. He came in every day at first, and he gave me his private phone number and told me to call him if necessary.

Shanks's executive secretary asked if she could stay on for three months while she looked for a job, so I kept her on, and it was mutually advantageous. Meanwhile I posted the chief deputy position with the personnel department for public dissemination and within the state agencies. When I received a list of candidates who qualified for the job requirements, the former executive secretary saw the name Doug Meagher among them and said, "You don't want him. He's gay." I found that disrespectful, irrelevant, and so insensitive.

Meagher had a master's degree in public administration from Indiana State and had been working six years in the computer division of state government. Not being very knowledgeable about computers at the time and realizing how important they would be in the future in the operation of the system, I thought, "Great!" Doug presented himself well during the interview, and I hired him. He was very bright and a hard worker who made significant contributions toward the success of my tenure as chairman. He was my go-to person, and we made a great team. By the end of the year I felt I was up to speed.

Then, with chief of staff Bill Moreau as the contact person, Governor Bayh created a seven-member Workers Compensation Blue Ribbon Committee. Moreau appointed Bill Bowling, a retired autoworker from New Castle, Indiana, as our executive liaison. Bill had a master's degree in public administration from Ball State University and was a very hard worker. He was extremely helpful and committed to helping bring about meaningful reform to the worker's compensation system. Bowling and I became good friends and remain in contact to this day.

The committee's charge was to review the entire scope of the laws and then create a fair system with reasonable benefits. I was the chair, and the governor appointed an equal number of members from labor and business, including representatives from the AFL-CIO, the United Auto Workers, the Chamber of Commerce, the National Association of Manufacturers, and the Indianapolis Power and Light Company. A nationally known consultant from Florida, John Lewis, guided us through the process. I'd consult with my board members on issues and have the Republicans, such as John Shanks and Richard Noel, be emissaries to the business committee members and the Democrats funnel information to the labor representatives.

Subcommittees studied various aspects of the package. At one point the business representatives said, "Why don't we leave the system in place but add more money to the benefits?" I said, "No, that won't work unless the process is streamlined. If unfair roadblocks prevent injured workers from receiving benefits, the rest is meaningless." I told them, "It's not up for negotiation."

We started in March of 1990 and submitted our recommendations by October. We retained the parts of the system that worked and replaced or modified the antiquated parts. We improved the benefits and eliminated unfair roadblocks. Our package wasn't pie in the sky but reasonable and practical. In the end the committee voted unanimously on all the component parts. What it came down to in the end was that employers didn't mind paying benefits so long as the person was deserving and the process fair and reasonable.

Governor Bayh and Bill Moreau were pleasantly surprised, to say the least. We were able to dispel myths perpetrated by insurance companies and other special-interest groups. When asked how I managed to get such consensus, I praised my staff and said, "We just worked hard to help guide the process along." Perhaps it went back to what my dad taught me about trust and integrity and being a "good man" and my mom's doggedness when she knew she was in the right. I was pleased at how well it was received and believed I had earned the faith Joe Manley, Bill Moreau, and Governor Bayh had placed in me.

Still the package needed to pass the General Assembly, and there were conservative elements opposed to any change in the system and Republicans anxious for the Bayh administration to fall on its face. The House was evenly divided between Republicans and Democrats, and Republicans controlled the Senate. I testified before the Labor Committee, chaired by Democratic state representative Rolland Weber, as did John Lewis and other committee members. In the end the package passed into law without a dissenting vote.

In the Senate the Labor Committee chairman, Republican Joe Harrison, was well known for keeping benefits low and killing legislation that would have helped workers; but the bill made it through his committee and passed the upper chamber with just three nay votes. It was amazing. Many people had hoped the whole endeavor would fail, but within just two years of Governor Bayh's taking office we had implemented a necessary reform that benefited the State of Indiana. The governor presided over a signing ceremony right outside the worker's compensation office. It was the first worker's compensation reform in sixty-two years!

## FAMILY LIFE

Veronica and Maria developed into charming, loving daughters. Veronica reminded me of my sister Maria in terms of her physical appearance and mannerisms. Betty dressed her up in frilly clothes, and I spoiled her, too. She attended kindergarten at St. Bridget's in Hobart. After we moved to Indianapolis, she went to Greenbriar Elementary. Her first-grade teacher, Miss Shonski, turned out to be from Gary and a Lew Wallace High School grad like myself. Veronica loved going to school and enjoyed her teacher.

Starting at the new school, Veronica wanted me to walk her all the way to her classroom rather than just drop her off. After several days I told her we couldn't keep doing this indefinitely. We worked out a compromise whereby I'd walk her to Miss Shonski's classroom for a week, accompany her to the school's front door for another week, and then by the third week she'd go into school by herself. On Monday of the third week, I took her to school as usual and said, "OK, now you're going to go by yourself." She was willing, but unfortunately it had been raining and the sidewalk was icy, causing her to slip and fall. So much for best-laid plans. I got out and escorted her to class, but next day everything worked out fine.

We enrolled Veronica in many activities, including a modeling class. She and other six-year-olds would demonstrate kids' clothes at malls. She joined a Mexican folk dance group and performed at the first Latino Fest in Indianapolis. Later Betty enrolled her in a Filipino dance group as well.

As a child, Maria was even more independent than Veronica. When she was two, we had a family portrait taken and wanted a photo of the girls by a table. Maria refused to cooperate until finally she grabbed a little chair and indicated she wanted to sit on it on top of the table. Then she climbed up, sat down, and folded her arms as if to say, "I'm ready now." Two years later in Florida at Christmas they were putting on a skit with Betty's niece Mary Beth. Betty's dad played the piano as their signal to come out into the living room. Maria refused to appear until she could do it her way – with a guitar and sunglasses on.

We were living in Crown Point, Indiana, when Maria began kindergarten at St. Mary's Catholic School. On the first day upon arriving at the school parking lot, I was about to get out of the car to walk Maria to class when she said she could go in by herself since she remembered where the classroom was located from the orientation we had all attended. I told her I wanted to walk with her on her first day, but she insisted that she'd be fine walking by herself. "Well, OK," I said. That was just Maria being Maria, loving a challenge and going about it on her own.

Maria resembles my mom in her features, mannerisms, and personality. They look at every little thing and don't forget. Maria makes friends easily and has always had compassion for people. In school she noticed students making fun of a classmate with disabilities, told them to stop, and befriended that child.

Following an exhaustive search in Indianapolis, Betty and I never found a house we liked well enough to purchase. One evening I said to her, "You know why we can't find a house. It's because we want to go back to Lake County and be near our family." It had just come to me like a lightning bolt. I did not want to see my daughters separated from their grandparents and other relatives, as my parents, who had to move north out of necessity, missed out on so much being away from their parents. Neither did Betty. So in July of 1991, after about two years residing in Indianapolis, we moved back to northwest Indiana, and I commuted to the state capital two or three days a week for the remaining three years I stayed on as chairman of the board.

By this time my folks were living on the north side of Crown Point, so we had a home built on the south side of town – close enough that they could play a meaningful role in our daughters' lives and that Betty and I could care for their needs. My dad was able to pick the girls up from school, take them to Dairy Queen, and do the things he could not do with his own children. My mom baby-sat while Betty and I worked. We cherish the fond memories of those years.

Around 1992, Maria and I were playing downstairs in our new home. Maria started to run, and I chased her. All of a sudden, I started slowly running after her. This was the first time I had run since the onset of Guillain-Barré in 1983. The illness had depleted my body's reflexes back then, and I had had trouble walking, let alone running. I called Betty and Veronica and demonstrated my renewed ability to run. We all were very pleased and excited.

With the exception of trips to Washington, D.C., and Spain, most of our vacations were to visit family. When visiting in Clearwater, Florida, where Betty's parents lived, we probably went to Disney World twenty times, including for the Christmas parade and the opening of Epcot

Center. We were also at the debut of Sea World and Universal Studios. We went sailing and fishing in the Gulf of Mexico and visited museums and other places of interest in Tampa, including its Cuban quarter, Ybor City. We also visited my siblings in Dallas, San Antonio, and Oklahoma City, as well as south Texas where my parents had lived. Our old Texas home and school were victims of urban renewal; the canal is gone, and a highway has replaced the dirt road, but the movie theater and a few other landmarks still remain.

I asked Betty if she wanted to visit the Philippines, but nearly all her family was either in the United States or deceased. She preferred to remember Manila the way it was when she lived there. In March of 1995, we visited my brother Eloy in Rota, Spain, located right on the Mediterranean Sea. Armando joined us, too. Veronica was eleven and Maria eight years old. One day the adults took a ferry to Morocco and a bus ride to the city of Tangiers. It was a scary experience. Even the merchants were unfriendly. As we were getting ready to leave, people literally surrounded our bus shouting "Yankee Go Home!" and calling us "American Jews." People were banging on the windows and rocking the bus so violently that I feared it might tip over. The driver had to drive slowly to avoid running people over.

We boarded a bullet train to Madrid, where each restaurant had its own recipe for sangria. Compared to Mexican food, Spanish main dishes were bland and included many fish entrées. We toured Columbus Square, numerous museums, the royal palace, a memorial to victims of the Spanish Civil War, and a monastery where crypts of former kings were located. Betty and the girls vetoed attending a bullfight. In Toledo, the original Spanish capital, was a church that took over three hundred years to build. The area near the altar was pure gold. It hit me that the precious metal more than likely had been stolen from the Mayans and Aztecs, who had been enslaved and murdered by the conquistadores.

## PRACTICING ATTORNEY

In 1991 I opened a private practice in the Gainer Bank Building at Fifth and Broadway. I wanted to go back to my Gary roots and give something back to the community. Being at that location kept me grounded in reality. I had my own law office but shared space with Chuck Graddick, Willie Harris, and Karen Freeman-Wilson, all three of whom were interested in government and politics. I practiced criminal and personal injury defense work for the most part. Over half my cases were pro bono – representing people being taken advantage of by landlords, business companies, or employers. So I was working for free a good deal, but it was my way of acknowledging, quite frankly, God's gift of life and his blessings to me and to help others in need.

In January of 1994 on my last day as board chair, Doug Meagher invited me out to lunch. On my advice he had gone to law school and now was a member of the Indiana State Bar Association. Betty and the girls loved him, and we had become close friends, but the subject of his being gay had never come up. At lunch he gave me as a gift a bust of John F. Kennedy, whom he knew I admired, and then said he had something to tell me – that he was gay. I said, "Doug, I always knew that" and told him the story about his predecessor saying I should not hire him. Then he told me he was married to a man in a civil union and put on a ring that he had never worn at work. Doug remained executive secretary and then was appointed to the board by Governor Bayh.

We worked hard and had fun during our tenure in state government. I believe our success is a tribute to Governor Bayh's ability to select good professionals and public servants. I remained affiliated with the board for eight more years as an administrative law judge, hearing disputes in Lake and LaPorte counties and rendering decisions.

While working as chairman of the Worker's Compensation Board, I ran into my old law school buddy Mark Bailey, he of the cowboy boots and kind heart. He had become a trial judge in Decatur County and was hoping to be appointed to the Indiana Court of Appeals. At the time a vacancy existed, and applications were being accepted. A judicial panel interviewed the prospective candidates and forwarded the names of three finalists, including Mark, to Governor Bayh for his consideration.

Mark asked if I would write a letter of recommendation on his behalf. Betty said a prayer and lit a candle for him. I was honored to write a reference letter for such a worthy friend and also talked to the governor's legal counsel on his behalf. In 1998 Governor Bayh selected Mark as the next judge to the Indiana Court of Appeals. After he was appointed, he called and thanked us, especially for Betty's prayers and lighting a candle for him. Mark Bailey was retained in an election two years later, and currently still presides on the Indiana Court of Appeals.

Church at the Dominguez ancestral farm, Relampago, Texas.

Roy's maternal great-grandfather, Luis Castillo.

Abelardo Dominguez, Roy's paternal grandfather.

Roy's paternal grandmother, Maria Treviño Dominguez.

Roy's maternal grandmother, Vicenta Castillo Mata.

Roy's maternal grandfather, Hinijio Mata, with tomato bushels.

Roy's mom, Inocensia, age thirteen.

Roy's dad, Jesus (Jesse), while he was in the U.S. Army, 1945.

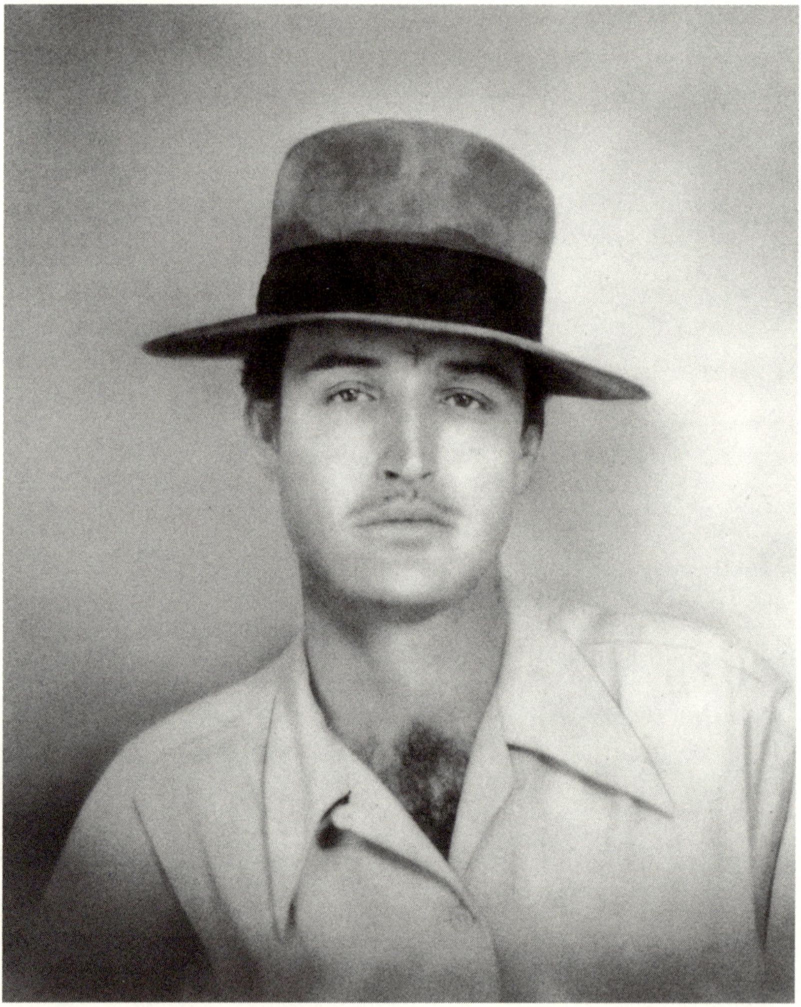

Uncle Felix (Roy's father's brother).

David Dominguez, who died while serving in the Korean War.

Roy's sister, Maria, with his brother, Jesse. Jesse is in braces due to polio.

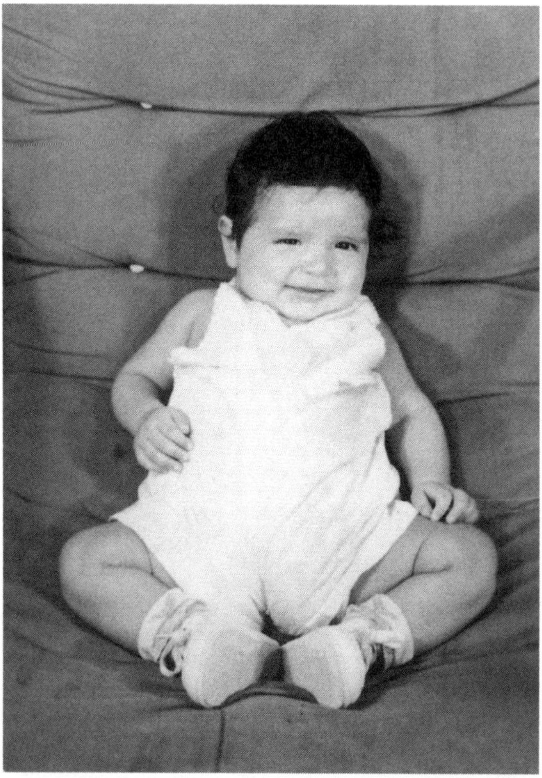

Roy at three months.

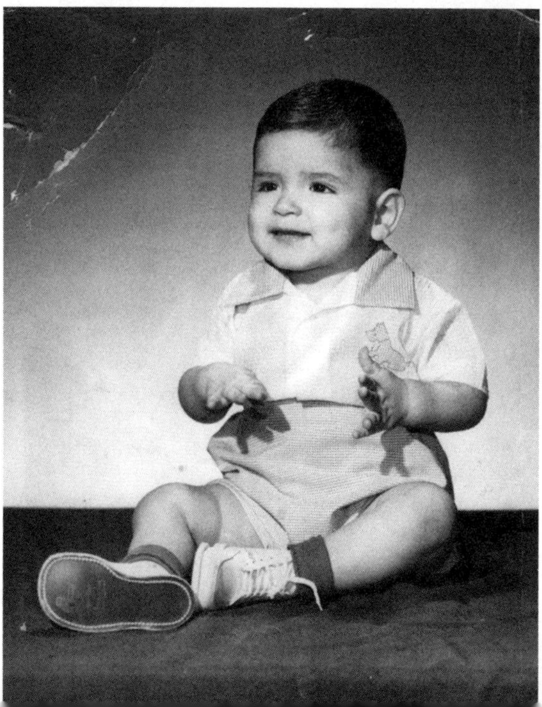

Baby Roy.

Roy (in suspenders) with his parents and Hector in Mercedes, Texas.

Roy and his brothers in Mercedes, Texas: (*back, from left*) Eloy, Jesse, Armando, and Roy; (*front*) Hector.

Roy (behind Yolanda) and his siblings on Durbin Street.

Roy in eighth grade, Edison Junior High.

Roy's 1972 high school graduation picture from Lew Wallace High School.

Lieutenant Andy Lazar (*center front*) and the Indiana University Northwest Campus Police Department, circa 1975. Roy, backrow, second from left.

Betty Olayta, circa 1975, while dating Roy.

Roy at Betty's house in Miller in 1975.

Roy with his sister Maria, October 1976.

Roy with Indiana Attorney General Theodore L. Sendak,
October 15, 1976 at State Police Academy Graduation.

Roy and Betty with Roy's parents on their wedding day in August 1978.

Roy with former U.S. Supreme Court Justice
Arthur Goldberg, at Valparaiso Law School, 1981.

Valparaiso Law School graduate Roy Dominguez with his parents, May 1982.

Dominguez family picnic, June 1988.

Roy being sworn in as Chair of the Worker's Compensation Board by Indiana Governor Evan Bayh, March 1989.

Roy with Indiana Lieutenant Governor Frank O'Bannon, 1991.

Roy and Betty on their 25th wedding anniversary at St. Maria Goretti Church in Dyer, Indiana.

Roy's parents' 50th wedding anniversary, 1998.

Campaign cartoon from 2002. *Used by permission of the* Times of Northwest Indiana.

Roy celebrating his election as sheriff in November 2002.

Roy and U.S. Senator Evan Bayh in 2002.

Roy with former Texas governor Ann Richards.

Roy's daughters in Mexican garb.

Dominguez Christmas photo with nephew Alex.

Roy campaigning with Hillary Clinton in 2010.

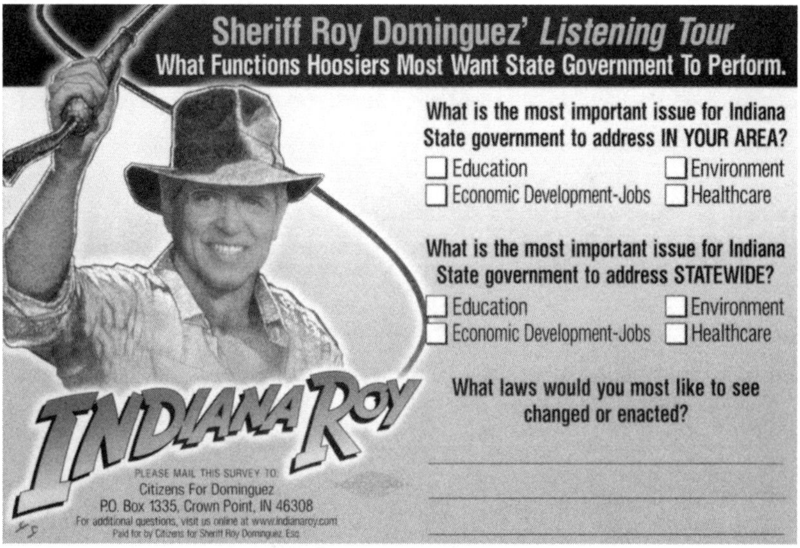


Campaign materials from Roy's listening tour.

Sheriff Dominguez with a new EC120 helicopter. *Photo by Kyle Telechan. Used by permission of the* Times of Northwest Indiana.

Roy at the Dominguez family cemetery at Relampago, Texas, January 2011.

Sheriff Dominguez honoring women in law enforcement. *Photo by John Luke. Used by permission of the* Times of Northwest Indiana.

The Democratic Machine rolled on unimpeded during the 1980s. Federal investigators had no difficulty filling prison cells with crooked officials. Citizens marveled at the list of jailbirds named on a bronze tablet commemorating the dedication of the county government complex.

LANCE TRUSTY, *Steel Shavings* 38
("The Uncertainty of Everyday Life")

I don't promise you ease. I don't promise you comfort. But I do promise you these: hardship, weariness, and suffering. And with them, I promise you victory.

GIUSEPPE GARIBALDI

EIGHT

# 1990s Political Campaigns

*Korean War veteran Eliseo Castaneda, active in East Chicago American Legion Post 508 and the* UBM*, had the nickname Vitamins. He once said, "Roy, just call me Vitamins." I replied, "No, Mr. Castaneda, my dad can call you Vitamins, but I don't think I can." I felt honored that he was comfortable enough to allow me to refer to him by his nickname, but in respect I continued to call him Mr. Castaneda.*

## CAMPAIGNING FOR SHERIFF

In 1994 I ran for Lake County sheriff because I thought I'd be able to promote a level of professionalism that was sorely lacking in that office. In fact, many regarded it as a political police force. Because of other obligations, I was not able to announce my candidacy until February. I wanted to finish up projects with the Worker's Compensation Board before taking a leave of absence. With the primary the first week in May, it was essentially a ninety-day campaign, and perhaps a month too short.

There were a total of twelve candidates, including the favorite, John Buncich, who had been a fourteen-year supervisor of the sheriff's civil office in Gary and adopted the late Sheriff Chris Anton's dubious slogan, "A policeman for a policeman's job." Buncich began campaigning and securing endorsements the day after Sheriff Stephen R. "Bob" Stiglich was reelected in May of 1990. As a result, he garnered the support of most Fraternal Order of Police (FOP) groups and unions, including the Teamsters and most of the building trades. Many thought his main rival would be county assessor Peter L. Benjamin, who had the political backing and support from then Sheriff Stiglich and other political rivals of Mayor Robert Pastrick. Amase Colby, a retired Gary police officer, was also a credible and serious candidate.

I first met Mayor Pastrick during the Jack Crawford and Evan Bayh campaigns and helped him when he ran for an unprecedented sixth term in 1991 against Vincent McCutcheon. He was extremely well mannered, polished, and gentlemanly. Even though he indicated he'd support me, it was more vocal than substantial in terms of providing financial contributions or campaign workers. More than anything, he wanted Benjamin defeated. Many of Pastrick's supporters were backing Buncich, probably with Pastrick's approval, because they thought he had a better chance than I did.

I think Pastrick meant it at the time when he indicated he'd support me, but he had other political agendas. He was polished and wanted to be fair to candidates, but you couldn't always rely on his full support because of his other interests. Bobby Cantrell backed Buncich because he didn't think I could garner support outside the Hispanic community. Frankly, he considered me a newcomer and doubted that a guy named Rogelio Dominguez would get support in the white southern part of the county. Although officially a Republican, Cantrell was a behind-the-scenes force who, to use a sports analogy, wanted to play on everyone's team at the same time.

Longtime Lake County behind-the-scenes political operative Bobby Cantrell was a complex and intelligent person with a PhD and a love of sports. In fact, he viewed politics as a combat sport of sorts. He was a person never to be underestimated or taken for granted. He made deals irrespective of party label or principle. To him politics was about power, deceit, deal making, competition, and intimidation, and he loved it when people groveled to him. Even with friends, he enjoyed playing all sides so he could undeservedly take credit for either candidate's victory. He appeared to thrive on creating chaos and to relish spreading rumors to enhance animosity amongst political camps.

Perhaps Cantrell's strongest personal motivation in contriving political battles was his need to feel of value to elected officeholders. Once such "political value" was achieved, he would then commence to arrange his political machinations. One of Cantrell's strategies was to covertly contrive political opposition for officeholders in the form of throw-in candidates and then find it strange that they would take it personally. Of course when directed at him, it was personal and not sport.

My ninety-day campaign was a grassroots effort. We raised a significant amount of money, but it was mostly all from small contributions of less than a hundred dollars. My family was very involved. Sandra Shoemaker, an African American who worked for the Teamsters, was campaign chairperson. Her husband was a former state trooper, and both are dear friends. We put on a very strong effort in Gary because I had lived my formative years there and had many long time friends.

Mike Higgins, a retired twenty-five-year veteran county police officer, had thought of throwing his hat in the ring himself but joined my campaign and was my treasurer. He was a jovial, bright friend who at a moment's notice could produce a joke or anecdote that would have everyone laughing. He had a good deal of common sense and knowledge of the traditional operations of the sheriff's department.

On April 24, 1994, in the *Post-Tribune* I published a "Dominguez for Sheriff" ad entitled "New leadership in the '90s." In it I promised that "as sheriff, I will dedicate my educational and public service experience to crime prevention and reduction. . . . My commitment [is] for a 'Safe and Progressive' Lake County."

On Election Day Buncich garnered 1,700 more votes than I did. Benjamin finished a distant fourth. Ironically, had he done better, I might have won since he and Buncich were going after the same voters. We didn't get all the votes we were entitled to, I believe, because political operatives placed four Hispanic "sham candidates" into the race to confuse the electorate and to divert votes that otherwise probably would have gone to me. In fact, the Arredondo organization threw in their nephew Andrew Solis simply to siphon votes from me. All told, these throw-in candidates tallied approximately 6,000 votes, most of which would have gone to me. My opponents knew that I would promote good government and was unapproachable in terms of controlling my agenda, and their strategy worked.

That evening my brother Hector convinced me to accompany him to Casa Gallardo. Well-wishers congratulated me on my campaign and reinforced my feeling that I had done my best. It was a great campaign, more successful than anybody but my inner circle would have predicted, and I learned a lot. No doubt had I started a bit earlier, it would have made a difference because I didn't have enough time to develop a sufficient enough name recognition. Even so, I think I earned the trust of most voters who knew me. The main thing that hurt my candidacy was the entry of the four throw-in Hispanic candidates. I didn't harbor any ill will but didn't forget a lesson learned. That's just part of life, a learning experience, as my parents would say.

From my perspective it is never a loss if you are trying to bring about positive change. Maybe there is a delay but never a loss. I don't necessarily believe it was fate, but maybe it wasn't yet my time. I thought I was pretty mature at forty but was probably more savvy and capable by the time I did win at age forty-eight. I think I lived up to my parents' admonition to "work hard and do it right." I never cared to be slick and was not fearful of the political powers aligned against me.

Rather than brood over the questionable verdict, I said to myself, "Keep working. Get to know more people and talk to voters about their concerns." So I continued to gain more experience in the political campaigns of others, even though, as I came to realize, there's a vast difference between working on a campaign and being the candidate.

In 1995 I continued my involvement in politics. For instance, I supported Mayor Pastrick in his primary battle against former sheriff Robert Stiglich. I built up my association with Hispanic organizations, becoming an active member, for example, in the Latino Historical Society. There was a time when the Mexican and Puerto Rican communities in northwest Indiana were not as harmonious as is the case today. The acrimony had to do, I believe, with an evolving society. The Mexican American community has been in northwest Indiana a generation longer. Although the two groups speak the same language, albeit different dialects, we're separate cultures, each with its nationalistic pride and desire for its own cultural identification.

There were people who exploited the differences between the two Hispanic communities because they didn't want there to be a single powerful Hispanic voting bloc. That was the motive in getting an East Chicago retired police chief of Puerto Rican ancestry to run for sheriff in 1994 even though he didn't campaign.

## LATINO HISTORICAL SOCIETY

I was asked to volunteer as the legal counsel for the Latino Historical Society. Jesse Villalpando Sr. was the driving force behind the organization, whose main goal was to preserve for posterity, in conjunction with IU Northwest's Calumet Regional Archives, the rich contributions of Hispanics to the heritage of northwest Indiana. Jesse said, "I want to put your name on the society's letterhead because then more people will show up and join." He asked that I draw up the incorporation papers and offered to pay me for the filing fee, but I said, "No, I'll be the first contributor to the organization." In addition, I drafted the by-laws for the society.

Louis Vasquez Sr., an active member of the Latino Historical Society, wrote his autobiography, which he called "Weasal," his childhood nickname because of his diminutive size. Most people of his generation, it seemed, had nicknames. Like Mr. Villalpando, he was a valuable community resource who helped young people move ahead and got them to better understand their heritage. He had known my father and when I called him Mr. Vasquez, he said, "Just call me Weasal." It was similar to a conversation I had had with Mr. Castaneda. I told him, "Mr. Vasquez, with all due respect I don't think I can do that." He replied, "Fine. I can accept that."

In his quiet way Abe Morales, a Latino Historical Society member from my old Brunswick neighborhood, was intimately involved in volunteer activities on behalf of the community. My dad and Mr. Morales, as I called him, knew each other from being active members in the VFW and other organizations and were personal friends. Both were proud of their military service. Without fanfare Abe would collect pencils and paper to take along on visits to VA hospitals.

For decades Abe Morales taught English as a second language at area migrant camps. He helped workers get transportation, medical care, and other practical needs, including information on how to become an American citizen. He'd persuade priests to hold pastoral services at migrant camps. A retired postal worker, he facilitated other Hispanics in applying for government jobs and promotions. One way he promoted cultural awareness was through writing letters to the *Post-Tribune* documenting the historic contribution of Hispanic Americans to our country. We all looked forward to reading them.

## CELEBRATING THE HISPANIC HERITAGE

For more than a quarter century I've been involved in the East Chicago Mexican Independence Day and Puerto Rican parades. The former takes place on the Sunday on or before September 16; the latter is usually held on the third Saturday in July. Recently Lake Station has started holding similar parades honoring these holidays. The sheriff's department typically sends a police car, motorcyclists, and a tactical truck. Walkers, often employees and their children, pass out candy, balloons, educational brochures, and pencils that contain our anonymous 800 hotline number as well as positive messages such as "Stay in school" or "Report a crime." If asked, we provide a flag honor guard and our pipes and drums unit to play patriotic songs.

One custom in the Hispanic community is the *Quinceñera,* a coming-of-age celebration for young women at age fifteen. Some families hold individual parties, and organizations put on a group event to spare people the cost of food, a band, hall rental, and the like. Veronica attended one hosted by the Filipino Professional Association, a group Betty belonged to that honored seven or eight girls at their annual banquet. It's a tradition common to cultures, including Mexicans, Puerto Ricans, and Filipinos, who once were under Spanish rule. A court of honor, usually consisting of young men, escorts the ladies, who commonly are dressed in gowns and wearing tiaras. Members of the procession perform a carefully rehearsed group waltz, followed by a Latin-flavored "fun" dance such as a salsa or merengue. Then there's a father-daughter first dance before other guests join in the fun. The music is usually a dance-friendly blend of Latin and American pop tunes.

## CAR ACCIDENT

In February of 1996, I was driving our Dodge Caravan along State Road 55 in Crown Point near St. John's Church on the way to Southlake Mall without utilizing my seat belt. It was a frigid winter day. Betty and I were taking our daughter Maria and a school friend to a place where they could run around and expend energy while we shopped. Suddenly an oncoming vehicle cut in front of us to turn east and hit the left front fender, sending us off the road and into a big oak tree. The airbags activated; otherwise I'd have gone clear through the front window. As it was, without a seat belt on, my head hit the windshield hard enough to shatter it and render me unconscious. I woke up with blood all over my face and asked Betty, who was screaming, if she and the girls were all right. Then after sitting back into the seat, I lost consciousness for over four hours.

All I recollect is hearing my deceased sister Maria's voice saying, "Russ, wake up. Russ, wake up." When we were children, she called me Russ sometimes when we were playing because my name began with "R" and it was short for "Russian." Those were Cold War days when the Russians were adversaries. Also in the background I could hear "American Pie" by Don McLean, which had been a favorite song of ours with its references to the deaths in 1959 of popular recording artists Buddy Holly, Ritchie Valens, and the Big Bopper. The lines that I heard repeated over and over went, "So bye, bye, Miss American Pie / Drove my Chevy to the levee but the levee was dry." What I did not hear was the remainder of the verse, which ends, "This'll be the day that I die."

I wondered, "What did that mean? Maybe I will live through this." Some spiritual things aren't necessarily explainable, but it was as if my sister Maria had been looking out for me and was waking me up. The message to me was that my life and work here on earth were not yet done. That near-death experience further motivated me to live an inspired life, not shrink from life's challenges, and be sure to use my seat belt.

## POLITICAL CONSULTANT

In the summer of 1994 Julia Jent, my friend from law school, had opened a law office at Forty-ninth and Broadway, and I had accepted an offer to join her there in 1995. Judge Nicholas J. Schiralli also offered me a job, as a superior county court public defender. He was in a tough fight for reelection in 1996 and wanted my help. I told him I didn't need a job in order to support him. As my parents always said, "Support those whom you'd like to help, not because you received something in return." He said, "No, you don't understand, Roy, I want you in my office so I can talk with you and be the recipient of your advice."

Judge Schiralli was from Gary's Glen Park neighborhood, and I was friends with his family. Being a public defender in his courtroom added a dimension to my professional career. It was a chance to be on the other side from the prosecutor and gave me a broader perspective and appreciation for the legal system. I handled mainly traffic tickets, DUIs, and public intoxication – misdemeanors and Class D felonies, not major violent cases.

Schiralli's father had been a justice of the peace, and when that office had been replaced by statute in 1974 Governor Otis R. Bowen appointed young Schiralli, still in his twenties, to the bench. Unlike other superior court judges, who were approved by a yes or no retention process, county court judges faced potential political opposition when they went before the voters every six years. This, however, was the first time Schiralli had faced a serious challenge. He was essentially a nonpolitical person whose campaign committee was basically inactive, so I was pleased to assist him, especially in view of those scheming to replace him. It is said that Bobby Cantrell, East Chicago councilman Joe De La Cruz, Judge Lorenzo Arredondo, and others persuaded former county court judge Paul Stanko to enter the race, promising him both campaign funds and political muscle. Stanko had been previously appointed to the county court division-two bench (Schiralli was in division one) when Judge Bielak was forced to step down, and he subsequently switched from the Republican to the Democratic Party, much to the chagrin of Republican county chair Joe Kotso.

Early on, Schiralli wanted to sit down with De La Cruz and Cantrell to find out their concerns. I told him that I had learned a long time ago that candidates should not negotiate from a position of weakness because the opposition will jump at the chance to take advantage of their vulnerability. All they wanted was to play political games that were inconsistent with good government, so I was certain the meeting would be counterproductive. I said, "Let's build our team and just win the campaign." I was telling him to be a fighter, like my mom instilled in me. He agreed, saying, "OK, Roy, I'm with you."

Together Judge Schiralli and I went to various organizations throughout the county, and I advised him on how to organize a winnable campaign. He was easy to counsel because we got along personally, he trusted me, and he is a gentleman, very charming and well liked in the Lake County community. Many times it's difficult for judges to get out and campaign, but once reinvigorated, Schiralli loved campaigning. He proved to be much more proficient at it than Stanko and won by a landslide.

In the fall of 1996 forty-year-old Evan Bayh was finishing his second term as governor after winning reelection in 1992 against Attorney General Linley Pearson by the largest margin in the Hoosier state's history. His manner of public service, I believed, was second to none, and he was a role model for me. He had a keen sense of determining how societal issues might best serve the public. Some say he waited to see in what direction the political wind was blowing, but I interpreted the method as staying in tune with public sentiment, unlike some who make decisions and then hope to persuade a skeptical public to go along. Evan was thoughtful, careful, honest, deliberate, and frugal. His ability to do more with less was truly impressive and worth emulating.

Running for governor in 1996 was sixty-six-year-old Lieutenant Governor Frank O'Bannon. A native of Corydon in southern Indiana (the state's first capital), he had a folksy, outgoing, down-home style that reminded one of an endearing uncle or grandfather. I drove O'Bannon to local events on many occasions, introducing him to various ethnic groups and service clubs, advising him on their particular traditions and history much like Jack Crawford had done with me a decade earlier. He'd say, "This is what I have on my schedule. Now how best can I maximize my time?" So I'd help arrange an itinerary for him along with his aides.

I also accompanied O'Bannon's wife, Judy, on various occasions when she visited Lake County. She was an intelligent, well-informed lady whose acquaintance I was honored to make. O'Bannon went on to defeat Stephen Goldsmith, the mayor of Indianapolis, by a margin of 52 percent to 47 percent. In 2000 he won reelection against Congressman David McIntosh.

Like me, O'Bannon suffered from a great deal of neuropathy in his extremities, which causes limited mobility. It made me respect him all the more for his determination to remain in public service at a time many people his age would be retiring from what can be an exhausting profession. When there are times when my feet get swollen or I have balance problems, I fondly think of Governor O'Bannon or of my grandfather Hinijio Mata working the fields into his seventies even though he had battled asthma for forty years, the result, in all likelihood, of being exposed to dangerous insecticides. In fact, growers used to spray chemicals on crops while he was in the field. Despite it all, they continued down the path of a better life. The sacrifices the previous generation made inspired me to continue pursuing my dreams despite the adversity I might face.

## 1998 ASSESSOR RACE

After Judge Schiralli's reelection, Lake County assessor Paul Karras called. "Hey kid," he quipped in his endearing way, "I want you to come work for me. And by the way I'm up for reelection in 1998." Again, I told him I didn't need a job in order to support him. Like the Schirallis, the Karras family was from Gary, was allied most of the time with Mayor Pastrick, and knew my parents. Paul had good name recognition, being the brother of football stars Alex and Ted, the latter being a fixture in local politics.

I told Karras I knew nothing about tax assessments, but the position he had in mind for me was to be legal counsel for the county property board of review, which conducted administrative appeals for people contesting their property tax assessment. My role would be to ensure that the board conducted its hearings legally and in compliance with law and due process. With my experience as an administrative law judge I knew I was qualified to perform in that capacity and accepted the job.

It appeared that Karras's opponent would be Peter Benjamin, who had held office as assessor between 1987 and 1994 but had decided not to seek reelection and had run, unsuccessfully, for sheriff. A lawyer by trade, Peter was aching to get back into county government by running for either auditor or assessor, whichever race he thought he had a better chance of winning. He was supported by the Stiglich camp and had great name recognition.

Even though not related to the late, beloved Congressman Adam Benjamin, Peter Benjamin would never dissuade anyone of that fact. He often claimed, much to the displeasure of Adam's family, that they were cousins. At the time of Adam's sudden death, still believing they were related, I offered Peter my condolences, asked how he was holding up, and he said he was on the way to the hospital for a cardiac checkup because weak hearts run in the Benjamin family.

Peter Benjamin was an aggressively negative campaigner. One day with great fanfare at a press conference Benjamin accused Karras of corrupt practices in the county assessor's office and claimed he was submitting evidence of criminal wrongdoing to the U.S. attorney's office. Realizing that Peter was probing to see how Karras would react, I advised Paul to denounce the outlandish and unsubstantiated accusations in the most forceful of terms. In fact, we learned that Peter had not turned information over to the U.S. attorney, and that it was all public grandstanding. We prepared a strong public statement and scheduled a press conference. Rather uncomfortable in the glare of the spotlight, Karras came close to calling it off. I told him he needed to be strong and expose the lies; otherwise the attacks would escalate. Remembering my parents' fighting spirit of not allowing others to disrespect you, I told Karras that it was time to do battle.

The message I wanted Karras to send to Peter was, "If you are going to attack, you better be ready for a fight." Karras said, "Hey, kid, I hope you're right" and went on with the press conference. He distributed material that proved not only that Peter's assertions were false but that Peter knew they were false.

In the end Benjamin chose not to challenge Karras, who won reelection easily. Afterward, Paul told people that holding the press conference on my advice was the turning point in fending Peter off. Instead, Peter ran successfully for auditor after the incumbent county auditor, Sam Orlich, decided not to seek reelection when faced with Peter's challenge. Perhaps sensing that my political star was rising or maybe for reasons of diversity, some months later Peter's auditor's office gave me a job offer to help defend the county against what some believed was an unconstitutional tax imposed upon the county for indigents' health care costs. I knew nothing about tax litigation and told them so. They intimated that it was not a problem. Remembering what my parents taught me, I replied, "No, I do not submit vouchers for work that I didn't do."

After I declined Peter Benjamin's offer, someone else accepted the position and, not surprisingly, ended up with legal problems. Later on, Peter Benjamin went to jail for sundry illegal activities.

After Julia Jent got elected to a Porter County judgeship, I went to work in Hammond with Barry Sherman, a top-notch personal injury lawyer. He was about seventeen years my senior, and we had worked on a case together. He suggested I come work with him. I said, "I'd be honored, but I didn't know you were looking for another lawyer." He replied, "I'm not, but I'd love to have you in my office." We practiced law together for about five years until I started phasing out my private practice once I won the May 2002 primary for sheriff. Living in Crown Point, I had a real chore to get to the Hammond law office because of the traffic and trains, but the opportunity to learn from Attorney Sherman was one I couldn't pass up.

## EAST CHICAGO CORPORATION COUNSEL

In late 1998 I got a call from Mayor Robert Pastrick, requesting a meeting with me. He was up for reelection, this time against political nemesis Stephen "Bob" Stiglich, and asked me not only to work on his campaign but to manage the office of corporation counsel for the city of East Chicago. I told him I was not a trial litigator, and he said what he needed were my administrative skills. My duties entailed managing the city's legal affairs. Assigning lawsuits properly at their outset is critical. If you don't immediately marshal the facts correctly, the consequences can be very detrimental to your case. When a lawsuit is filed against the city, you have a certain number of days in which to respond. If you miss the deadline, there might be a default judgment or other difficulties.

City attorney Jesse Villalpando Jr., whose father was founder of the Latino Historical Society, worked closely with me, handling cases in city court, advising department heads, and assisting in day-to-day matters. I would assign cases to various contract lawyers depending on their specialty, whether it was public safety, marina issues, the water department, housing, or whatever. The pattern of who would receive the cases was already set when I started work. These lawyers were Pastrick's friends, of course, because he wanted people he could count on to carry out their responsibilities. And, I must say, they were very good at what they did.

I had no part in the so-called Sidewalk Scandal involving allies of Mayor Pastrick. The program was in place years before I became corporation counsel. With the help of an Indianapolis law firm the city had negotiated a contract with Showboat casino that earmarked a percentage of gambling revenue (eventually totaling more than $24 million) for economic development and beautification projects. Much of the money went for trimming trees and installing sidewalks and driveways on private properties in anticipation that the owners would support the mayor in his race against Stiglich. Not only did this raise the issue of whether the program was being used to procure votes, but also the companies hired to pour the concrete and trim the trees received contracts without competitive bidding.

A federal investigation eventually ensnared fourteen of Pastrick's allies, including several council members and his closest political aides. Near the outset of the probe, one of Pastrick's legal assistants brought me a memorandum of law detailing the contract between Showboat and the city and asked me to sign it. I said, "Why would I attach my signature to a memorandum of law that I have never drafted, have no knowledge of its particulars, is outside my area of expertise, and was clearly the work product of another lawyer?" I asked who had worked on it, and he replied, "James A. Shanahan of Ice, Miller, and Donadio." Shanahan was an expert on municipal finance. "If Shanahan wrote it, he is the one who should sign it," I told him.

A few days later the legal assistant came back with the identical memorandum, only this time typed on official East Chicago legal department letterhead. He said Indianapolis attorney James Shanahan recommended I sign it because I was corporation counsel. The way he said it, I got the feeling that he was implying that if I wanted to keep my job, I better sign it. Even so, I told him, "As I said before, I didn't draft it, so I am not signing it." As I was informed, ultimately Shanahan did sign it – rightfully, since it was his legal analysis – and the document became the centerpiece in subsequent litigation.

In retrospect, had I signed something after the fact that I hadn't drafted in the first place, it would have tarnished my reputation and possibly placed me in legal jeopardy. So I felt good about sticking up for my values. Suffice it to say, when you do the right thing, you can go home and sleep at night.

There were no ramifications from Mayor Pastrick or his staff when I refused to sign the memo, but, in any case, I wasn't worried. I've always been able to make a living and know that if times get tough, I will survive just like my folks managed to do as migrant workers by doing, in their words, "an honest day's work for an honest day's pay."

## EVAN BAYH FOR U.S. SENATOR

In 1998 Evan Bayh was the overwhelming favorite when he ran for the United States Senate against Paul Helmke, a former mayor of Fort Wayne, Indiana. Naturally I campaigned for the former governor, whom I had worked for as chairman of the Worker's Compensation Board. Bayh garnered 64 percent of the vote. It was the largest margin of victory for a Democrat in an Indiana Senate race.

Evan Bayh was a guest on a weekly talk show called *Indiana Now* that I cohosted with attorney Larry Evans on Lakeshore Television. The public broadcast station was seen throughout northwest Indiana and the Chicago metropolitan area. Larry, my senior partner, taught me a great deal. He had the patience of Job and was a sincere, intelligent, and welcoming person. During our five years together on the air starting in 1996, we interviewed local and state newsmakers, including political candidates and officeholders, as well as authors and sports legends such as Coach Hank Stram, a graduate of Gary Lew Wallace High School.

## ELOY'S DEATH

After twenty-three years of service in the U.S. Air Force and having fond memories of time spent there, Eloy decided to live in San Antonio following his retirement. Dad and I attended his retirement ceremony at Hurlburt Field in Fort Walton Beach, Florida, and helped him, wife Kathy, and their two daughters, Kelly and Monica, relocate to Converse, Texas, a suburb of San Antonio. Jet mechanics, especially military retirees, were in high demand there. Eloy's work had taken him all over the United States and, for that matter, the world, including England, Germany, Spain, and North Africa. In 1996 when a C-130 plane carrying Commerce Secretary Ron Brown on a trade mission crashed into a mountainside in Croatia, Eloy's crew was part of the team of investigators.

Within a year of retirement in April 1999, Eloy was diagnosed with pancreatic cancer. Our family recoiled at the thought of the ordeal ahead. Like Maria, Eloy fought his battle and underwent chemotherapy and prayed for life for the sake of his wife and two daughters. In the ensuing nine months my tall, fun-loving, well-built, cherished brother lost his hair and became weak, bedridden, and exhausted.

During my last visit with Eloy, I asked if he wanted to be buried next to Maria in Merrillville. He said, "You know Roy, I always said that after my military service, I wanted to live in San Antonio so I have made arrangements to be buried here."

On January 10, 2000, Eloy passed away at age forty-eight, and days later he was buried with full military honors at Colonial Chapel Hill Cemetery in what residents call the "River City," known for its famous River Walk. Eloy was justly proud of his family, his military service to his country, and his life. He attained the rank of master sergeant and earned numerous meritorious service awards as well as tons of friends.

Eloy's ordeal seemed to the family like living through another nightmare. It was tough to accept, especially for my parents. Now they had lost two of their beloved children. With prayers and faith we carried on, but the dark shadow of the loss never has completely gone away. Mom stayed strong for all of us, but Dad went into another deep depression emotionally, from which he never fully recovered. By now a diabetic, Dad refused his doctor's orders to take his insulin and watch his diet. He could not rid himself of painful memories of loved ones lost.

Grief-stricken by the deaths of Maria and Eloy, I vowed to carry their passion for life in my heart. By giving my best, I honor their memories and sacrifice. When my life comes to a close, I pray I'll see them and ask if I made them proud. With this in mind I hope family members can also give life their very best. I hope they will be inspired by those who came before them, just as I have been by those who came before me, and for a brief moment in time hold the torch for their future.

My brother Armando was a big help during these times of grief. Living in Oklahoma City, he came home from time to time, rarely in winter but always when needed. He and his first wife, Teresa, had two children, Alejandro and Elicia. Though he was the brawn behind the family, he had good common sense, accepted responsibility, made no excuses, and didn't look for trouble but took no stuff from anyone. He loved his motorcycle and sports, especially wrestling, boxing, handball, racquetball, and football.

Mando was a real charmer, with plenty of friends and a love of family first. He struggled with his divorce from Teresa but always provided for his children. He was there in both good and bad times and always there when you needed him. He is happily remarried to second wife Debbie, and they live in the Fort Worth metro area of Texas, enjoying mild winters and plenty of hot weather.

Mando's children Alejandro and Elicia both reside near us in northwest Indiana. Both are smart and personable like their dad. An attorney, Alejandro is married with children, and we all enjoy each other's love and company.

## CROWN POINT AND FAMILY LIFE

In 1999 I saw my grandmother Vicenta one final time. She was ninety-four, her body had literally given out, and she was dying of cancer. We expressed our loving affection, and I told her how much she meant to me. She told me how she always prayed for me, especially when I was so ill. Her parting advice, as always, was "Take care of yourself so you can care for your family."

I am very family-oriented, and even though pursuing and holding office is time-consuming, I'd like to think I had been able to balance the two. But it is something one needs to be mindful of or clearly family discord can result. I've seen it happen too many times. My priorities are family first, then my life. I've tried to monitor my professional life to make sure it didn't overstress me to the extent it detracted from my role as husband, father, and family member.

Even though Crown Point was not ethnically diverse compared to some areas in northwest Indiana, my parents felt comfortable there, as did Betty and I. It was a little more difficult for my daughters, especially Maria, who at times felt ostracized by virtue of her Mexican-Filipino heritage. When she was in kindergarten at St. Mary's, she'd come home and say, "The teacher always makes me go last in line even when I start out at the front."

Betty and I thought perhaps she was exaggerating but attended the school's Christmas holiday production and, sure enough, when her class came out, there was Maria at the back end of the line. Betty made an appointment to talk with the teacher and did not get a satisfactory explanation. In fact, she came home very angry, and we did not send Maria back to that school. If parents and teachers do not respect other cultures, prejudice is passed from one generation to the next. In the Crown Point public schools there were hardly any African American or Hispanic teachers. The city has come a long way since the Ku Klux Klan was active during the 1920s, but the schools and agencies of city government have not made much of an effort to make their staff more diverse.

Maria started first grade at Eisenhower Elementary. Normally I'd drive her in the morning and Dad would pick her up after school. One day when she was in second grade, I told Dad I'd get her. When she didn't see Dad's car, she went back into the school unnoticed by anyone. Instead of going to the office, she decided to walk home and exited a side door. We lived about two miles away, and she would have had to cross a busy street.

When I couldn't find Maria and the school monitor had no idea where she was, I was quite frantic, especially after discovering that she was not inside the building. I started driving down a side road looking for her and fortunately spotted her before she had left the school grounds and started across State Road 55. By now frantic, I asked why she was walking home. In a nonchalant way that was quintessentially Maria, she said, "I can walk home, no problem."

We introduced the girls to many sports, including baseball, soccer, and basketball. I think athletics are important in developing teamwork, staying physically fit, and being exposed to competition. Veronica approved of my cheering for her, but Maria would allow me to watch her play only if I kept quiet. Once I yelled to Maria some words of encouragement from the bleachers, and she just stopped. I knew immediately that I had made a mistake and promised not to repeat it. We enrolled the girls in a karate class, and they lasted all of two weeks. When they told me they wanted to stop going, I said, "OK, but maybe when you are older, you might want to take it up as a means of self-defense." Veronica said, "OK, maybe when I'm older," whereas Maria said, "No, Dad, not even when I'm older."

The sports the girls liked best were swimming and tennis. We took them to the pool at the YMCA, and Betty's dad taught them the basics of tennis when we were in Florida. Later on, they were both on the high school tennis team. Veronica was a little more competitive in terms of getting bothered if she lost, while Maria took things more in stride but usually won next time.

The one thing Betty and I insisted they stay with was piano lessons. We believed it would help in mental development, eye-hand coordination, and staying focused. They went twice a week and practiced at home as well. It's kind of a Filipino tradition to have a piano in the house. Betty and her sisters all played. At times the girls had to be coaxed, but at other stages they enjoyed it. Now when they are at the house, they'll often sit down and play first thing. It is relaxing and brings back memories of when my dad would say, "Hey, play a song" and then praise their talents.

Veronica played the trumpet and was in band, starting in fifth grade. Maria had no interest in joining, marching at football games and the like. Taking up the violin, she was in the orchestra. She also taught herself to play the guitar and drums. I got her an electric guitar and amplifier, and she'd play with friends.

Betty and I are baptismal godparents to my brother Armando's son Alex (Alejandro). After he finished high school, he left home to find his own way in the world, just as his father had done years earlier. I kept in touch and urged him to consider college, offering to let him come live with us if he did. One day he called, inquiring whether the offer was still good. "Absolutely," I replied. So at age nineteen Alex moved in with us. It was seamless. He was a great addition, almost like the son I never had. My daughters loved him like a big brother. His dad took care of most of the college expenses.

Alex's initial goal was to teach in elementary school. At IU Northwest he majored in education. His last semester he student-taught, and afterward he told me, "Uncle Roy, I don't want to be a teacher." Intending eventually to study law, after graduation he got a full-time job. I said to him, "The agreement was that you could live with me as long as you were in school. I think it's time you moved on." He was good with that and found an apartment, but Betty and the girls were thoroughly upset with me. I was in the doghouse for a while.

About six months later Alex asked if he could move back if he attended law school. He had taken the LSAT and had admission letters from DePaul, Valparaiso, and IU law schools. He was especially impressed with the welcoming atmosphere at DePaul and the school's 98-percent graduation rate, whereas Valparaiso warned that only two-thirds of incoming students would graduate. DePaul offered him a scholarship covering half his tuition (totaling close to $50,000 over three years); that sealed the deal. Alex commuted from our house in Crown Point, taking the South Shore from Gary's Adam Benjamin Transportation Center back and forth to Chicago. The third year he lived with fellow students in an apartment near campus.

Alex later passed the Indiana Bar Exam and secured a deputy prosecutor's position under Lake County prosecutor Bernard Carter before opening his own private legal practice. He is married to Angie Pomales, and they are loving parents to two sons and a daughter.

Our mission at the Lake County Sheriff's Office is to enhance the quality of life in Lake County by serving and protecting our community through excellent law enforcement services.

Lake County Sheriff ROGELIO "ROY" DOMINGUEZ's website

What about it? Any of you got guts enough
to stand up and take sides?

ERIC "HOSS" CARTWRIGHT,
*Bonanza,* season 1, episode 13, "Vendetta"

NINE

# Becoming Lake County Sheriff

*One day I took my teenage daughter Maria to the animal pound after school to adopt a kitten. We arrived around 3:30, an hour before the Lake County animal pound was scheduled to close, and asked if we could take a close look at the kittens. The director said curtly, "Don't you see the sign? We do not show cats after three o'clock. Come back tomorrow." I thought to myself, "How unfortunate" and "Such a bad attitude." As we were leaving, Maria asked what happened and I said, "What you have just witnessed is a lack of concern for public service." That was the nicest way I could put it. She understood.*

## 2002 RACE FOR SHERIFF

Realizing my previous campaign for sheriff in 1994 was too abbreviated, I decided to announce in May of 2001, a year in advance. Starting early would allow me sufficient time to promote my reasons for seeking the office and communicate those ideals and principles successfully. During my predecessor's seven years in office, the sheriff's department had become more politicized, and its morale and reputation had suffered grievous damage. Pilfering and corrupt practices had occurred to the extent that several federal criminal investigations had taken place. It was so bad that a sheriff's police officer assigned to the Lake County Drug Task Force was under federal investigation for criminal activities while on duty. After a lengthy federal probe, Officer Alex H. Richardson was indicted for several federal criminal offenses, found guilty, and sent to a federal penitentiary. After serving his prison sentence, Richardson wrote a book titled *Lines Crossed,* published by Author House. In it he discusses his activities and those of the Drug Task Force. He wasn't the only one convicted.

I decided to make my announcement outside the Crown Point sheriff's office at the Lake County government complex, similar to when mayoral candidates stand on the steps of city hall, a tradition that is about as American as you can get. Upon hearing of my plans, Sheriff John Buncich threatened to have me arrested if I went through with the announcement. My reaction was, "He's got to be kidding." No, in fact he told the local media that his attorney, John Bushemi, had advised him that I couldn't make my announcement on county property without permission. Never mind that it was public property and that so long as I was not being disruptive, I would not be guilty of trespassing.

Finding such a position distasteful and vulgar, the local press wrote stinging articles and editorials denouncing his threat. I'm sure it sold a lot of newspapers. Asked if I intended to go through with the plan, I declared, "Absolutely." Reporters billed it as the showdown at high noon, like in the western movie of that name starring Gary Cooper. It was not that I wanted to go to jail, but I was willing to risk it in order to defend my freedom of speech and candidacy. I recalled that my dad and brothers had served our country in the military and that Dad's cousin gave his life fighting in Korea. I wasn't about to let anyone bully or intimidate me or my family. In Lake County, politics is hard-fought and not for the faint of heart, but this threat had reached a new low.

As the twelve o'clock hour approached, I was with wife Betty, daughters Maria and Veronica, and my mom, who was all for me standing up to Buncich and wouldn't have missed it for the world. I think my mom might have duked it out with my adversary had he shown up. My dad was too ill to attend but knew I needed to make a stand. He was there in spirit. The ravages of diabetes, including muscle loss and occasional signs of dementia, had reached the point where he needed frequent medication and constant monitoring in a nursing home. Still, whenever we visited him, his parting words were, "Be sure you take care of your mom."

I made the announcement that I was a candidate for sheriff on a green pathway between Buildings B and C of the Crown Point county government complex. Police cars were all around, as well as about seventy-five supporters and curiosity seekers. The whole thing went off without incident. Although I was unaware at the time, Buncich at the last minute issued a press release saying he wasn't going to arrest me and claimed that he had never implied that he would. Since I didn't retreat in response to his threat, all he could do was deny, deny.

Unable to run himself because of the term-limits law, Buncich was supporting Mike Arredondo, who had been chief of police during his tenure. Mike and I had different circles of friends because he was reared in East Chicago and I was from Gary, but respected each other. We just happened to become competitors for the same position. Fortunately I never had to run against Mike because Buncich made himself the issue. He was a negative lightning rod. Without bothering to inform Mike, he announced that he would be chief of police if Mike won and therefore would still be running the department. It was a colossal mistake, but apparently Buncich wanted to embarrass me in a big way. It backfired enormously, as voters do not want their elected officials beholden to others. In fact, I think he wanted to do more than beat me; I think he wanted to humiliate me. The reasons for his unwarranted attacks were foreign to my way of thinking. Suffice it to say, he and his close allies failed to respect people of different racial backgrounds.

Ironically, twenty years before, Mike's uncle, Joe Arredondo, had been a victim of the same sort of aggressive animosity filled with racial overtones and lost a reelection bid to Chris Anton, part of the same ethnic coalition that supported Buncich. I was not intimidated but took precautions and steered clear of Buncich. He had always been aggressively negative toward me ever since 1994. I'm told people would get his goat by saying, "If it wasn't for those Hispanic throw-ins, Dominguez would have beaten you." The police bodyguards around him all the time might try to gain favor with him by creating problems for me. If we happened to be at the same function, I would not go up and shake his hand. I recalled what my dad told me: "You give respect when respect is earned; but if someone disrespects you, you don't need to respect him."

Unlike 1994, my opponents did not throw in sham candidates, because they thought Arredondo would beat me one-on-one. Most unions and all local Fraternal Order of Police chapters supported him; in fact, the national FOP leader came in to attend one of his rallies. Mayor Pastrick went to the same church as the Arredondos but told me he was not going to get involved and kept his word, unlike 1994, when in his zeal to defeat Peter Benjamin he accepted the lesser of two evils. That taught me a lesson: that a pledge is something not to take for granted. On the other hand, Pastrick's political enemies – Stiglich and Cantrell – supported Arredondo.

As corporation counsel for East Chicago, I knew that many of Pastrick's supporters who had not supported me in 1994 were with me now. For the past seven years, since my previous sheriff's race, I had stayed actively involved in community events. Mindful of my parents' advice – "It's always about the people" – I was determined to make it a people campaign.

There were many new supporters who helped in 2002. This time I had the assistance of Lake County surveyor George Van Til, who had been involved in county politics for decades. He was once a staffer for U.S. senator Vance Hartke, and, in my opinion, the most savvy campaign strategist around. He knows well the history of county politics and the shenanigans that go on. Like me, George believes in good government for our citizens. We became good friends. He is very methodical and attributes his attention to details to his Dutch family background. His charming, intelligent wife, Patti, is a retired lieutenant from the Lake County Sheriff's Department and also a valued supporter.

I won the May primary decisively. It was a major upset. Immediately afterward, Buncich started telling people that he would be running in four years, so, in other words, don't make friends with Dominguez or support his administration. I learned through the grapevine that many officers feared that he'd retaliate against them later if they cooperated with me, should he again become sheriff four years later. In fact, in February of 2003, a month after I was sworn into office, Buncich held a fund-raiser, billing it as in support of his reelection three years hence. While the Indiana constitution forbade sheriffs from serving more than two consecutive terms, they were free to run after four years out of office.

## SELECTING A CHIEF

One of the first important decisions awaiting me as the presumptive sheriff-elect was to select an able chief. While I would be setting policy and overseeing the office in a general sense, the chief was responsible for implementing policy decisions. In a technical sense the person appointed to the post is not simply chief of police but chief of all three divisions, including correctional officers and the administrative staff. I decided that it would be presumptive to make a selection prior to the November general election, but I certainly knew I wanted someone who was bright, energetic, and knowledgeable about police work, and who would have the trust of the community – in short, an honest career professional who would inspire respect.

About a dozen people expressed an interest in the position and sent me resumes. I also asked several people if they wished to be considered. My goal was to appoint someone who really wanted to make a difference in the post, not one who felt he was entitled to it because of either years of service or political support. Several men in particular represented my idea of an ideal candidate. One was state police major Jerome Ezell. He turned down an opportunity to be considered, saying simply, "I'm not ready to retire" from his present job.

That same day I also asked IU Northwest criminal justice professor Gary Martin, who had served for a quarter-century with the Gary Police Department in various capacities, including assistant chief. He knew how to fight for his principles and had seen just about everything that might confront a police agency. He was a strong advocate of diversity. He had also been a trusted friend for many years.

I invited Gary to have lunch at the Cracker Barrel Restaurant in Merrillville, Indiana, and out of the blue popped the question to him. He said, "Naw, naw, absolutely not" with that Southern drawl of his and quipped that he had retired from police work ten years before and didn't want to go through what had happened in 1991, when Crown Point's first Democratic mayor, James Metros, had nominated him to be chief, only to have the appointment blocked by a Republican-dominated city council. The argument used against him was that he was from the city of Gary, and that hurt him deeply. Having experienced some discriminatory difficulties myself, I knew at the time how tarnished he felt and called him up to commiserate and convey my regrets because he would have done a great job. It was Crown Point's loss.

I responded to Gary's reply by saying, "Can't we just talk about it?" He said OK, and we didn't leave the Cracker Barrel until nearly six hours later. Spiritually and mentally we were on the same wavelength. Gary grew up in a poor section of Nashville, Tennessee, and was from a large family. We both had many similar life experiences, coming from humble beginnings, enduring grief of family members who had died from illnesses, struggling to accomplish our dreams, having love of family and integrity, and both being aware of the fragile, precious gift of life. We both knew the important role law enforcement played in community safety. Gary also had vast experience in police work, was a hard worker, and valued integrity and trust. He asked me a series of questions, and by the third or fourth one I sensed that he was hooked. He loved new challenges.

At the end of our six-hour marathon conversation Gary Martin said he wanted to talk things over with his Russian-born wife, Olga, whom he had met when the two of them worked at U.S. Steel. He loved teaching and knew he'd have to cut back to part-time. That evening about nine o'clock Gary called the house. His first words were, "Are you serious?" I replied in the affirmative. Then he said, "Do you have the power to appoint your chief?" Recalling the Crown Point fiasco, I knew why he asked that question. By statute I had sole discretion to appoint the chief; it did not require approval by any other entity. Satisfied with my affirmative answers, Gary said, "OK, count me in" and added, "I wouldn't come out of retirement but for the opportunity to work with you, Roy." I was honored that he put it that way because I knew he meant it, and I was honored by his friendship.

While examining the dossiers of other candidates, the measure of my deliberation was "Would this person be a better choice than Gary Martin?" He was the upper bar for me, but I wanted to feel comfortable knowing that I had made myself receptive to others. During this time, in the media speculation about whom I might select, Gary's name was never mentioned among the leading candidates. I was pleased that there was a discussion within the community over the appointment and believed it would help me bring the department back in the fold in terms of its becoming more professional and public service–oriented.

In the end the choice for chief came back to Gary. Betty and I invited him and Olga for dinner, and I officially extended the offer. He accepted.

In early December of 2002, a few weeks before I assumed office, I scheduled a press conference at the law office conference room of longtime friends Jim and Leon Sarkisian. At 10 AM members of the media were in attendance when I presented my selection for chief. Prior to that day Gary, as perhaps befitted a college professor, wore a diamond-studded earring in his right lobe and wore his hair in a ponytail. I never asked him to get a haircut or remove the earring but hoped that he would. When he entered the room from a side door, it was without the earring and ponytail. We both knew that, especially in police work, image is important.

My selection of Gary Martin was extremely well received, and reporters later told me that it was one of the best-kept secrets they could recall. One reporter asked whether Gary was a political supporter and if that played a part in my selection. I was able tell the press that Gary had not voted for me. The truth was, he had been so nonpolitical he hadn't voted at all. Feigning shock when he first told me that, I said, "You mean you didn't vote for me?" "I'll vote for you next time," he promised with a smile. I picked Gary Martin to be chief, I told those attending the press conference, because he was a professional who had the integrity and skills to repair the morale and enhance the mission of the sheriff's department.

## TAKING OFFICE

In December of 2002, we held a swearing-in ceremony at Indiana University Northwest's theater. U.S. District Court judge Rudy Lozano, a man of impeccable integrity, administered the oath of office. Some of my political partisans wanted me to demote Mike Arredondo, but I wouldn't do that. He didn't remain police chief, of course, but he was appointed to the rank of commander, whereas I could have reassigned him to his merit rank of sergeant. He was courteous and helpful during the transition. I respected the Arredondo family for all their accomplishments and didn't want them to think ill of me. Mike was finishing his last semester in college and wanted to avoid shift work, so I left him on days and allowed him to keep his police car, which avoided financial difficulties for his family. His wife, Letty, and two sons are wonderful people, and I hoped to earn their friendship by showing respect to Mike. We were friends then and now.

From the beginning, John Buncich and his friends never stopped concocting ways to create problems for me and to disrupt what I was attempting to accomplish. He had hired over half the police officers I inherited and tried to ensure that they remained loyal to him and didn't befriend me. Among them were many good officers, but some were involved in sweetheart contract scams or held second jobs on county time. In October of 2002, he convinced the County Council to adopt a collective bargaining agreement in order to create difficulties for me. He had had eight years to do this, but now he was prepared to skillfully use the FOP and police unions and allege that my agenda was anti-police. What nonsense and waste of time, and they did not achieve their goal. The onset of the October 2002 collective bargaining agreement was in large measure an attempt to emasculate the authority of the sheriff-elect. The county ordinance did not include the elected sheriff in collective bargaining negotiations.

There is a tradition that on Christmas Day the outgoing sheriff relinquishes his office and turns it over to his successor. When I got there, the outgoing administration had sanitized the files and the computer memory banks were deleted, including personnel records for those officers he favored. Within a week I received a letter from thirteen members of the police canine unit demanding reimbursement for three years of back pay, totaling over a half-million dollars. Never mind that they had volunteered to be canine officers, had not documented their alleged overtime hours, and had never brought this matter to the attention of the previous sheriff. The department had paid to purchase the canines and had sent the officers to specialized training at a combined cost of approximately $15,000.

Under the prior administration the department had allowed officers to charge veterinarian bills, various equipment, pet food, and other expenses at will. Even so, the K-9 officers had set up a private bank account from individual donations solicited from fund-raising activities in which the sheriff's police emblem was employed to play upon people's goodwill toward police officers. This went on unchecked with no administrative procedures in place, and there was no accountability for the monies and expenditures. When I demanded an accounting, they refused on the grounds that their fund was private and not officially part of the sheriff's department. I ordered them to stop using the sheriff's logo or claiming any association with the department and implemented a detailed K-9 procedural set of rules of conduct.

In short, the lawsuit was an initiative launched to create problems for me and to raid the taxpayer's county treasury. If I caved in, I would be compromised and Buncich would claim the victory. If I held firm, politicos would allege that I was anti-police. What they failed to realize was that I was more dedicated to public service than to political expediency. So I rejected their demand even under pressure from other local politicians who threatened not to support my initiatives unless I settled the lawsuit.

Because National Labor Relations Board standards require that canine officers are entitled to so many days off for the care of their police dogs and that the officers are entitled to pay even though they volunteered, I realized that legal precedent required some sort of negotiation. Our legal counsel ultimately reached an out-of-court settlement. There was a nondisclosure clause, so I cannot reveal the exact amount of compensation, but it was significantly less than first demanded. We saved the taxpayers a considerable amount of money, but Buncich's allies claimed they had forced me to settle, even though some of the original canine officers separated themselves from the litigation when they realized it was a political ploy meant to undermine my administration and to raid the taxpayers.

I couldn't remove many of those malcontents because merit board rules and a collective bargaining agreement were in place that made termination very difficult for reasons short of criminal actions. I believe in checks and balances and realize that everyone makes honest mistakes, but the rules and collective bargaining agreement were amended to protect those who were intentionally insubordinate or looking for a means to get out of work. I am pleased to say, however, that Buncich's cronies did not derail my progressive agenda even though he was brazen enough to come into the sheriff's office at times and huddle with them. What a waste of energy.

My team and I had a lot of work ahead of us. When I first came in, I met in the government center auditorium with the police officers, then the correctional officers, and finally the civilian employees. I let everyone know that I wouldn't tolerate unprofessional conduct. If they were not dedicated to public service employment, I recommended that they seek employment opportunities elsewhere. I did not force them to give up part-time jobs but emphasized that it was illegal to work second jobs on government time. In other words, the days of doing nothing for eight hours were over. I told officers to arrive at work in uniform. They knew I meant business. Some resigned or retired, realizing the gravy train had ended and accountability would be reinstituted. I did not set a uniform dress code for the civilian staff but expected them to look neat and professional.

If I were going to do more than talk the talk, I realized that I had to walk the walk, so to speak. That is why, in order to set an example, I gave up my successful private law practice of twenty years even though not legally required to do so. I had done well and represented my clients ably. I had a good reputation and have never been disciplined by the Supreme Court. My action symbolized that I was on duty full-time, that my energies would be fully devoted to being sheriff, in other words that public service was my number-one priority.

As a step toward reform, my first department order was to remove politics from departmental operations. Employees were forbidden to engage in political activities during working hours. There would be no wearing political buttons, selling campaign tickets, or soliciting votes or support for any political candidates whatsoever. Breaking with precedent, I announced that no employees would be allowed to contribute money to my political fund. Previously, there had been a so-called two-percent club whereby employees were required to donate that proportion of their pay – one percent to the county Democratic Party and one percent for the sheriff.

Many of my political advisers thought these measures were ill-advised and would leave me politically vulnerable, but I wanted to set a new ethical standard of operations. Believing in good government, I challenged the staff to redirect its activities toward public service, not political services. Reform was critically important and necessary to reinstitute trust with our citizens. Also I wanted the staff to know that meritorious conduct, not political loyalty, would be the measure for promotion. The vast majority of staff members cheered this new attitude and went to work enthusiastically. If they were faithfully serving the community, no longer would they need to fear political reprisals.

## DEPUTY CHIEF MARCO KUYACHICH

I told Gary Martin that he should select the deputy chief. According to the merit rules, the appointee had to come from within the departmental ranks. I hoped it would be someone just like him in terms of being trustworthy, energetic, intelligent, and experienced. He selected Lieutenant Marco Kuyachich, who was highly respected by his peers and had served in a wide range of capacities. A distinguished career officer with almost twenty-five years of experience in numerous capacities, he had grown up in Glen Park and was an honest, solid, bright, hard-working family man. Chief Martin assured me that Marco was the man who could best assist him in implementing our mission, policies, and goals. Informing me of his choice on a Thursday, Gary said that he hoped to make the announcement at a Saturday conference luncheon in Indianapolis hosted by the Indiana Association of Chiefs of Police.

I did not know Marco personally and told Gary I wanted to think it over. Suspecting correctly that I intended to respect his choice, Gary said, "Boss, unless you tell me no, I'm going to announce it at the luncheon." I said, "I think that is a great idea." To Marco's surprise, at the luncheon Gary called him up and gave him his new uniform insignia of two stars to be worn on the collar. Marco got a standing ovation. Deputy Chief Marco, as we call him, proved to be a good friend, an asset to the team, and a great selection.

## RETIRED MAJOR DON PETERS

One afternoon in the spring of 2003 my staff assistant informed me that a retired major named Don Peters had come to see me. An elderly retired police officer who walked with a cane, he stated that he wanted to meet the man he had voted for. Major Peters had been appointed to the sheriff's department in 1954. He proceeded to tell me stories about the history of the department while he worked there. During the 1960s, he helped FBI agents representing the U.S. attorney's office investigate corrupt practices, which were all too common then. He seemed eager to offer suggestions on making the sheriff's office a better department, and we talked most of the afternoon. One comment in particular stayed with me, and that was that if the people elected an honest sheriff, there would be more honest government countywide.

I was honored that Major Peters would share his life experiences with me and that he trusted I was honest and could return the sheriff's department back to the community and restore its integrity and trust. If I abided by the values my parents taught me, I could not fail.

Administering an office is a complex step-by-step process involving give-and-take. One thing that is not complex and doesn't come piecemeal is honesty. It just doesn't. I might be on cordial terms with many people, as all elected officials have to be, but I don't hang around with those who I suspect may be involved in unethical activities. That doesn't mean that everyone who hangs around with me is always honest or that I am overly judgmental. But I'm very mindful of what Major Peters imparted to me and try to live up to his standards.

## SETTING A NEW TONE

There was a perception that the sheriff's department was the biggest burglary unit in the county. It was alleged that on police raids some officers at times simply helped themselves to the contents of the house. Beforehand, as a private lawyer, I deliberately shied away from cases involving the sheriff's department because I didn't want to be seen as suing out of sour grapes because I didn't win the 1994 election. However, while I was in private practice, clients would tell me how they believed some officers stole their rings and other personal valuables. The department's reputation was so tarnished that federal agencies shied away from working with its officers. As sheriff, I changed the supervisor and some of the officers. You create a different mindset by setting a tone and appointing professional administrators who were men and women of integrity and dedicated toward public service.

Many good officers, who had felt tarnished during the previous regime, wished us well. Others were resistant to change and vehemently obstructionist. I expected difficulties and political animosity from the Buncich organization. The former sheriff's legal counsel, Stanley Jablonski, sued me, for instance, at every turn. But I proceeded forward. As a lawyer, I knew the legal ramifications of political discrimination lawsuits. The key precedent was known as the Richard J. Elrod decision, named after a former police officer paralyzed in 1969 during the so-called Days of Rage when he attempted to tackle a protestor. Elected sheriff of Cook County, Illinois, defeating Under Sheriff Bernard Carey, Elrod terminated various officers when he took office in December of 1970. Their subsequent lawsuit went all the way to the Supreme Court.

Previously, it was common for newly elected officials to bring in their own staff people under the justification, dating back to the age of Andrew Jackson, "to the victor belong the spoils." The Elrod decision gave career employees protection against retribution for not aligning themselves with the successful officeholder. On the other hand, the decision recognized the right of officeholders to bring in their own staff in confidential or policymaking positions. I believed this was a sound decision and was careful not to cross the line in terms of my authority. Nonetheless, appointees who previously held discretionary positions filed nuisance lawsuits to distract me from moving forward and create as many political landmines as they could.

Many hangers-on had "straw" jobs that entailed little work. They'd come in during the morning and set out for the coffee shop or a local restaurant for the rest of the day. We eliminated quite a few of these positions, again not without a legal fight. Some council members and commissioners had a stake in the status quo in terms of either contracts or personnel. I set to work to remove these entanglements in the belief that police work required protecting the community, not providing political benefits. When I eliminated superfluous positions of employees who were not doing work, a number filed lawsuits claiming they were dismissed for political reasons. All told, however, we were very successful and never lost a trial, thanks to attorneys John M. Kopack and John Dull and their staff.

I reviewed all the contracts the sheriff's department had with vendors and did not renew those that were not in the public interest. For example, one politically connected person with only a bachelor's degree was being paid $10,000 a month to provide additional counseling to inmates. Incredibly, Buncich had proposed to the county commissioners that this contractor should receive a raise of $12,000 to boost his annual salary to $132,000. He did not maintain an active private office and had literally no overhead to speak of and only a part-time secretary.

On several occasions I asked this vendor to let me see documentation of his work product, as required under terms of the contract. He refused to comply, so I canceled his contract. He claimed my action was politically motivated, but I had documented my requests for his records and his refusal. I believe strongly in providing counseling or help for offenders since eventually they go back into the community, but I had no confidence in this private vendor. We found a competent replacement at half the salary who filed quarterly reports and provided counseling for drug and alcohol addiction as well as anger management.

State statute empowers Indiana sheriffs to issue at their discretion special deputy commissions to individuals, who then have full police powers, including the authority to make arrests and carry firearms. In some instances, police deputy commissions were given for legitimate reasons to court bailiffs, school resource officers, and investigators for the coroner or prosecutor's office. All told, there might be two or three hundred people involved in protecting legitimate government entities. When I took office, however, there were approximately two thousand special deputies, many of whom had contributed $1,500 into the sheriff's political fund or received the commission as a reward for political loyalties.

On my first day in office I stopped the outdated practice, sending a letter out that all previous deputy commissions would expire in three months. That gave officers working for government entities time to apply for a renewal. I required applicants to get authorization from their employer. In other words, it would be up to the judge, prosecutor, coroner, or school superintendent to determine if the employee needed a police commission.

Every occupation has its professional courtesies, such as, for police, being let through security if one is late for a flight or being let off from a possible speeding ticket with a warning. With minor discretionary matters that might be OK, but some people would flash their badge to get out of DUIs, domestic battery incidents, and a whole host of serious things. That was simply wrong, and if these people created a legal liability, the sheriff's department and ultimately the taxpayers are parties to lawsuits. Equally important, police officers train very hard to earn the right to don the uniform with pride, and it is an affront to them for politicos to be able to buy that privilege and possibly tarnish the profession.

When I terminated the deputy commissions as a reform initiative, my political enemies would tell those whose commission expired words to the effect, "If Dominguez had been defeated, you'd still have your commission, but this guy is no good."

## BOARD OF COMMISSIONERS

Serving as the executive branch of county government is a three-member board of commissioners, elected in staggered four-year terms. Typically one is from Gary, a second from Hammond, and a third from south county. In the past sixty years virtually all were Democrats except for Ernie Niemeyer, who lived in Lowell.

During my first term Rudy Clay, who later became mayor of Gary, was the county commissioner from District One. Being from Gary myself, I had known Rudy for years. He was always supportive. The same cannot be said for all commissioners. The son of one of them was a canine officer. At one point he had three K-9 units assigned to him, which was unheard-of, and in the lawsuit brought by members of his unit he claimed he was entitled to up to triple the amount of damages. Though she never said so, it was clear by her actions that this commissioner wanted me to settle the lawsuit on terms favorable to the plaintiffs. As things progressed, we became good friends, and I am happy for our association.

Serving as the legislative branch is a seven-member council representing various districts and responsible for drawing up an annual budget, setting salaries, and acting on special appropriation requests. Most members traditionally are Democrats, but a Republican from Crown Point, Larry Blanchard, served on the council and was supportive, as were most council members. Of course, we had our debates, but that is healthy in the process of government.

I believe in diversity. If you are assembling a team to serve the public, it should have a variety of perspectives reflective of the constituents. To use a baseball analogy, you don't want all pitchers; you need some infielders and outfielders. Diversity is our nation's strong suit because people of different backgrounds bring a pluralistic view of issues and imagination. This was especially true in northwest Indiana. Furthermore, we as Americans are composed of a multiplicity of cultures, and we can best respect and appreciate each other by interaction and not segregation.

In the sheriff's office when hiring police, it is important to have officers who are representative of the entire community, including race, class, gender, and ethnicity. County-wide geographic diversity is also important. I want police officers and staff members who are comfortable talking to farmers as well as officers comfortable in an urban setting. I didn't hire individuals who I believed failed to understand the importance of cultural sensitivity and respect.

One tactic I used successfully when I started a good government initiative was to put the proposal in writing and release it to the media as well as to the commissioners. That way, if others attempted to put roadblocks in my way, they would have to answer to the press and the voters. They objected to my method, but I stood my ground, and at times the threat of going public was quite effective.

I was able to get most things through, thanks to a great staff led by Chief Gary Martin, Deputy Chief Marco Kuyachich, and legal counsel John Kopack, whose experience and legal acumen were second to none. Well respected in our legal community, John is also a tough litigator. To date, we have never lost a lawsuit. John reveres good government, and many of our new initiatives were successful because of his legal and practical advice.

New positions of administrative chief of staff and deputy staff chief were created in order to implement civilian staff management and community services. John Key was selected as administrative chief of staff and Patti Van Til, a retired lieutenant from our sheriff's department, was chosen administrative deputy chief of staff. Both are intelligent, community-oriented, and dedicated to public service. They were given the responsibilities of staff training, human resources, community outreach programs, domestic violence prevention, drug-free programs, and animal shelter adoption initiatives. The overall goal was for the department to do its very best in advancing our motto "To Serve and Protect."

Our officers have jurisdiction anywhere in the county and in particular provide police services for those in unincorporated areas that lack police departments. In addition, we have specialty units for several initiatives. A countywide Drug Task Force allows us to form a metro unit for which we get officers from various police agencies to combat drug-dealing gangs. We have a helicopter unit, and a marine unit patrols the shores of Lake Michigan, both of which respond to requests from neighboring counties. If there is a drowning at Dunes State Park in Porter County, for instance, we get involved and do not charge for police services. Our job being to protect the public, we, as police professionals, provide assistance regardless of jurisdictional boundaries.

## MAINTAINING THE COUNTY JAIL

In addition to 168 police officers, about 180 correctional officers maintain the county jail. One of the sheriff's statutory responsibilities, in conjunction with the warden, is to maintain a constitutional jail. On average the inmate population is between 850 and 900, including those awaiting trial and some serving sentences of three years or less. The old wing is linear, whereas the newer wing is set up in a circular pod that gives correctional officers a better view from which to provide for inmates' protection.

For those serving sentences of more than twelve months, the Indiana Department of Corrections pays the county a stipend to house them and therefore relieve overcrowding at state prisons. We maintain a jail medical facility, but if inmates require more than immediate care, we take them to Methodist Hospital. We provide prescription medicine (probably 75 percent of inmates are on some type of medication), dental care, psychological counseling, and, of course, a kitchen. We serve three thousand meals a day to prisoners and staff, who cannot leave during their eight-hour shift. We employ a dietician and provide a proper daily menu that usually includes eggs or cereal and bread for breakfast, lunch-meat sandwiches at noon, and a hot evening meal.

In the jail is a commissary unit. Like a general store, it sells products. Friends or relatives can deposit money on behalf of an inmate, who can use a certain amount per day on such items as toothpaste, slippers, soap, combs, brushes, juices, potato chips, Doritos, gum, candy, Twinkies, and in the old days cigarettes and chewing tobacco.

Before I took office, middlemen with political connections would sell products at inflated prices to the commissary, which in turn boosted the prices even higher, and the "straw man" kept the profits. Such a deal. I canceled those commissary vendor contracts. Our correction officers assigned to the commissary unit now shop for the products wherever we can get the best price. Therefore, by eliminating the middleman, all commissary profits accrue to the sheriff's department to be used to buy equipment, building repairs, training of personnel, and other department necessities. The net effect reduces our operating budget and is a huge savings to taxpayers.

Since most inmates smoked cigarettes when I took office, profits from the sale of tobacco were enormous. During my first year we announced that the jail would become a smoke-free facility within three months, the date to coincide with National Smoke-Out Day on November 20. Thereafter cigarettes, cigars, and even chewing tobacco would be considered contraband, with the offender subject to disciplinary procedures. Some warned that the inmates would become agitated and riot and that many staff members would quit in protest, but we instituted smoking cessation programs and paid for professionals to come inside the jail and for the staff to attend stop-smoking sessions. Many had wanted to quit previously but had lacked the wherewithal to make the commitment voluntarily. The American Cancer Society made guest speakers and booklets available, and our program received local and national publicity.

When November 20 arrived, the experiment went seamlessly. Only one inmate needed special medication, and there was no uprising or mass resignation. We did lose quite a bit of commissary profits, but that was OK because we took the profit out of a dangerous and addicting habit.

When I took office as sheriff, there was a work-release program in place that allowed nonviolent offenders to retain their jobs and in that way help their family survive and perhaps retain their medical insurance. They'd stay in jail overnight and be responsible for getting to and from work. Some 20 percent of their net pay went toward running the program. Under my administration we expanded the program to provide placement services, training in resume writing and computer skills, and a GED program. I also instituted a community service program where certain nonviolent offenders could work at county parks, governmental facilities, Lake County Fairgrounds, and buildings owned by not-for-profit agencies such as the YMCA, the YWCA, and the American Legion. We bought the necessary tools and a truck to haul in the equipment, such as mops, paint, window cleaner, and the like. An outdoor crew cuts grass, prunes trees, rakes, picks up litter, and does other necessary tasks.

## "NO-KILL" ANIMAL SHELTER

In 2003 the county animal pound was under the auspices of the county commissioners. The sheriff's previous role was to appoint a representative to an advisory board charged with setting policy and oversight responsibilities. Over its twenty years in existence there was a history of conflict and acrimony between the staff, the board, and members of the community. No one seemed to have the ability to change that attitude. Dogs and cats were euthanized within days of being rounded up, and then their bodies were placed in an incinerator. Some were pets that had strayed away from their home. Staff members seemed to have little sympathy for the animals or their owners.

As problems continued, Commissioner Gerry Scheub and Larry Blanchard, the advisory board member representing the county council, asked if I would take over the animal pound. They were so eager for me to say yes that I think they would have accepted any terms. I certainly had enough to do but agreed on the condition that it become a no-kill animal shelter. I told them it would need more funding but that I would not ask for an exorbitant amount of money. The three of us visited a no-kill facility in Detroit and decided it was feasible. So the board of county commissioners voted to transfer the animal pound to the sheriff's department. Some wanted to hold on to the hiring and firing of personnel, but I insisted that for things to work you couldn't have two chiefs, so to speak, and they agreed.

Many observers thought I had committed political suicide and had been hoodwinked by Scheub and Blanchard. Since I had never operated an animal shelter, what did I know? Well, I hoped that we could do better, and, for me, it was important to save the lives of these pets, pure and simple.

I talked to the director and her staff, consisting of two or three full-time and a half-dozen part-time employees. They were very antagonistic. I told her to send the personnel files to my office and that I wanted to meet with her at 10:30 the following morning. No files were forthcoming, and she did not show up for our meeting. The next day I ordered her to come to my office immediately with the files. Commander Dennis Heaps happened to be with me discussing other administrative matters, and I asked that he remain as a witness. The director came over with another lady and literally threw the files onto my desk. I told her to have a seat and asked who her companion was. She said, "My lawyer advised me not to meet with you without a witness." I said to the so-called witness, "Ma'am you're to leave my office now." She had no authority to be there and left without a fuss.

The director got up. I told her to remain seated because we were going to have a meeting. She declared, "I'm not staying." I said, "I'm ordering you to stay." She stormed out anyway, so I fired her and also changed the entire staff. Commander Heaps, who has a wry sense of humor, quipped, "Thanks, dad, this is just what I needed."

During the ensuing weeks we hired new staff members who loved animals and instituted new procedures and operations. Within a short time we instituted a "No Kill of Adoptable Pets" policy. Adoption, spay, and neuter programs became our main operations. Unlike the past we placed pets for adoption/rescue almost 98 percent of the time and euthanized only upon the recommendation of a veterinarian. Pets are occasionally so ill or injured that the most humane course is to put them to sleep. We won national awards for our new standards and "Can Do" attitude. Each year we placed approximately two thousand pets in adoptive homes and/or rescue facilities. On fliers we had photos of cats and dogs along with the slogan, "Help Us, Help Them."

The staff came up with a bumper sticker for those who adopt pets at the shelter. It reads: "Animal Lovers Love Sheriff Dominguez." I tried to discourage them, but they did it anyway, and there's no denying that it helps publicize the no-kill facility. The community has enthusiastically supported the shelter in a big way. We have an annual spaghetti fundraiser. In 2009 between 1,200 and 1,500 people in support of the shelter attended the dinner.

## ENVIRONMENTAL CRIME TASK FORCE

Protecting the environment is a big public service issue for me. Being against polluters is a natural extension of protecting the community. With the area so industrialized, I wanted to overcome the feeling of fatalism among some citizens, that nothing could be done about these conditions. I'll never forget that industrial pollution affected my older brothers directly and kept us apart from Dad for three years. My concern deepened during the 1960s and 1970s, when the ecology movement was part of the civic activism of the times. Sprayed upon while in the fields, my grandfather suffered for decades with an asthmatic condition. When I lived with him, at night I'd hear him wheezing loudly. That vivid memory stayed with me. I recall speeches where the charismatic labor leader César Chávez concluded that pesticides were a danger not only to farmworkers but to everyone as the chemicals worked their way into America's food chain, water, and air.

In conjunction with the prosecutor's office and the Solid Waste District I helped create an Environmental Crime Task Force. It was a citizens committee representing groups as diverse as the Izaak Walton League and the Northwest Indiana Forum. We also sought business input. I firmly believe companies can protect the environment and still prosper. Will there be some pollution? Yes. Can it be monitored? Yes. Do some companies see it in terms of dollars and cents? Sadly, yes. But can we strike a balance in favor of people and public health? Yes.

I believed that with law enforcement involved, polluters would respond quicker. Environmental agencies had civil but not criminal authority. Working with a consultant from Indianapolis, our lawyers drafted an ordinance approved by the council and commissioners. There were only two other such police environmental task forces in the country, and the only other one emanating from a sheriff's department was in Dade County, Florida.

The intent was not to supersede IDEM (the Indiana Department of Environmental Management) or the EPA (U.S. Environmental Protection Agency) but to supplement what they did and contribute additional resources to the common effort. IDEM, for example, had just three investigators for the entire state. Lake County alone could have kept a whole team of investigators busy. Rather than try to enforce laws as related to major industries such as steelmaking and oil refining, which was the EPA's responsibility, we concentrated on second-tier areas such as junkyards and auto salvage dealers.

Before vehicles are crushed and the scrap taken to steel mills, the law requires the removal of mercury, transmission fuel, and engine oil. A small amount of mercury can cause serious illness to anyone and birth defects to unborn children. The state statute places liability not on mills buying the scrap but on the salvage yards, many of which had neglected to remove the hazards. In those cases when the crushed vehicles were put in the furnace, noxious fumes went into the air and polluted the environment.

We informed salvage yard owners of their responsibilities, including record keeping. Surveillance teams monitor the companies involved and have authority to make periodic inspections without warning. We have filed charges against violators and businesses that illegally dump tires. There's a temptation for tire companies to keep the service fee (around $2.25 a tire) for disposal of their old ones and just dump them illegally.

Feddeler Landfill in Lowell had been closed for five years, supposedly under the supervision of IDEM. We discovered that IDEM never required that shields be deployed and that seepage from underneath was rising to the top. The Solid Waste District brought the situation to my attention. Many suspected that industrial waste had illegally been dumped into Feddeler's, but the owners were big Republican supporters and benefited from the diminution of staff funding and enforcement authority of environmental agencies both statewide and nationally. Kids were riding mopeds and motorcycles in close proximity to potentially deadly fumes. After holding a community forum and hiring career professionals to monitor air quality and well water in the area, we notified the EPA, the state attorney general's office, and IDEM of the situation and our actions. Declaring that an emergency existed, at a cost of $80,000 we placed an eight-foot cyclone fence around the landfill and put up signs warning folks to keep away.

The EPA and the attorney general's office were more helpful than IDEM, whose chairman, Thomas W. Easterly, reflected the pro-business attitude of Governor Mitch Daniels's administration. Before being appointed to head up IDEM, Easterly had been a steel industry advocate of deregulation. He refused to meet with me or even discuss the matter on the phone.

Claiming his agency had sole jurisdiction over the landfill, Easterly ordered us to remove monitoring equipment or else be subject to a fine of $25,000 a day on the flimsy grounds that our equipment might puncture sheeting used to cap the contents of the landfill. I replied that my view of the law was that IDEM may have had primary jurisdiction but not sole jurisdiction and that since the landfill had not been capped – there were no sheets – their safety argument was without merit. In fact, it was ludicrous.

Still seeking to be cooperative, I asked for a meeting with the governor's office. Chief of staff Earl Goode and policy director Neil Pickett met with four of us on behalf of the governor. Commissioner Easterly did not attend because, in Goode's words, he was predisposed in his opinion and the governor's office wanted to have a fresh discussion from our point of view. After we presented them with a summary of the facts, Goode, a well-seasoned professional, turned to Pickett and inquired, "So what is the sheriff doing that he shouldn't be doing? And why hadn't the landfill been capped? And why does the IDEM commissioner want to fine the sheriff $25,000 a day?" All Pickett could say was, "I don't know."

Goode then asked what we wanted the governor's office to do. I said, "Frankly, I wasn't worried about the fine." Goode replied, "Yeah, I wouldn't have been either." Then I said, "All I want is for the attorney general to ensure the landfill is properly closed and that the area be monitored for at least a year." He replied, "That sounds reasonable. In fact, Sheriff, we will monitor it for two years." I said, "Will you folks incur the costs?" He replied, "That's our job. We'll pay for that. What else?" I asked that we be notified about any meetings or new developments. He agreed that we should be.

As I was walking out, Goode was still questioning Neil Pickett about why IDEM had been so uncooperative. Soon afterward, I received a letter from Pickett confirming what we had agreed upon and, of course, that there would be no fines. Both Earl Goode and Neil Pickett were professionals and great to work with.

The attorney general's office filed a lawsuit requiring Feddeler to comply with the law. While they turned down the task force's request to participate in the lawsuit, they kept us abreast of developments. We asked the EPA office in Chicago to monitor the operation in addition to IDEM. I believe in checks and balances, and what one agency doesn't discover, maybe others will. Commissioner Easterly gained more notoriety when without the proper hearings, IDEM gave permits to BP Amoco allowing that company to increase the amount of pollutants they emitted, as part of a plant expansion program. Shortly after that fiasco, he resigned and was replaced.

In the spring of 2007 the Environmental Crime Task Force held a community awareness conference at Gary's Genesis Center. We had booths and displays, and brought in environmentalist Robert F. Kennedy Jr. as keynote speaker. His speaking fee was $20,000, which we raised entirely through private donations, but his appearance generated a great deal of media attention. He eloquently spelled out the connection between corporate polluters and key members of the George W. Bush administration, and he decried the unhealthy influence lobbyists had on legislators from both major parties. It was my intent, by bringing in

Kennedy, to alert our community to the devastating effects of pollution. We did not have to surrender our precious land, water, and air to special interest groups of polluters. That is our responsibility: to protect the environment for our future generations.

The better part of one's life consists of his friendships.

ABRAHAM LINCOLN

Gary Martin was a great storyteller with a zest for life. I talked to him about personal issues, and he was a great help.

I.U. Northwest student CASSANDRA OGLESBY,
*Steel Shavings* 35 ("Educating the Calumet Region:
A History of Indiana University Northwest")

TEN

# Triumph and Tragedy

*My dad had been ailing for some time, but it still was a blow when he passed away in 2006. At the cemetery as the casket was being lowered into its final resting place, Mom sang his favorite song, "Amorcito Corazón" ("my love, my heart"), made famous by Pedro Infante. There wasn't a dry eye in the crowd as eighty-one-year-old Chencha sang it in perfect tune from memory.*

## NEAR-DEATH EXPERIENCE

On March 13, 2004, Officer Robert Bridgeman was driving me to Indianapolis in a marked police car. We were in the I-65 passing lane just south of the Crown Point exit. Its being spring break, my nephew Nicholas, a Purdue University criminal justice major, was in the back seat, and I was checking my schedule on a handheld organizer. A truck driver suddenly cut us off the road. The officer swerved onto the grassy median strip and then accelerated to get back onto the highway. Slickness from the rain caused the vehicle to turn sideways and then flip over violently four or five times before finally landing off the west side of the road, upright but with the roof caved in. The truck driver later admitted that he had not used his signal light when he crossed into our lane and had been at fault.

The accident seemed to happen in slow motion, and I thought we were going to die. The vehicle had a full tank of gas and could have easily exploded and caught fire. I said to myself, "This is how it's going to end. That was a quick fifty years." It was three days before my fiftieth birthday, and my life passed before me as if in an overnight dream. I said a prayer that I might live, as my family needed me and there was so much work I still wanted to do.

The officer got on the police radio. Chief Gary Martin was home showering but heard the radio dispatch and was among the first on the scene, wearing a jogging suit and slippers. It was typical Gary – right there for me all the time, taking charge in the midst of pandemonium. There were county, state, and city police from Crown Point, Merrillville, and Gary as well as rescue vehicles, fire trucks, and ambulances.

Chief Martin located us halfway down a ditch and yelled, "Are you guys all right? Are you bleeding?" I told him we were OK, but he kept talking to make sure we stayed conscious. The roof had collapsed so much that neither the doors nor windows could be opened. We were hunched over and unable to sit up. To ease Gary's mind I started bantering with him about my driver, who had been his student at IU Northwest. When Chief Martin said, "Look what you all did," I replied, "Not me, Bridgeman." Chief Martin turned to Officer Bridgeman and joked, "As soon as I get you out, I'm going to kick your butt." Officer Bridgeman replied, "Please, Chief, we are hurt, don't make us laugh." The bantering kept us alert until the fire department rescue team arrived. In actuality, had Officer Robert Bridgeman not taken evasive action, the semi would have run us over, and we would have been crushed under its wheels. His defensive driving saved our lives.

Fire department personnel finally cut us out with saws and steel jaws, and an ambulance took us to St. Anthony's Hospital, whose staff had been alerted of our arrival. The three of us survived the traumatic ordeal without serious injuries, but I was very sore along the chest where my seat belt had been. When my family arrived with worried looks and tears streaming down their cheeks, I was hooked up to all kinds of monitoring devices and tubes. They had cut my clothes away, and to ease Betty's and my daughters' minds I quipped, "You remember the underwear with the holes you told me to throw away? Well, I have a pair on." I really didn't, but she smiled, called me a brat, and told the medical staff I was OK.

They all laughed and then Veronica and Maria said, "Dad, you're famous, you interrupted Oprah!" Both had been watching TV in the waiting room when ABC News broke into regular programming with the story. A Channel 7 helicopter was transmitting the accident scene. Afterward a sheriff's court security officer Albert Rodan, a talented musician, wrote a song about the accident titled "There Must Have Been an Angel." Perhaps my sister was still watching over me.

As was the case eight years before, when our Dodge Caravan collided with an unmovable oak tree, the experience was additional motivation to tackle challenges that hopefully will make a difference in people's lives.

## 2004 DEMOCRATIC NATIONAL CONVENTION

In 2004 I was a delegate at the Democratic National Convention in Boston. By that time Senator John Kerry had wrapped up the nomination, but still it was a once-in-a-lifetime opportunity. Betty, Veronica, and Maria went with me. At times when delegates opted not to be on the floor they'd trade off credentials, so there were times when Betty and my daughters could be there with me. What a spectacle! We were next to the Illinois delegation and got to talk with Senator Dick Durbin, Chicago mayor Richard Daley, and Jesse Jackson, Senior and Junior.

Along with Lake County chairman Stiglich and Porter County chairman Leon West I had been a coordinator in selecting a balanced delegation that would represent the First District. Mayor Richard Hatcher had informed me that his daughter Rachelle desired to serve as a delegate. Hatcher was a towering figure who withstood many difficulties and calumnies but stayed steadfast in the arena. I was delighted that his daughters inherited his love for public service. I discussed it with the county chairmen and they agreed. The former mayor was not a delegate but was an invitee by virtue of having been a former Democratic National Committee vice chair – but he did not have credentials to be on the floor.

On the evening of Senate candidate Barack Obama's keynote speech, nobody was giving up their credentials. Earlier in the year he had won a landslide victory in the Illinois Senate primary. Everyone wanted to hear it. I told former mayor Hatcher, "I would love to hear Barack Obama, but I would love it more if you joined your daughter on such a momentous night." So I loaned my credentials to him. He first said, "No, no, Roy, you should go" but I insisted. As a dad myself, I knew it would be a special moment for him and Rachelle. Afterward, he sought me out to thank me for that unforgettable opportunity. I told him it made my heart feel good that he and Rachelle would have that memory.

## WEED AND SEED

I have tried to give back to IU Northwest because of the opportunities it gave me to reach my potential and achieve my dreams. I established a Roy Dominguez Scholarship and have worked with the Calumet Regional Archives and student organizations such as ALMA (Alianza Latina del Medio-oeste de America). I have also been involved in several initiatives to redevelop the Glen Park neighborhood where the university is located.

The U.S. Department of Justice sponsored a program called Weed and Seed that seemed perfectly designed for IU Northwest. Randy Jacobs, an energetic university administrator, put together a task force to secure federal funds for redeveloping the area around the university. I was one of the first people he called. He argued that if I would agree to participate, other community leaders would follow. I said, "Randy, do you think so? Then count me in." Chief Martin later told Randy in my presence, "If the sheriff had said no, I would have kicked his ass." I quipped, "You didn't need to convince me. Whatever you need, let me know and I'll send Chief Martin."

We held a series of meetings at the IU Northwest Conference Center. Mayor Scott King and Congressman Peter Visclosky sent representatives. We ultimately secured funds for purchasing property, tearing down abandoned buildings, enhancing security, doing drug prevention, and beautifying the neighborhood.

## DIRTY TACTICS

Once again in 2006 my opponents had "sham" candidates file in an attempt to confuse the voters. One of them, Anthony Dominguez, had not voted in a Democratic primary since 1984. Another, Roy Del Rio, was mad at me because I revoked the special deputy commission he had obtained from Buncich and I would not issue a new commission.

Anthony Dominguez worked at Inland Steel, dated the sister of a close Buncich ally, and once had lived next door to wheeler-dealer Bobby Cantrell. When I accused Cantrell of orchestrating his candidacy, he denied it until I brought up that fact. "Oh, you knew that?" he said. My legal counsel, Jim Weiser, filed a petition to the five-member election board challenging the propriety of Anthony Dominguez remaining on the primary ballot since proof that he was a registered Democrat was lacking. Two election board members were Republicans, two were Democrats, and the chair was county clerk Tom Philpot, nominally a Democrat but one who held a grudge against me.

Philpot was a bright fellow, and we once had enjoyed friendly relations. When he had been coroner, he had use of a county car. Upon taking office as clerk, he asked that an unmarked vehicle be assigned to him. There was no precedent for the clerk getting a vehicle, so I turned him down. He went over my head and persuaded the county commissioners to authorize me to issue him a vehicle. Though the cars came out of the sheriff's budget, in a technical sense they were the property of the commissioners.

We had confiscated a Mercury Grand Marquis in a previous drug raid. It was four or five years old, but I had our garage mechanics make certain it was clean and mechanically sound. I offered it to Philpot, and he drove it for a while, but then demanded a new Ford Crown Victoria with lights and even a CD player. I told him, "Mr. Clerk, you will get the vehicle I have assigned to you. The new vehicles are for officers on patrol every day. And if you want a CD player, you can do what some officers do – buy one at a local store." Philpot got so angry, he decided if he couldn't have a new Crown Victoria, he didn't want the Grand Marquis, and within a week he returned it.

The episode illustrates, I believe, how petty politics can be. I recognize that officeholders need to balance means and ends and that one cannot be constantly apolitical. Good relationships with other governmental entities are important, and I thought my offer was reasonable. I tried to reach a compromise but refused to bow to Philpot's every whim when it would detract from police work. Suffice it to say, a required attribute of public servants is the fortitude to say no on a consistent basis when things are not in the public interest. It goes back to what my dad and mom said: "It's always about the people."

Prior to the election board hearing, realizing that Philpot would vote against me on the Anthony Dominguez case, I contacted Republican county chair John Curley and expressed the hope that his representatives would be impartial and afford me a fair opportunity to present the facts. He replied, "You know, Sheriff, I like you but am happiest when the Democrats are fighting." At the hearing two Democrats voted in favor of removing from the ballot the name of Anthony Dominguez, who was represented by Buncich's attorney Stanley Jablonski, but Philpot and the two Republicans voted against removal.

After losing that hearing, my attorney Jim Weiser announced that upon the urging of my family I was considering not running for reelection. They feared that the confusion would be too insurmountable a hurdle to overcome and that other dirty tactics would be forthcoming. In addition to respecting their advice, I believed that if I simply accepted this insult to the voters (that, in essence, is what it was), the public might not be aware of the fraudulent tactics that were corrupting the political process.

The Buncich organization heard of my possible intent not to seek reelection and rejoiced. Their premature victory party, however, soon came to a screeching halt. To my relief what followed was a barrage of newspaper articles exposing the ploy for what it was. Both the *Times* and the *Post-Tribune,* the two daily newspapers serving northwest Indiana, objected to such corrupt practices and encouraged me not to withdraw my candidacy. One such headline read: "Sheriff Must Run!"

During my first term I had developed a level of trust with the press, which I recognized had a special duty to be the watchdogs of government. I didn't hide from reporters and tried to be candid and truthful because once you lose their trust, you can forget it. I met with several editorial boards whose members knew that I was working for good government and that many politicos were not. They encouraged me to stay in the race. After a couple weeks, satisfied that the electorate was sufficiently educated about sham candidacies, I announced that I was remaining in the race.

When I had first indicated I might not stand for reelection, Chief Martin was adamant that I remain in the race in order to preserve the reform initiatives we had instituted. He knew how hard we had worked and the political retribution that would follow if that happened. He exclaimed, "You're running, and I'm going to resign as chief and campaign with you every day." There was no prohibition preventing him from remaining chief and still campaigning while off duty, but he wanted to set a different standard so nobody could criticize what he was doing. That was an awesome sacrifice on his part. He picked me up every morning, and we campaigned day and night. As always, he was like a big brother.

There was no limit to the gutter tactics and fabrications employed against me and my family. False rumors circulated that Betty and I were under federal investigation by the FBI and IRS because I allegedly had hid her on the sheriff's payroll. They spread the lie that my Guillain-Barré, which had previously caused some disability, was out of remission and therefore I was unfit for a second term. They claimed that I was under FBI investigation for the East Chicago Sidewalk Scandal because I was the city's corporation counsel, even though lawyers don't make policy and they knew the sidewalk program was enacted by the East Chicago City Council and promoted long before I joined the Mayor Pastrick administration. It was pure nonsense and false. Betty and my daughter Veronica were able to handle the lies better than Maria. She was seventeen and a junior in high school.

Some holdover officers from the previous regime, I learned later, even had a "Maria Watch," where they'd shadow her, hoping to catch her staying out late or doing adolescent things. In fact, they spread untrue rumors that made it difficult for her to attend school. Ultimately, she became angry and her grades suffered. To get her out of harm's way Betty and I sent her to live with my sister Yolanda in Oklahoma City to finish her junior year.

Since the 1980s my brother Hector has been a bailiff in the Lake Superior Court juvenile division. When people introduced him as "Roy's younger brother," he'd say, "Some people call me Hector." During the 2006 campaign, one day, when the court was not in session, he was alone in the courtroom taking care of filing and paper work when an ardent

Buncich supporter engaged him in a few minutes of small talk. Then the officer said with a trace of sarcasm, "How is your brother and his family doing?" Hector looked him in the eye and said words to this effect: "I know you don't care for my brother, much less his family, so don't confuse me with Roy. He's the nice one in the family, but I'll kick your ass if you don't get out of the courtroom." Had the person not immediately left, Hector, who was strong and wiry, would have made good on his threat. That was quintessentially Hector. It doesn't take much to get his ire up. The guy never bothered him again.

Opposing me were remnants of the old Club SAR crowd that had controlled Lake County politics during the previous generation. Gary mayor Scott King came out for Buncich after I refused to contribute $5,000 to his campaign war chest. Nonetheless, as Election Day approached the momentum had swung our way. We emphasized what my administration had accomplished, what we'd do in a second term, how Buncich had corrupted the ballot process, and the ramifications of a return to the politics of yesterday.

Election day was filled with hope and anxiety. As the returns came in, it was clear early that the voters supported my candidacy by a landslide. We carried virtually every community in Lake County. Only Whiting and Lake Station were close. I won by almost 10,000 votes. It would have been even more of a landslide had Anthony Dominguez not received 6,000 votes and Del Rio almost 2,000. Given all the roadblocks, I cherished the victory as much as the one four years before. I am eternally grateful for the voters' affirmation of our public service and the way we provided reform to the sheriff's department.

Our success was a tribute to my family, campaign supporters, and political strategists, including George Van Til, attorney John Kopack, John Key, Chief Marco Kuyachich, Deputy Chief Joe Kumstar,[1] and my steadfast and dear friend Chief Martin. The campaign had tremendous "people support" from across Lake County. Among the hundreds of workers were Elsie Franklin of Gary, Mary Morris Leonard of East Chicago, and Willie Mae Durr of Hammond. Betty worked tirelessly, and, of course, my mom campaigned for me every day and would not have missed the fight. My dad, who was ill, rested in a senior citizens' nursing home but was with us in spirit, and we carried him in our hearts.

That evening we held a victory party at the Patio Restaurant in Merrillville. As I walked toward the entrance, there to greet me stood Betty, Mom, Veronica, Chief Martin, attorney Kopack, and others. On the side was George Van Til. As photographers from the local newspapers started taking photographs, I grabbed George and had him join my family because of his friendship and invaluable advice. Next day he was in the group photo that the *Post-Tribune* chose to print.

Hundreds of supporters and members of the media crowded into the hall. In my victory speech I thanked my supporters and the voters of Lake County and promised to continue the progress we had initiated along the lines of good government. Also I thanked my dad and my daughter Maria, who were with us in spirit. My supporters knew why Maria was living in Oklahoma City, so from my cell phone I broke the good news to her as the crowd began chanting, "Maria! Maria!" That brought tears to our eyes. Thereafter, we sang and danced the night away with well-wishers.

The next few days were filled with phone calls, letters, flowers, and other expressions of congratulations from friends around the county, state, and country. Our first decision was to bring Maria home, now that the danger from my opponents had subsided, as soon as she finished her junior year in Oklahoma City. Mom cooked one of her favorite meals for her and the entire family. As the saying goes, "All's well that ends well." The following year Maria went on to graduate from Crown Point High School.

After Maria returned in the summer, I explained why she had come under attack and added: "God is presenting these difficulties while you are under my and your mom's care, so later in life after you go off on your own and run into similar difficulties, you will be prepared to deal with it."

I asked Pastors Steve and Melodye Munsey if they would host the second inaugural ceremony at their nondenominational Family Christian Center in Munster. It has seating for over two thousand and is often filled to capacity during weekend services. The congregation is very diverse. At Easter the center puts on a spectacular production of *The Passion of Christ*. The Munseys convey insightful religious messages about living a useful life, frequently mentioning the vision and dreams of Martin Luther King Jr.

## DEATH OF GARY MARTIN

After Marco Kuyachich took over Chief Martin's duties, Gary became my chief deputy sheriff who worked on special assignments. He was such a trusted adviser and seemed to harbor no animosity against those who disagreed with him. Sometimes when I was tempted to react rashly to one of my opponent's stratagems, he'd say, "Now what good would that do?" He'd make me consider a more tactful approach. He threw himself into activities and was a marathon runner and an avid biker.

One of Chief Martin's most passionate causes was an organization called Concerned Officers for Police Survivors (COPS). Every year he participated in the Indiana COPS bicycle trek throughout the state to raise funds for the benefit of families of officers killed in the line of duty – everything from emergency support to college scholarships.

On August 20, 2006, Gary Martin led a contingent of about a dozen bicyclists. Following close behind was a bread truck carrying equipment and provisions. The truck had a big banner and blinking lights to warn motorists of their slow-moving caravan. When they stopped in Merrillville, we provided them with a police escort and arranged a dinner for them. The Radisson provided overnight accommodations at a reduced rate and my department sponsored a free breakfast for the cyclists and staff. Other than Gary, the most experienced rider was state police lieutenant Gary Dudley, a physical fitness instructor. He and I were often the recipient of Gary Martin's jokes about the state police. He was merciless. As the group left the Radisson's parking lot, I told the others what I had always said in years past, "Be sure you take care of our Chief."

On Wednesday, August 22, the bikers were trekking down U.S. 41 north of Terre Haute on Indiana Highway 63 and stopped for lunch. The contingent that was to escort them on the next leg of their journey phoned them to say they'd be late. The group decided to push on and have the police escort join them en route. It was a bright, sunny day. The bikers were in the right lane of U.S. 41 heading south when the driver of a semi tractor-trailer failed to realize how slow the bread truck was going. By the time he put on his brakes it was too late to prevent his vehicle from plowing into the bread truck, which lunged forward and ran over Chief

Gary Martin and Lieutenant Gary Dudley, killing them instantly. Several other riders sustained injuries. Martin and Dudley had just moved to the back of the group to encourage stragglers to pedal faster. They were always everybody's cheerleaders, even to their last breath.

That afternoon, I was in my office when I got a call from Lieutenant Larry Kaiser of the Lowell Post of the Indiana State Police. We had been shift partners with the state police, so I knew him well. At first I didn't want to believe what I was hearing, so I put him on speakerphone and asked him to repeat what he had said. He proceeded to tell me again what had happened. It was very, very difficult. I started to cry when the horrible truth registered. I asked whether the families knew the terrible news. When Lieutenant Kaiser said no, I knew I had to find Olga and their family before they learned about the accident from anyone else.

After notifying Betty, I assembled a team of officers to locate Gary's son Greg and his wife, Stephanie, daughter Jennifer, and Jennifer's husband, Zack. I had Olga's cell phone and found her shopping and getting ready to drop off a niece she was baby-sitting. I said, "When you're done, I need to see you." She agreed to meet me at the Grand Café on Mississippi Street in Merrillville, which was convenient for her.

When Olga pulled up in her car, I went outside to give us more privacy. As I approached her, she immediately joked, "OK, what hospital is he in?" She was used to the occasional spills and scrapes that come from Gary's bicycling. Summoning my courage, I said, "Olga, Gary was involved in a bad accident and isn't in a hospital. He went home today." Fear entered her eyes, and she collapsed. I remember catching her. She was so full of life and happy-go-lucky, like Gary. I still get emotional thinking about it. We were able to get the whole family together.

Chief Marco Kuyachich and I flew by helicopter to the crash site. I'd estimate it took less than an hour. The bodies had been removed, but police investigators and media personnel were at the sealed-off area, and their crushed bicycles were still in place. At Gary's last place on earth I said a prayer and thanked him for everything he had done. I took some solace from the fact that he probably never knew what happened and didn't suffer. Gary Martin and Gary Dudley went home doing what they enjoyed doing, being police officers and helping others. I like to say that they biked their way to heaven.

Our department took charge of escorting Gary's body back to Lake County, assisted by a state FOP critical incident team trained in helping in these situations. The procession route was made public, and civilians, as well as police, fire, and emergency services personnel lined the roads and highways. Gary was an army veteran, so members of a veterans' motorcycle club joined in the escort, as did many different police and fire agencies. It was a long procession.

In the city of Gary the hearse carrying the body of Chief Martin stopped at the new Gary Public Safety Building on Fifth Avenue and then at the former police headquarters at Thirteenth and Broadway, where Gary had worked for twenty-five years. He had joked that one regret was that when they knocked down that obsolete building, he was not there to press the button. He felt the Gary police officers and staff deserved a new facility to better serve the public.

During the two days that the body of Chief Gary Martin lay in rest at Burns Funeral Home in Merrillville, law enforcement representatives arrived from as far away as New York, California, Canada, and Nashville, Tennessee, Gary's hometown. The crowds represented all walks of life. Former students said they would never have gone to college, much less graduated, had it not been for Gary Martin. Many others said they would not have been police officers without his guidance and encouragement. Gary's family and out-of-state relatives were overwhelmed by the expressions of love and the turnout.

Before the burial there was a service at the Russian Orthodox Church. Gary liked to tell people that he was the only hillbilly member of the congregation. I'd say, "Now, Gary, the proper term is Appalachian American." He'd laugh and say, "I'm a hillbilly and can say hillbilly." He never lost his Southern drawl and could ham it up and make it thicker when the situation called for it. If someone noticed his Southern drawl and asked where he was from, he'd sometimes say, "I'm from the South" and after a pause, "South Boston." He had a great sense of humor in addition to his intellect and wealth of common sense.

The procession to St. Mary's Cemetery on Ridge Road was, if anything, even longer than the one two days earlier. As it passed by the county government complex, we had the vehicle he had driven while chief in front of our police memorial along with a replica of the bike he had been riding. There was an honor guard, and the county helicopter flew overhead. Pipes and drums units from several communities met the hearse near the cemetery entrance, and the sound of bagpipes greeted those arriving at the gravesite.

It had been showering off and on all day; but as officers started with the twenty-one-gun salute, it started to pour. It was a deluge, but nobody left. I told people, "I'm sure Gary is upstairs and turned on the water faucets to have his last laugh." Those who knew Gary concurred. I'm sure Gary would have said, "This is what you get for burying a hillbilly in a Russian cemetery." I told that to Olga; she laughed and said, "You're right."

Outside of my family, Chief Gary Martin had been my closest friend, confidant, mentor, and trusted adviser. In fact, we were as close as brothers. He was always there for me. Now, whenever I have a tough decision to make, I think to myself, "What would Gary do in this situation, and what good would it do?"

## NOTE

1. In 2011 Kumstar and two other officers would be indicted for illegally selling weapons on the Internet, and subsequently they pleaded guilty. That they would betray the public trust and my personal trust in them constituted the biggest disappointment of my tenure as sheriff.

Death Before Dishonor

Motto of military units dating from Roman times

Always do right! This will gratify some people and astonish the rest.

HARRY S. TRUMAN's favorite Mark Twain quote

ELEVEN

# Second Term

*A primary reason I sought a second term as sheriff was to continue the good-government policies I had started to depoliticize the office and reprofessionalize the police force. I feared that these initiatives, so important in providing for public safety, would be in jeopardy if former sheriff John Buncich succeeded me. As sheriff I planned to continue to pay special attention to protecting victims of domestic violence, an area of interest to my wife Betty as well. In 2007 the Indiana Coalition against Domestic Violence named me officer of the year.*

## JAIL SUICIDES AND BEATING

In March of 2002, before I took office, my predecessor had appointed a longtime corrections officer from Gary to be warden in hopes to garner political support among African Americans. I reappointed her and, wanting her to succeed, tried not to micromanage the jail and let her pick her staff. Perhaps in retrospect I should have replaced the warden with someone with undivided loyalties. She had potential, but unfortunately I had more hope than she had desire for real reform. She pledged to carry out my policies, but her actions did not match her statements. I think she was torn between wanting to support my initiatives and at the same time do what she could for fellow correctional officers. I do believe she cared, but despite additional assistance she was overwhelmed by jail issues.

A main concern of mine was the number of suicides at the jail. Even though they averaged about one a year, that was too many. Suicides are difficult to prevent because by nature they are secret and deceptive. We tried to identify high risks and put them in special rooms with safety features. Most suicide victims hang themselves using a bedsheet or T-shirt, for example, but one inmate smuggled a razor blade inside a fresh cut from hernia surgery and when nobody was looking cut the vein in his leg, bleeding to death. We don't conduct strip searches, but at any rate we'd have never discovered that. A suicide expert from the National Correctional Officers Association made several recommendations, and the warden insisted that she implemented them. The hangings continued. I'd say, "Why aren't you talking to Southlake Mental Health and trying other initiatives?" I'd send many directives to that effect, to no avail.

In December of 2007, a group of correctional officers beat an inmate almost to death. I was on Christmas vacation when it happened but was available via cell phone. Nobody notified me for fifteen days. There is a code of silence among correctional officers. The man was so seriously injured he was in intensive care for seventy-two hours. After somebody asked if I knew about the incident, I called the warden's office. She claimed to be unaware of what happened. In that case, I said, you either are being deceitful or are incompetent. I removed her from her post and launched a criminal internal investigation. I immediately contacted the FBI office in Indianapolis and asked the special agent in charge of operations in Indiana to initiate a criminal and/or civil rights investigation. They assigned FBI agents from their Merrillville office to conduct the investigation.

This is what happened. The inmate, a convicted murderer, was being taken in handcuffs from one location to another. He and a correctional officer started talking trash, and the officer threatened him. The inmate allegedly replied that the guard wouldn't be talking so bravely if the handcuffs were off. The officer proceeded to remove the handcuffs, and a fight ensued. The inmate got the best of it, so other officers intervened, re-handcuffed the inmate, and pummeled him at a location where there were no surveillance cameras.

There was no way the warden could not have known of the beating, and it was clearly her responsibility to take the requisite review and notify me immediately. I reassigned her to sergeant, her former merit title. She subsequently quit to take a job with the Gary Park Department. Her successor, a former correctional officer and current deputy police chief, is very competent. The FBI investigated what happened, and a federal grand jury took testimony. There was an administrative hearing before the merit board. Some officers quit, and others, found to be negligent, were terminated. The federal investigation is still pending with the U.S. attorney's office.

We've never had a jailbreak. On rare occasions correctional officers have let prisoners out inadvertently. Someone may have posted bond on one criminal charge, but there were other charges that escaped notice. A couple of mix-ups came from similar names, such as a Stan Smith versus a Stanley Smith.

Do people let you down? For sure. Sometimes subordinates fail to perform as hoped for. But, for the most part, we stopped the nonsense by sending out a strong message that illegal activities won't be tolerated. On numerous occasions we have submitted to the prosecutor's office information on officers who we believed were dishonest. Things were not swept under the rug. In 2007, for instance, FOP treasurer Mitch King was charged with stealing. As a result, a small group of nineteen officers out of a total of approximately three hundred members met with the executive board and revoked my FOP membership. They believed the matter should have been settled in-house. To them the code of silence was paramount.

The FOP criminal case went to trial, and Mitch King was found guilty. The jury was out less than half an hour. An old axiom advises, if the facts and the law aren't with you, make it personal. That's what King's attorneys attempted to do, but the strategy, lame as it was, failed. Had I swept the thefts under the rug and allowed him to continue arresting people for comparable offenses, it would have signaled an acceptance of the so-called code of silence and put police officers above the law. The public needs to know that is not the case.

When the FOP revoked my membership, the agenda was not announced beforehand, nor were the procedural due processes adhered to. Many officers encouraged me to contest the ouster, but I told them I did not become sheriff to join the FOP but rather to serve the public. After the episode received media notoriety, the governing board of the Indiana State Troopers Association voted to make me an honorary lifetime member. I was only the second person so honored. Members came to my office and presented me with a plaque attesting to their action. I was very flattered, especially given my pride in having been a state trooper.

On another matter, a custody officer had received several write-ups. Rather than terminate him we transferred him to court security. One thing that I have been emphatic about is court security officers not walking around with phones to their ear. They should be paying full attention to their job – security. In addition, it leaves a poor impression on people who come in and ask for services. One day this officer was walking down the hall with a phone to his ear. When I told him to put it away, he claimed to be on a break. "Then go to the cafeteria where people won't assume you're on duty," I told him. In the afternoon I spotted him at our information booth talking on his cell phone. So it was time to let him go. He later claimed discrimination because he was white, over sixty years of age, and a John Buncich supporter. Nonsense, once again.

### JUSTICE DEPARTMENT REVIEW

Shortly before I assumed office, the county jail facilities had expanded, but the number of staff remained stagnant even though the inmate population eventually almost doubled to a peak of 1,250. My pleas to the council and commissioners for additional correctional officers and resources to modernize certain procedures basically fell on deaf ears. Realizing that the situation was intolerable, in 2006 I requested that the Department of Justice conduct a review of jail conditions even though we had recently passed inspections by state and national correctional officer associations with flying colors. The Justice Department investigators wrote an unflattering and rather unrealistic report that did not, in my opinion, take into account how hard we had worked to comply with state and national standards despite being woefully understaffed and underfunded.

I had a tough decision to make: either challenge the overly negative federal review or make it the justification for garnering more cooperation and support from county officials. I toiled with that dilemma, but since the goal was to secure funds for implementing improvements, I left the review unchallenged, even though I realized that it would definitely leave me open to criticism. Almost immediately, the strategy paid off. I obtained several hundred thousand dollars to renovate shower facilities. Not lined with stainless steel, the walls inevitably attracted mold that made inmates more susceptible to asthma attacks, skin rash, allergic reactions, and other health threats. I also secured funds to computerize the facility's medical records. Beforehand, it took an entire large room to hold the handwritten records, boxes and boxes of them. It was almost impossible to access files efficiently. One part of the Department of Justice cooperative agreement that I strongly endorsed was for a professional jail administrator to be appointed warden rather than have the position remain a political appointment. We worked diligently on the details for over a year, and in December of 2010, the board of commissioners approved it.

To reduce the jail population I augmented a "book and release" program for those charged with misdemeanors and certain Class D felonies who clearly were not a threat to the community. Historically, those awaiting trial had to post bond even for nonviolent offenses such as speeding, driving without a license, or Class D felonies likely to be plea-bargained down to misdemeanors, such as possession of marijuana, shoplifting, or passing bad checks. Otherwise, they'd remain warehoused in jail. Some judges and bail bondsmen didn't like the new practice, but we had little alternative. Besides, it just made sense and did not compromise the department's primary mission, public safety. For every new inmate, medical, psychological, and prescription reviews were required. An expansion of facilities would easily cost $100 million. Through "book and release" and electronic monitoring, using ankle bracelets that restrict those arrested to their home and workplace, we ultimately reduced the number of inmates to around seven hundred. Though my political opponents criticized these practices, the "book and release" and electric monitoring programs remained in effect after I left office.

## AUTO THEFT AND DRUG TASK FORCES

According to our auto theft unit statistics, incidents involving stolen vehicles have declined compared to thirty years ago. More antitheft devices are on the market, for one thing, as well as alarms built into the vehicle. It's more difficult to interchange auto parts due to new systems of identification and better trained police officers. But auto theft still goes on. When the cost of steel and steel alloys rises, we'll send our officers to check the auto salvage and junkyards.

The Lake County Drug Task Force receives funding from the Byrne Justice Assistance Grant. We applied for the grant every year, supplying work product statistics and administrative costs for the previous year. The task force is a county-wide metro unit in which local police agencies and the county share resources and personnel to combat drugs and gangs throughout Lake County. We deputize the local police officers to avoid possible legal entanglements or potential liability.

If drug purchases are going on in a certain house, it's a big deal for residents on that block. If customers are coming and going from other places, perhaps armed, parents are afraid to let their children outside. It terrorizes the entire community. Our undercover officers employed video monitors, followed the traffic patterns of cars not from the neighborhood, and arranged bogus drug buys. After assembling enough evidence, we obtained search and arrest warrants and raided the house, ideally at a time when people were inside buying drugs. We confiscated the drugs and seized contraband that might be the results of profits from illegal sales, including vehicles and even the house itself.

In civil court, when a judge ruled in our favor, the contraband items were awarded to the sheriff's office to be sold at public auction, with the profits used for law enforcement purposes. We could use confiscated vehicles for up to three years, sometimes as part of undercover operations.

County prosecutor Bernard Carter and his staff, including chief deputy Barb McConnell and first deputy assistant Pete Villarreal, were extremely cooperative. Prosecutor Carter and I were friends in law school, and I have the utmost respect for him and his staff. We'd present them with cases along with possible charges. Clients and dealers, or those working for them, might receive a reduced charge or lesser sentence in return for agreeing to testify against the suppliers. The main objective was to get drug dealers off the streets, but we were also looking to nab the so-called drug kingpins.

The sheriff's department is also part of the federal initiative HIDTA (High Intensity Drug Trafficking Areas program). Since 1996 Congressman Peter Visclosky has obtained about $3.2 million annually for its operation. On the board are representatives from the FBI, IRS, ATF, DEA, the U.S. attorney's office, and the U.S. marshal's office, as well as local police agencies. HIDTA's initiatives usually involve interstate operations, in particular intercepting and arresting major drug dealers and suppliers driving through Lake County from places like Mexico and Texas or, closer to home, Chicago and Detroit. We intercepted one huge shipment that was headed for Toledo, Ohio.

One HIDTA unit concentrates on procuring intelligence, including the interrogation of dealers under arrest about where they're getting their drugs. If a dealer has a prior felony conviction and had a gun in his possession, we can threaten him with additional charges if he does not cooperate.

Police in uniform working for HIDTA drive unmarked cars. They are on the lookout especially for out-of-state drivers who are acting suspiciously. When stopping such vehicles, perhaps for speeding or some other offense, officers are trained to ask a series of questions designed to size up whether the person is, in police parlance, a "mule," a transitory transporter of illegal substances or drug money. Those unable to fashion a reasonable explanation as to why they are in the area will have their vehicles searched. Minorities are not targeted, but many times operators use undocumented workers because they have fewer ties with the community or local drug dealers. Specially trained K-9 units sniff out drugs that may be hidden in the impounded vehicle.

One time we confiscated a car carrying almost a half-million dollars in twenty-dollar bills. That's several thousand bills. One cocaine seizure had a street value of $1.5 million; another time the value was an estimated $1.3 million. After major drug busts, I think of all the lives saved as a result of people who won't use that cocaine or be victimized by drug users who commit crimes to feed their habit. One time we caught a Russian immigrant who was hauling a huge load of untaxed cigarettes from out of state. Counterfeit movie DVDs are also a major illegal enterprise. In one case they were being produced locally and sold at different area flea markets.

So-called crack houses are the bane of declining urban neighborhoods. If it's not a major enterprise, HIDTA lets the Lake County Task Force deal with it. Otherwise the agencies might work in tandem. Crack houses are all over and so mobile that after we target one neighborhood, they often relocate to another. Where you have abandoned buildings, especially in out-of-the-way areas, they are more likely to go unnoticed.

We haven't encountered much crystal meth production in Lake County. Because labs emit such a foul odor, these are located in rural areas. They are very dangerous and toxic. Once they're raided, a special state police unit is called in to dismantle them. We are on the lookout, however, for the new methods of meth manufacturing that do not require elaborate labs.

A Calumet College survey of inmates housed at the Lake County jail who volunteered to participate in the study found that the overwhelming majority of substance abusers went from marijuana to hard drugs. I don't see decriminalization benefiting society. I never used marijuana because I was brought up to believe that if I smoked a joint, I was literally going to go nuts – that it would make me crazy. What did I know? So I was never tempted by drugs, but I don't consider myself morally superior to those who briefly experimented during a time when it was commonplace among the young. In fact, I admire Barack Obama's refreshing candor on the subject in his autobiography.

## REOPENING COLD CASES

Advances in the technology of DNA "fingerprinting" allowed our department to solve several infamous cases that had long been inactive. Some retired police officers asked my staff and me to reopen the Kenny Conrick case. On October 15, 1979, the eight-year-old boy disappeared. When his naked body was finally discovered two weeks later tied to a tree, it was badly decomposed but showed unmistakable signs of mutilation and sexual deviancy. At the time police focused their investigation on the Native American boyfriend of Kenny's mother, Myrna. During the 1970s many people looked down on interracial dating, and both the boyfriend and Myrna believed he was being targeted for that reason. After the couple separated, he suffered from depression and committed suicide.

I had the detective bureau commander and his officers look at the case and get back to me. Two pieces of evidence drew our attention and caused me to give them the time to work on it. For one thing, the rope used to bind the victim was found to contain seminal fluid. Secondly, in 1992 the sister of Myrna's sixteen-year-old paperboy, David Bruce Bowen, told police she suspected that her brother had committed the crime. Detectives discovered that Bowen had carried out a molestation prior to Conrick's death but it had been dealt with privately, with an agreement that Bowen seek counseling. Had charges been brought, Kenny's life might have been saved.

A combination of legwork, in-depth interviews, and forensic tests broke the Conrick case. The state police crime lab did a tremendous job. The suspect's sister provided them with a DNA sample, which was similar to her brother's and matched in important respects the sample from the rope.

Our detectives obtained a warrant from a Lake County judge to take hair samples and saliva swabs from Bowen, who was living in an apartment in Portland, Maine, and working in construction. Some time passed between the day we took the samples and when we learned that it was a certain match, so perhaps he believed nothing had come of it. We sent detectives to provide surveillance and follow his patterns. He seemingly lived a quiet, solitary life, spending virtually all his time in his apartment when not at work. Neighbors and fellow workers said they had no reason to suspect he was a sexual deviant and murderer.

Our officers and Portland police officers were at the apartment the night before, intending to arrest him when he left for work. That morning the lights did not come on, and nobody exited the apartment. Bowen's crew, they learned, was working on a project several hours away and being housed at a nearby hotel. The Maine state police got in touch with their counterparts in that location, and Bowen was arrested at his workplace.

On December 16, 2007, announcing the arrest at a press conference, I said, "For Kenneth Conrick, I pray and hope his spirit is here with us and that he knows that we never gave up on him." Bowen subsequently confessed and was transferred to the Lake County Jail, where he was put on suicide watch. The successful resolution reminded me how very important it is to have honest, competent police work and dedicated officers doing their job. It took twenty-eight years, but those detectives and retired officers never gave up trying to bring this murderer to justice.

At the sentencing hearing Kenny's mother testified before Judge Clarence Murray. Though not an elderly woman, she lived in a nursing home and entered the courtroom in a housedress and slippers. After she took the stand, the prosecutor asked, "Now you *were* Kenny Conrick's mother?" She answered, "No, ma'am, I *am* Kenny Conrick's mother." You could feel a hush go through the courtroom as she proceeded to give one of the most moving, organized, methodical, and intelligent testimonies I've ever heard. She talked about how she missed out on seeing Kenny grow up, finish school, date women, and become a man and how the heinous, unsolved crime had sapped her spirit. At the very end she turned to Bowen and in a loud, impassioned voice said, "I hope you rot in hell." Tears were flowing in the courtroom that day. It was so, so emotionally gripping.

The same month the Conrick murder was resolved we reopened the case of twenty-two-year-old Linda Bennitt, abducted a quarter-century before from her Tiberon Trails apartment and then brutally raped and murdered. The body, with its throat slashed, was found on May 5, 1984, on the property of Riley Elementary School in Glen Park. A Purdue graduate from the small town of Vevay, Indiana, located in Switzerland County near the Ohio River, Linda had recently accepted a position at L. S. Ayers in Southlake Mall. Her apartment was in unincorporated Ross Township between Gary and Merrillville.

Forensic analysis helped lead detectives to Mark Erler, serving time in California on numerous charges, including rape and attempted murder. Commander Shaw Spurlock and the detective bureau did a splendid job of interviewing people of interest. Due to that legwork, they eventually identified fourteen possible subjects. There was a fingerprint in the evidence, and, making use of a national database of felons incarcerated in prisons around the country, they discovered that it matched one of them, Mark Erler, who had once attended Riley Elementary.

After identifying a prime suspect, we contacted Linda Bennitt's mother. Years before, she had been told that water damage had destroyed the evidence and that the police would never be able to find her daughter's killer. Well, that was totally untrue. I cannot begin to fathom how someone could be so heartless as to say that. She told us that she'd given up all hope of having her daughter's murderer brought to justice. She asked to be informed of every court hearing so she and other family members could be present.

We obtained an arrest warrant and governor's extradition papers to bring Mark Erler to Lake County, Indiana. Linda Bennitt's family asked to be present when we transferred Erler to the county jail. I pondered the request long and hard and discussed it with my legal counsel. Certainly Erler had no right to privacy. I came to the conclusion that the family deserved to see the wheels of justice finally working to apprehend their loved one's killer.

We decided to position the immediate Bennitt family in the sally port, the enclosed garage adjacent to the jail where an unmarked car would bring him from O'Hare, escorted by a marked police vehicle. They would be approximately thirty feet from where Erler would exit the car. We'd provide chairs and had a nurse and an EMT on hand with an oxygen tank in case anyone was overcome by emotion. After securing the family's permission, we also invited the media to be present. My view, and theirs, too, was that throwing a spotlight on the scene, so to speak, might bring some solace to families that had endured similar tragedies and inspire other police agencies to pursue cold cases aggressively.

Entering the sally port came a marked car, followed by the unmarked vehicle carrying Erler and three officers. The back doors could only be opened from outside. Before Erler emerged from the car, the sally port doors were closed by remote control. I asked various officers to keep an eye on specific family members, and I positioned myself next to Linda's sister Bobbie Marksberry. To my alarm I could see Bobbie turning flush red and starting to hyperventilate. I suggested she take a seat and take deep breaths. When Erler was in sight, someone yelled, "Murderer," and Bobbie collapsed. She didn't lose consciousness, but her legs gave out under her.

Two of us caught Bobbie before she reached the ground. The nurse and EMT put a blanket under her, laid her down, and administered oxygen. After she composed herself, we got her to sit in a chair. The whole procedure probably took no longer than five minutes before Erler was locked up inside the jail, where the family and the media were not permitted.

Erler denied having been in northwest Indiana at the time of the murder, but we had proof to the contrary. He had served his prison sentence for sex offenses committed in California but had been detained in a mental institution until such time as it would be determined that he was not a danger to the community. He was assigned a very competent attorney, Ted Page. Unexpectedly, at a procedural hearing before Judge Diane Boswell, Page got up and said, "Judge, my client wishes to address you. He has been informed of his constitutional rights that he does not have to say anything, but he's demanding to address you."

After Judge Boswell agreed, Erler announced that he wanted to plead guilty to the charge of murder but not guilty to the charge of criminal sexual deviancy. He claimed to be doing this in order to spare the Bennitt family the ordeal of a trial. What hogwash. In his twisted mind he thought if he could win sympathy from the family or judge, he might be sent back to California, where he'd fare better than in an Indiana prison.

Attending the subsequent sentencing hearing was a large contingent of family, friends, clergy, and reporters from Vevay, Indiana. Days before, Linda Bennitt's mother, Joan King, had surgery on the lower part of her leg. She refused to have the operation until assured that she'd be cleared to attend the hearing. Nothing was going to prevent her from making the trip. She arrived in a wheelchair in the care of a nurse. She gave a very descriptive and emotional statement about how brokenhearted the family was at the loss of Linda, and by such violent means. She thanked the sheriff's department, the prosecutor's office, and all the police agencies that assisted in bringing Linda's killer to justice.

Among those testifying was Linda's younger sister, Bobbie Marksberry, who talked about the terror and trauma that caused her such reoccurring nightmares and unending grief. The last time she saw her older sister, she testified, Linda was laughing and smiling as she drove away. Then she added: "If I could chase that car today, I would grab her and never let go." On Friday, May 28, 2009, about eighteen months after the case was reopened, Judge Boswell, unmoved by Erler's plea for leniency, sentenced him to the maximum prison term of sixty years.

Afterward Linda's mother said to me, "Sheriff, this crime against my daughter has tormented me for twenty-five years. When your office called, it gave me hope. Now I can die in peace." I immediately thought of how hard it had been on my mom and dad when two of my siblings,

Maria and Eloy, died of cancer. As a parent, I can only imagine the torment Mrs. King and other family members went through. Even today when I think of her parting words to me – "Now I can die in peace" – it fills me with emotion. With such thoughts I continue doing the best I can do to protect the community and bring murderers and other felons to justice, with the purpose of serving the public to the best of my ability.

## JUDICIARY SQUARE SPEECH

On May 15, 2009, I gave the keynote speech at the National Law Enforcement Officers Memorial Day ceremony at Judiciary Square in Washington, D.C. The purpose was to honor local, state, and federal law enforcement officers who made the ultimate sacrifice in the line of duty. The tradition dates back to 1962, when President John F. Kennedy signed into law a bill creating the observance. Subsequent legislation set aside National Police Week, and a candlelit vigil took place on the eve of the May 15 event. The Lake County Sheriff's Pipe and Drum Corps had been chosen as the host band, and it was through that organization that my name was suggested. Being chosen was an honor and a humbling experience. Not only was I the first Hispanic keynote speaker but the first sheriff and first from Indiana. By tradition the keynote speaker selects the guest speaker who introduces him, and I asked Senator Evan Bayh, who readily agreed. Members of the Emerald Society, which planned the event, were very pleased. They had never had a sitting senator speak before. Betty, Maria, and Chief Marco Kuyachich joined me, and with the bagpipers performing, Indiana was well represented that day.

## MICHAEL JACKSON TRIBUTE

I grew up listening to vintage Jackson 5 hits such as "ABC," "I Want You Back," and "I'm a Big Boy Now." The group played at my sister Maria's prom at Marquette Park Pavilion in Gary before they were nationally discovered and signed a record contract with Berry Gordy's Motown label. My children grew up listening to Michael Jackson's songs such as "Billie Jean" and watching his pathbreaking music videos like "Thriller."

He was bestowed with God-given talent. He deserved the title "King of Pop." Obviously he had his personal difficulties, but there's no debating that he was one of the world's greatest entertainers.

After Michael Jackson's death on June 25, 2009, Gary mayor Rudy Clay and police chief Reginald Harris asked if the sheriff's department would assist in providing security and traffic control services for a tribute show at the Steel Yard, the baseball stadium that was home to the Rail-Cats. We said, "Absolutely." The state police also provided tremendous help. Over ten thousand people attended, the largest Steel Yard crowd I've ever seen. Michael Jackson look-alikes were everywhere, and many ladies and young men wore white gloves. Somebody handed me one, and I put it on. It was my way of paying tribute to a local icon. The gesture even made the local news. Other men started doing the same. It caught on like wildfire.

Chief Marco Kuyachich and I met up with two of the sponsors, Pastor Steve Munsey from the Family Christian Center and Chicago TV executive Joseph Stroud. Their wives, Melodye and Yvonne, joined us as well. The Strouds own the popular Christian channel WJYS and put on a half-dozen religious-oriented programs. Scheduled to perform an exciting version of "Thriller" were dancers from Family Christian Center, a megachurch located in Munster, Indiana. Pastor Steve's parents, founders Bishop Frank and Ruth Munsey, through their lifelong dedication gave hope and spiritual guidance to hundreds of thousands of people not only in northwest Indiana but, as a result of their support of missionary work, in Latin America and Eastern Europe.

When we arrived, the seats set aside for us were already occupied. Rather than create a fuss and make the folks move, I had some officers get eight folding chairs, and we created a row even closer to the stage. I told Pastor Munsey, "Look here, the Good Lord provided us with the best seats." An officer stood by us, so we wouldn't be disturbed. We were joined from time to time by such celebrities as the Reverend Jesse Jackson and Joe Jackson, Michael's father.

The celebration of Michael Jackson and his musical legacy clearly showed Gary at its best. Tribute was also paid to Gary native Karl Malden, who had passed away earlier in the summer and is best known for his Academy Award–winning role as a priest in *On the Waterfront.*

Froebel graduate Fred "The Hammer" Williamson talked about how the actor born Mladen Sekulovich helped him break into Hollywood after he retired from his famed football career.

## WINFIELD STANDOFF AND HONEYBEE CASE

In 1993 Winfield incorporated as a town. By law the community should have set up its own police department or made arrangements to compensate the Lake County Sheriff's Department for continuing services. Yet for seventeen years Winfield refused to pay anything. After their public officials ignored my warnings, in October I called their bluff and stopped all nonemergency police services. After realizing that it was in my power to do so, they agreed to pay a nominal sum for six months, at which time an evaluation would be rendered as to what their fair assessment should be. So I ordered police patrols to be resumed.

In October of 2010, a shooting occurred in Beecher, Illinois, located in Will County. Three fellows were remodeling a house when a stranger asked if they had any extra plywood and if they knew anything about breeding honeybees. He left, then returned and shot two of them, one fatally. Then the shooter came to a farmhouse in Lowell, Indiana, and asked a farmer about honeybees. Without warning he fired three shots at the man's head. The farmer ducked and got wounded in the shoulder. He was able to describe the shooter's vehicle as a light blue Chevrolet Cheyenne with discoloration on the passenger side. After ballistics confirmed that the bullets were fired from the same gun, we formed a bi-state task force with Will County to share information about what the press had dubbed the "Honeybee Killings." They subsequently arrested a police officer identified by their witness, but the suspect was released after being able to prove he was at home on his computer at the time of the crimes.

Six weeks later Gary Amaya walked into a tanning salon in Orland Park, demanding money. As Amaya was tying up the woman on duty, Jason McDaniel walked in and found himself facing the barrel of a gun. After pleading for his life and offering Amaya six hundred dollars cash, McDaniel was told he was going to be tied up. As Amaya reached down to get rope from his bag, he set the gun on the counter for a moment.

McDaniel was able to get hold of the gun and then fatally shot Amaya as he moved toward him. We came to find out from Illinois authorities that the bullets matched the Lowell shooting and that Amaya had been driving a light-blue Chevy Cheyenne with discoloration on the passenger side. Also the victim from Lowell positively identified Gary Amaya as the person who shot him. A search of his house revealed map directions to Beecher and Lowell, but nobody could fathom his motive. He had no history of a violent past. Although it appeared that Amaya was the "Honeybee Shooter," we waited for further forensic examination results to confirm our suspicions.

If one advances confidently in the direction of his dreams, and endeavors to live the life which he has imagined, he will meet with a success unexpected in common hours.

HENRY DAVID THOREAU, author of
*Walden, or a Life in the Woods*

Have faith and pursue an unknown end.

FRANCIS BACON

TWELVE

# Dreaming Big

*In August of 2009, I spoke to the editorial board of the* Kokomo Tribune, *and someone said, "There's never been a governor who came from Lake County." I pointed out that there never had been a candidate for governor from Lake County either. In other words, I don't think it's a legitimate issue. On another occasion* Times *publisher Bill Nangle asked me, "Don't you think this Lake County issue could be very difficult to overcome?" I replied, "My coming from Lake County is as much an issue as my being Hispanic." He argued that my ethnic background was not an issue. "Then neither is my being from Lake County," I replied.*

GOVERNOR MITCH DANIELS

At a January 2005 Gary Frontier Social Club's breakfast honoring Dr. Martin Luther King Jr., newly elected governor Mitch Daniels was one of the main speakers. I wished the incoming governor well and told him that even though I was a Democrat, I believed in good government and would help him in any way I could since he was our governor. He was cordial and receptive. From time to time thereafter, before he'd visit Lake County, his staff would ask whether I was available to join him. I made every effort to accept his invitation and was honored to be asked. He was always a gentleman and had his strong points as a politician, but, in my opinion, he was not a natural like Evan Bayh or Frank O'Bannon.

Although opposed to the selling of the toll road and the privatization of the state welfare services, I agreed with some of Governor Daniels's ideas on local governmental reform. Sharing resources and eliminating duplication of services, for example, is simply good government. I was even open to discussing whether sheriffs should be appointed rather than elected. You should not start a discussion on how to streamline and reform government without putting everything on the table without preconditions and exclusions.

In the spring of 2008 I talked to the governor, along with other county officials, about plans to hold a taxes and economic summit. He had been pressuring Lake County to pass an income tax or face dire consequences. He agreed with the concept of a summit and promised to attend. Meanwhile, party primaries were taking place. Republican Daniels was running unopposed, while I was supporting Jill Long Thompson against Jim Shellenberg in the Democratic contest. Jill asked me to introduce her at the Jefferson-Jackson Unity Dinner. Also in attendance were presidential candidates Barack Obama and Hillary Clinton, both of whom I respected greatly. As South African Bishop Desmond Tutu said, what a difference his election would make in terms of America's leadership position in the world.

In my presentation to the party faithful, I concluded, "And Jill Long Thompson is the only candidate who can privatize Mitch Daniels and make him a private citizen." I didn't mean anything personal, of course, but it was the type of partisan rhetoric the situation demanded.

Soon afterward, Pat O'Rourke, president of the Hammond Teachers Union, got a call from Neil Pickett saying that the governor had read the quote about privatizing him in the *Indianapolis Star* and was not pleased. In fact, he had decided to torpedo the upcoming summit. Pat reiterated that I hadn't meant to insult the governor and compared politics to a game of basketball. You compete hard, hoping to win, but that doesn't mean you hold hard feelings once the election is over. O'Rourke suggested I call Neil.

I placed the call. Neil Pickett reminded me that Daniels had never run for political office until four years before and was not as thick-skinned as most veteran campaigners. Even so, forcing the cancellation of the summit was a setback for the forces of good government.

Governor Daniels had agreed to discuss taxes, economic development, and other issues with leaders from northwest Indiana. Consultants had prepared data. My remark was just political bravado, talking to the troops, so to speak; I'm sure when the governor is with Republican partisans, he is not telling them to support Democrats. He left us wondering if this was just an excuse not to have the summit.

## NEW HELICOPTER

In 2005, along with the Indiana Sheriff's Association, we obtained enabling legislation to charge a user's fee on foreclosures for services being provided to banks and insurance companies, including hosting the subsequent auctions, popularly known as sheriff's sales. The fund would reimburse costs to county government and be used, subject to council approval, to buy squad cars, weapons, bulletproof vests, laptops, and, most importantly, a new helicopter. Our helicopters were forty years old and not equipped with modern crime-fighting instruments, such as searchlights, infrared lights, recording devices, or a monitored GPS (Global Positioning System) navigational device. When assisting our aquatic team in night rescues at Lake Michigan or other bodies of water, our unit had to make do with a handheld spotlight.

When we first started collecting user's fees, council members were skeptical, but in less than two years we had over $1.2 million in our account. When the housing market collapsed, the number of foreclosures spiraled. We estimated that we'd have enough money for a helicopter within one year. Senator Evan Bayh procured a $500,000 federal grant to help pay for the helicopter, and the company agreed to a 20 percent discount, which equaled $460,000 in additional savings.

Then the council voted to transfer the user fee money into the general fund. Such a move was not unusual, given politics, fiscal difficulties, and the like, but it placed the helicopter purchase in jeopardy. Council president Christine Cid opposed the purchase, claiming if we rented the services from a former county helicopter pilot who worked out of Lansing, Illinois, it would cost only approximately $96,000 a year, if we did not go over the allotted hours.

In April 2008, I was preparing to defend my proposal to purchase a new helicopter when county councilman Tom O'Donnell, a supporter of good government, warned me that I only had three of the seven votes: his and those of the two council members from Gary, Jerome Prince and Elsie Franklin. A council member from Hammond had bowed to pressure from Hammond mayor Tom McDermott Jr. to withdraw his support. Councilman O'Donnell suggested the vote be postponed until the next month on the grounds that it's tough to change a no to a yes once a vote is taken.

I told Councilman O'Donnell that my office was ready to make a presentation and hoped for a positive outcome. There are times when a leader has to show political muscle and demonstrate inspiration, and I felt this was one of those occasions that demanded it. If people in pursuit of negativity think they can quash reform, they will try all means available.

We were the last agenda item for the April 2008 meeting. As I laid the groundwork for our presentation, I knew I had to be focused and convincing. We prepared statistical diagrams and printed handouts showing how we had accumulated the necessary funds and that the county would lose almost a million dollars (the federal grant and the 20 percent discount) if the council declined the purchase. Our financial consultant, along with attorney John Kopack, spoke, as well as our helicopter pilots wearing their pilots' uniforms.

During the questioning Christine Cid, arguing for her alternate rental plan, said, "I did my homework, and according to last year's statistics, the helicopters weren't used much." She had received her information from a retired sheriff's pilot who hoped to do business with the county. I replied, "Madam President, I really can't discuss the statistics, but our two helicopter pilots who are present will respond." They proceeded to inform the council that her statistics were not for the entire year of 2007, as claimed, but for less than four months of 2008, when the helicopters were inoperative much of the time because funding had not been approved for necessary repairs. Thus they could not go up in an uncertified helicopter. When she insisted the statistics were from 2007, our sergeant said, "No, the person who gave you those records gave you the wrong statistics. I know they're wrong because I compiled them. That's my work product." She had no comeback to that and her face turned scarlet.

Councilman Tom O'Donnell at that point called for the vote. Under his breath he whispered, "Here we go, Roy." The measure passed 5 to 2. The new helicopter finally arrived in August of 2009. Once you order it, it takes about sixteen months to receive it.

Earlier, in March of 2009, at the Governor's Breakfast in Indianapolis, I greeted Governor Daniels cordially. He joked, "Did you bring your helicopter down?" I replied, "No, the weather didn't permit it." He is a gentleman, despite the actions he has taken that have benefited the rich and hurt the poor.

## THE CLINTONS AND THE 2008 INDIANA DEMOCRATIC PRIMARY

I first met Bill Clinton in 1991. Governor Bayh invited me and other staff members to meet the Arkansas governor whom some were touting as a presidential hopeful. I was impressed by his willingness to interact with the so-called foot soldiers. I try to emulate that, and after a function I take time to thank the servers and cooks for a job well done.

During the 2008 Indiana Democratic primary race I met Kathleen Kennedy Townsend, the eldest child of Bobby Kennedy and the former lieutenant governor of Maryland, in Portage at a union rally in support of Hillary Clinton. She was bright and engaging. Later we were together in South Bend when she was with Bill and Chelsea Clinton. Chelsea was a poised young lady. If someone questioned her about the Monica Lewinsky affair, she'd say, "That's a private matter between my mom and my dad." Asked which parent was smarter, she'd respond, "At different times they both are."

Bill Clinton has the magnetism of a rock star. He doesn't put on airs and is down to earth, often turning a situation into a pleasant witticism. When speaking to crowds, he has an inspiring way of illustrating issues through personal stories. I have tried to emulate that. He's very accommodating when people want his autograph or a picture with him, and he would request that local officials be brought into a private reception room so he could shake everyone's hand and thank them for their help. I was in one such receiving line in Schererville when the woman next to me said, "Oh my God, I hope I don't pee in my pants." That was Bill. His charm would just melt the ladies.

I was sitting in a small plane across from Senator Hillary Clinton, flying from Indianapolis to Evansville. After giving her time to mentally decompress from her previous campaign appearance, I introduced myself and asked about her recent visit to Texas. She had just won the Texas primary, so I figured that was a pleasant topic. Learning that I was from Hidalgo County, Texas, she exclaimed, "You're not going to believe this but after graduating from Yale Law School in 1972, I went to work on a voter registration drive in Hidalgo County for the Democratic Party." She said she knew my hometown of Mercedes well and that Congressman Ruben Hinojosa was from there. I told her that his family and mine went back several generations. So we had an animated conversation, and I found her to be very bright and personable.

Prosecutor Bernard Carter and I were with Hillary at Washington Township School near Valparaiso. She had time for another stop before heading to Lafayette, so when Senator Bayh's office asked for a recommendation, I suggested Crown Point and alerted Crown Point mayor David Uran so he would be prepared. She wanted to do an informal, down-home event, and he suggested Bronko's Restaurant, where her drinking a shot of whiskey received much publicity. I was invited but thought it best to let the mayor have center stage. Rather than to crowd the limelight, I didn't go.

For Senator Clinton's appearance at the Hammond Civic Center, I was asked to warm up the crowd and introduce Mayor Tom McDermott, who in turn would introduce Hillary. Since I had been with her on several occasions and gotten her autograph and picture with me, I stood in the background and let other local officials get close to her. When it came time to enter the hall and walk to the stage, she stopped everything and said, "Where's the sheriff?" I stepped forward and she said, "Sheriff, you go first." Mayor McDermott was not pleased, and his envy was apparent.

After the 2004 presidential election, Evan Bayh had formed an exploratory committee to assess whether he should be a candidate for the 2008 Democratic nomination. He campaigned all across the country and raised over $12 million. In the end he decided not to run himself but to support fellow senator Hillary Clinton. Had Hillary won the Democratic nomination, I'm convinced Evan Bayh would have been her running mate. When asked about the possibility, she'd tell crowds, "What do you think, wouldn't he make a great vice president?" He was equally coy, noting, "It's way too early to discuss it, but if asked, it's always tough to say no to your party leader."

After Barack Obama became president, Hillary could have stayed as senator, but she apparently believed she could do more for the United States and the world community as secretary of state. I admire those who take on new challenges on behalf of creating a better society rather than to rest on their laurels or not put past differences behind them. Maybe that's one reason I decided to consider a campaign for governor or another public office. I am not one of those who are unwilling to leave their comfort zone in pursuit of an unknown end.

## MEETING BARACK OBAMA

The Friday before the 2008 presidential election Senator Obama appeared at a rally at Wicker Park in Highland. Polls indicated that he had a good chance to win Indiana, which had not gone to a Democratic candidate since Lyndon Baines Johnson carried the state in 1964 during his landslide victory over Senator Barry Goldwater. The Secret Service asked if the sheriff's department would help with security, and I replied that we'd be honored. When asked, I requested some reserved seats for guests I planned to bring aboard a bus and expressed hope that I might meet Senator Obama. The special agent promised to relay the requests, and that evening we were able to go into the secured area.

The crowd grew to over thirty thousand people. It was incredible. I had never seen so many people in Wicker Park. In addition to our officers, we had our helicopter on hand, as well as paramedics and an ambulance in case people needed medical attention. Everything went without a hitch.

Before Obama arrived, Senator Evan Bayh delivered an address to the audience. Afterward, the two of us were chatting backstage, waiting for the candidate to arrive, when a staffer approached us and rudely demanded that we leave the area. Obviously, he didn't recognize Senator Evan Bayh and seemed oblivious to the sheriff's pocket badge in my sports jacket and the green button on my lapel signifying that I had Secret Service clearance.

As Senator Bayh and I looked at each other in disbelief, the staffer said, "Did you hear me? You'll have to move."

I said, "Young man, I'm not going anywhere."

He threatened to get the Secret Service, and I told him, "We'll wait for you here." I was stern but more respectful than he was with us.

The young man came back with a Secret Service agent, who took one look at us and said to the aide, "Do you know who these people are?" Then the agent proceeded to tell him that if the sheriff were to leave and take his officers and support, this would be an unsecure place and Senator Obama would have to cancel the rally. I would never have done that, of course, but that cleared up the matter, and the aide left with a lesson in civility hopefully learned.

Another campaign staff member then invited Senator Bayh and me into the Wicker Park clubhouse to have some refreshments. Within ten minutes Obama arrived with a radiant smile on his face. He came up to Senator Bayh, who introduced him to me. Obama was very genuine, engaging, and easygoing as he thanked me for helping provide security. After he posed for pictures with Senator Bayh and me, I asked him if he would autograph two rally tickets I had for the event.

I said, "I have two of them because I have two daughters."

"Say no more," he replied. "I understand. You can't go home with just one."

As he started signing, he said, "What's your first daughter's name?"

"Veronica," I told him.

After he signed "To Veronica. Best wishes, Barack Obama," he repeated the process for Maria.

The election of Barack Obama was a culmination of our society becoming more open, thanks to the contributions of pioneers in many fields, not only civil rights and military service but sports, entertainment, labor, and business. A majority of people assessed him not as an African American but as someone with the talent and leadership skills to deal effectively with the nation's problems.

Obama carrying Indiana signified that the electorate has increasingly moved beyond voting against minority candidates simply for that reason alone. It was a seismic signal that the ground had shifted. Obama even did well in Republican strongholds such as Hamilton County. It gave me hope that if someone voted for a minority candidate once, he or she might do it again for a candidate who ran an effective, professional campaign.

After Barack Obama's historic election, friends of mine close to Senator Evan Bayh asked whether I would give consideration to becoming U.S. attorney for Indiana's northern district or a federal judge to fill a vacancy in South Bend. While I was honored at being considered, I told people that I was not interested in pursuing those options because it would have required me to be apolitical. My passion was to remain active in politics so that I could continue to have more of a voice in community, state, and world affairs.

## CONTEMPLATING A CANDIDACY FOR GOVERNOR

On Saturday, April 25, 2009, I spoke at the Third Congressional District Democratic dinner at Columbia City near Fort Wayne. The other featured speaker was Congressman Baron Hill, who reportedly was also thinking about running for governor. That day the *Fort Wayne Journal-Gazette* had run a front-page story mentioning what I had said at Valparaiso. I was told to expect a crowd of about a hundred, but almost four hundred people showed up.

I talked about the perceived stigma to Lake County politics and the struggles I faced in my efforts to get elected sheriff as a proactive candidate for good government. There are those who wish to keep northwest Indiana divided, I said, but added that it is a major force in state politics when united. I mentioned that one reason I was starting my "listening tour" early was to dispel the notion that being from Lake County tainted me. I reminded them that the reason Indiana went blue in 2008 was because of the plurality Lake County delivered for Barack Obama. I added that neither Evan Bayh nor Frank O'Bannon would have been elected governor without the large Lake County pluralities. Then I asked them to think back to 1968 when Lake County gave presidential candidate Robert F. Kennedy his margin of victory in the Democratic primary. "So in 2012," I concluded, "don't let anyone tell you that someone from Lake County can't win."

My speech was extremely well received. My wife, Betty, who is admittedly biased toward me but a good judge of when I'm on and when I'm just so-so, told me when I sat down, "Baron's in trouble, having to follow you." Congressman Hill, a good friend, actually gave a great presentation.

Some have asked how a sheriff can think himself qualified to run for governor. Here again I think my family values come into play – being a good person but passionate about serving the public with integrity, like my parents. My primary goals as sheriff were to protect the community and make it a better place to live. The thing that excites me about serving as governor is the opportunity to be a hard worker for the people. By making the state more economically sound and helping to create more jobs I would be making Indiana a better place to live as well. A governor, like a sheriff, wants a better, safer place for all citizens. As sheriff I talked to residents about their concerns and dreams. At the same time I worked on a multitude of issues that required precise results.

Under Mitch Daniels corporations were not paying their fair share of taxes. In 2009 U.S. Steel, for instance, paid just a third of what they had been assessed a decade before. That whole area needs to be revisited. The threat of corporations moving out of Indiana is something to be mindful of, but many companies have received tax breaks and then later elected to move overseas or to Mexico anyway. It has more to do with corporate greed than high taxes. Executives are making tens of millions of dollars while workers are left to fend for themselves. That's un-American. A corporate-friendly state is equally important, and I believe a balance can be achieved.

Manufacturing jobs have been shrinking at an alarming rate for the past twenty years. In August of 2009, for example, Whirlpool announced the closing of its Evansville plant, due to the opening of a new facility in Mexico. The three hundred remaining administrative jobs will undoubtedly follow. It is estimated that for every industrial job lost, four others involving suppliers, service personnel, and the like will vanish as well. That translates into families losing income, health insurance, college savings, and possibly even their homes. For the State of Indiana it means reduced tax revenue and increased family service costs. In 1992 Ross Perot predicted that if NAFTA became law, we'd hear a constant sucking sound of jobs leaving this country. Time has borne him out. Governing will be difficult during times of unemployment and decreasing revenues, but I remain confident in our country's resilience.

In assessing whether to run for governor, I wanted to determine if it was a realistic possibility. So many people would be sacrificing their time and money that I wanted to be certain that there is an opportunity to succeed. I estimated that to launch a credible campaign for the Democratic nomination would cost between one and two million dollars, and it would take at least an additional $10 million to be competitive in the general election. Those are daunting amounts, but they are achievable. Meanwhile, discussing issues and encouraging young people to pursue their dreams are worthwhile endeavors in their own right. I believe this is especially true within the overall community, where a possible candidacy has generated a good deal of excitement.

Times have changed in my lifetime in terms of social interactions. Minority groups in our generation have been participants more fully than most would have thought possible, and I have encouraged people I meet to dream of a brighter society. Intercultural marriages occur almost seamlessly. Ethnic groups have the same challenges when it comes to their hopes and prosperity. Where once the overwhelming majority of Hispanics in Indiana were from Lake County, now there are sizable Hispanic communities in Elkhart, Fort Wayne, South Bend, Indianapolis, Crawfordsville, and elsewhere. As a result of cultural and social interaction, the unrealistic bias against minorities has diminished.

There are still those who lack cultural sensitivity, but most of us, I think, have progressed. Yet the recent talk of tightening the immigration laws has had a whole host of negative consequences, ranging from demeaning identification checks if you look Hispanic to negative stereotyping. A Hispanic campaigning for the top executive position in Indiana, something unprecedented, would be making the positive statement, "This is our country, too, and we are productive citizens who deserve to be accepted fully as partners." Indiana once was a Ku Klux Klan stronghold and known as "the Northern-most Southern state." It is gratifying to realize the collective progress that has been made since that time. We as Americans and Hoosiers can take pride in our advancements and our desire to treat people with respect.

## TOM McDERMOTT JR.

In 2003 Hammond's Democratic organization had been in disarray and without a serious challenger to run against incumbent Republican Duane

Dedelow. The mayor had been in office since 1992 after his predecessor, Thomas M. McDermott Sr., became president of the Northwest Indiana Forum a year into his third term. Dedelow was a very good man, and many people urged him to switch parties since registered Democrats outnumbered Republicans by a wide margin. Instead it was former mayor McDermott's son Tom who bolted to the Democratic Party in order to run in the general election against Dedelow. A rule stated that only those who voted in the previous Democratic primary could seek office as a Democrat, but county chairman Bob Stiglich granted him an exemption in exchange, as the saying goes, for future considerations.

Although I admired Dedelow's accomplishments and commitment to good government and diversity, as a loyal Democratic Party official I endorsed McDermott and persuaded prosecutor Bernard Carter to do the same. A photo of the three of us in front of Hammond City Hall appeared on fliers and in a full-page *Times* ad that ran on Sunday before the election. Speculating that the *Times* favored Dedelow, I warned McDermott that the ad might appear misprinted and to be prepared to demand that the paper run a corrected version free of charge the following day.

Sure enough, even though we had given the paper a clear copy, the photo was blurred. The paper offered to reprint it on Tuesday, but I told McDermott to insist on Monday. The *Times* acquiesced, and McDermott won by a slim seven-hundred-vote plurality. Afterward, he profusely thanked Carter and me for enabling him to do well in Hammond and among Hispanic and black voters. I subsequently encouraged him on several occasions to appoint administrators from Hammond's minority communities, but he was largely deaf to those suggestions.

In 2006 Mayor Tom McDermott Jr. promised to support my reelection bid for sheriff during a meeting my adviser George Van Til and I had with him and city Democratic chairman David A. Hamm, who also served as Hammond's fire chief. Prior to elections the Democratic precinct organizations in Gary, East Chicago, and Hammond commonly hold caucuses and endorse candidates. Some believed that securing early endorsements from these groups would provide important momentum. McDermott and Hamm moved up the date of Hammond's so it would be first, and they emphatically stated that I would secure the precinct endorsement. That seemed fishy to George Van Til, who was an experienced veteran in these matters. Talking with various precinct committeemen, I learned that McDermott had not endorsed me. In fact, Hamm was covertly and actively supporting Buncich, who received the caucus endorsement. McDermott may have believed that if I were no longer on the political scene, his future would be brighter. Perhaps this explains the essence of his subsequent combative attitude toward me.

One week before the election, when it was clear that Buncich was trailing badly, on his own McDermott published a newspaper ad endorsing me. On election night there he was at my victory party. He claimed that Hamm had orchestrated the precinct vote without his knowledge, but to me it was far-fetched to think that Hamm would have gone against his boss's wishes. I did not make an issue about it, however, because it was water under the bridge. I was not interested in retribution. Sentiments of revenge don't foster positive public service. So I maintained cordial relations with McDermott in hopes I could influence him to promote good government and minority interests.

In 2007 McDermott did not solicit my help when he ran for reelection because he thought he was politically invincible. After barely defeating an opponent who had almost no funds or organizational backing, he chastised me for not having endorsed him. I reminded him I had offered my help but that he hadn't procured any assistance from me since he thought he was unbeatable.

With talk afloat that Mayor McDermott was considering running for governor in 2012, I met with him in May of 2009 and asked about his future plans. His top priority, he said, was winning a third term in 2011 because being mayor was his bread and butter. He said he enjoyed his name being bantered around for governor but denied any intention to run. He pledged to support me so that, in his words, Lake County Democrats would speak with one voice.

Given my past experience with Mayor McDermott, I did not jump for joy nor accept his promise of endorsement at full value. The previous year, for example, he had gone back on his commitment to support Oscar Sanchez for county commissioner. I told him I was appreciative but added: "You know, Mayor, I must admit, when you're around, I'm watching my back." I didn't mean any disrespect but believe it is important in private conversations to be candid. He said he would improve his conduct; however, the sophomoric insults and political attacks continued.

That same month, my old nemesis Bob Cantrell went to jail as a result of a scheme involving contracts between various government agencies and a counseling service, Addiction and Family Care, from which he received half the money it took in. Judge Rudy Lozano sentenced him to seventy-eight months in prison.

During the last weekend in August of 2009, I attended a function of the Indiana Democrat Editorial Association in French Lick, Indiana. The event was a combination golf outing, fund-raiser, and political gathering put on by the Indiana State Democratic Party. With me were Betty, my daughter Veronica, her husband, Jason Rebar, and about six others. Veronica was just a natural; she grew up with me in politics and didn't fall far from the tree, as the saying goes. She and Maria have taken turns going with Betty and me to functions. My family, knowing how I felt, was all for my making an effort to become governor. Having them next to me brought a great deal of comfort and enjoyment.

Veronica graduated from IU Northwest and is working on a master's degree in communication. She's very much "center stage," while Maria is the "behind the scenes" technician. Like the instruments they played, Veronica is flashy like a trumpet, while Maria is smooth like the violin. After attending IU Northwest for a year, Maria made friends with members of the crew filming *Public Enemies* in Crown Point in the summer of 2008. She even had a walk-on part and learned some of the technical aspects of filmmaking. She was offered a part-time job in Chicago and followed the company to New York City in hopes that the experience would lead to a full-time job. After it became apparent that it wouldn't, she returned home to pursue her education.

At the French Lick event my political staff hosted a hospitality open house Friday and Saturday night. We had food and beverages and passed out promotional items and CDs that contained information on how to motivate young voters and utilize voter registration lists. Scheduled to take place between 9 and 11 PM, our open house continued until 1:30 in the morning.

Mayor McDermott also hosted a hospitality open house. Since our May meeting, I had been aware that he had not revealed publicly or privately that he was supporting me. Indiana Democratic chairman Dan Parker held a breakfast meeting Sunday for gubernatorial hopefuls in order to set forth certain ground rules and emphasize his neutrality in the process. In attendance were Speaker of the House Pat Bauer, Evansville mayor Jonathan Weinzapfel, and Congressman Brad Ellsworth, and representing Congressman Baron Hill was his daughter. When I arrived, there was Tom McDermott. Just a week before, the *Post-Tribune* had quoted him to the effect that he wasn't interested in state office and was focused on the 2011 mayor's race.

During our group discussion with Chairman Parker, Mayor McDermott said, "I haven't decided what my future in politics will be" – meaning he still might run for governor. Not surprised, I thought to myself, "So much for your pledge to support me." Some say that politics is about taking advantage of opportunities. I say not necessarily; it's about the people.

On September 10, 2009, the Lake County prosecutor's office charged David Woerpel, a close ally of Mayor Tom McDermott Jr., and three other family members with felony counts after an aerial inspection by the state police revealed marijuana plants growing in the Woerpel backyard. A team of officers in the sheriff's office whose job was to check daily the outstanding warrants list then arrested the Woerpels. The next morning I got a message on my cell phone voice mail from McDermott, claiming that this was the dirtiest trick he'd ever seen. He evidently left a similar message with prosecutor Bernard Carter.

After collecting my thoughts, I called McDermott back and told him that our officers were required to arrest those with outstanding warrants, especially drug charges, and that from all reports they treated Woerpel's family with courtesy. I added that it was absurd to insinuate that the episode was some sort of politically motivated conspiracy and that he owed the others and me an apology. After he heard me out, he insincerely apologized for getting so riled up.

I released the mayor's phone message to the press because I thought he was trying to politically intimidate others and me into not carrying out our duties. The public had the right to know the full story, including what the mayor was doing. Just because a person's friend is powerful politically, that does not mean the person is above the law. The mayor's claim that there was a conspiracy against his friend maligned not only the sheriff's department but also the prosecutor's office, the state police, and the judge who determined that there was sufficient cause to authorize the issuance of an arrest warrant. I had no involvement in seeking arrest warrants or the investigation and subsequent charges because it was a state police investigation.

Mayor McDermott's reaction to my releasing the phone message was to call me a "weasel" and a "snake," which I found to be very immature. Invited to appear on WJOB, I replied that I would not engage in name-calling. I respect McDermott's family and always have had my hand out in friendship. He says that politics is a full-contact sport, and that's where we differ. I think such a view is egotistical and self-serving, whereas I believe politics should be about public service to the people.

## RAPPROCHEMENT

Because Indiana law prohibits one from serving more than two consecutive terms as sheriff, I supported my chief, Marco Kuyachich, who had been like a brother to me since the death of his predecessor, Gary Martin. Also vying for the office were a half-dozen other hopefuls, including front-runners Tom Philpot and John Buncich. Recognizing that there are times when doors might open for healing old wounds, in 2009 I invited Philpot to lunch and said I hoped we could be friends, as we once were. We had a good talk for about three hours and agreed to end our enmity.

In January of 2010, I got a call from Buncich, wanting to have dinner with me to resolve our differences. We met at Strongbow's Restaurant in Valparaiso. With me was county surveyor George Van Til; with him was county treasurer John Petalas. He apologized for his past negativity and asked me to convey his apologies to my family as well. He said he regretted what he did and that when he stopped to think about it, didn't know what had gotten into him, to go into such a frenzy of negativity. He seemed sincere. I told him that my regret was that for over seven years I did not have the support of him or some of the officers loyal to him. After the meeting union leader Dan Murchak, chairman of Local County Police 72, said he wanted to be friends with me, and Robert

Klasner, Buncich's stepson who is the local FOP president, agreed to reinstate me as a member.

There was a great deal of buzz about our meeting afterward, but at the end of the day I decided to move on and resist those emotions that would have me carry grudges. Philpot called me and said, "What's this I hear about you having lunch with Buncich?" I said, "It wasn't lunch. It was dinner. Seriously, I made peace with you. Why wouldn't I make peace with Buncich?"

I told both former rivals that I was for Marco Kuyachich. They said, "Well, Marco can't win." I said, "I don't know that. In any event that's an evaluation that Marco will have to make in deciding whether to remain in the race."

Marco solicited my advice about remaining in the race for sheriff. Rather than tell him what to do, I asked a series of questions: "How are you doing in Hammond?" "How do you see yourself coming out of East Chicago?" "Do you have support in Gary?" Sadly, he was pessimistic on all three counts. In the end politics comes down to whether you believe you can win. There's no point in finishing third, and Marco was up against two old pros. He didn't file. Some of his backers were defecting to Philpot and urging him to do the same. I told him not to make a decision to endorse Philpot while tired or emotional. I myself try, whenever possible, not to make decisions in anger or when fatigued. Even so, he endorsed Philpot, who in turn promised to retain him as chief if elected.

Several candidates subsequently sought my support. I believed that former National Guard colonel Richard Ligon, an African American, was clearly the best choice for sheriff, but I debated whether to stay neutral. If I endorsed somebody, I wanted it to be meaningful. Both Buncich and Philpot took the position that while Ligon was a good guy, he had no chance. I met with Ligon and thought that he had the right passion, integrity, and desire to be a viable candidate. In a statement of endorsement I referred to him as retired colonel Ligon and praised him as the "best choice" to be my successor. I sent my statement to members of the *Post-Tribune* editorial board, and shortly thereafter that board endorsed him, using the same phrase, "best choice." The *Times* soon followed. I attended his rallies in part because I wanted his followers to realize that he could win despite what the Buncich and Philpot camps were saying.

Had the campaign gone on two more weeks, I believe the momentum would have swung Ligon's way. In the end Ligon finished second and lost by about a thousand votes. Philpot finished a distant fourth; in fact, had Philpot done better, Ligon might have won, because he and Buncich were essentially competing for the same voters.

Despite my respect and fondness for the Arredondos, when it comes to politics, we sometimes have different perspectives and political allies. Judge Lorenzo Arredondo was very savvy. Considering retirement from the Lake County circuit court after thirty years on the bench, he asked if I would seek to be his replacement. When I replied in the negative, he said he was thinking of endorsing Richard McDevitt, a magistrate in his court whose Filipina spouse was a friend of my wife, Betty. That was quintessential Lorenzo – to put a potential rival at ease and off guard. Later Arredondo told me he was going to file. In that case, I replied, I'm certain you'll run unopposed.

Shortly before the filing deadline, I received word from several sources that Merrillville town judge George C. Paras was at the Patio bar bragging that Judge Arredondo was going to withdraw at the last minute so that Paras could file and run unopposed. The essence of the last-minute switcheroo was to keep control of the court, its docket, and its employees. Previously my nephew Alex Dominguez, a former Lake County deputy prosecutor, East Chicago city attorney, and public defender in Judge Nicholas Schiralli's court, who had lived with us after graduating from high school, had expressed interest in becoming a judge should the opportunity present itself. Not pleased with the surreptitious arrangement between Arredondo and Paras, I encouraged him to file. After all, he was more experienced than Judge Arredondo had been when he launched his judicial career. I told Alex that it would be a tough fight against a well-financed opponent but that there were some things in his favor. Paras was not well known and lived in Ogden Dunes in Porter County, although he used his Merrillville address to vote in Lake County. Had we not caught Arredondo off guard, the judge probably would have selected someone with better name recognition.

The filing deadline at the secretary of state's office in Indianapolis was noon on Friday, February 19. I advised Alex to arrive around 11:30 and expect Judge Arredondo and George Paras to be there. Be forthright,

I counseled, when asked why he was there, and do not let them detain or delay you. Alex went ahead and filed, and right before noon Arredondo withdrew his name and Paras filed. Meanwhile, according to Indiana law, candidates have until noon Monday to withdraw. Over the weekend John Buncich called with an offer: if Alex withdrew, leaving Paras as the sole candidate, Judge Arredondo and others would arrange for my nephew to fill the vacancy in the Merrillville town court. I replied, "No thanks, Alex's candidacy is not up for negotiation." If he became a judge, it would be through the electoral process, not the result of a deal. Buncich said, "OK, Sheriff. I was just delivering a message. We're still friends." The remark sounded like a Marlon Brando line from *The Godfather.* The next time I talked to Lake County prosecutor Bernard Carter, he told me that even Michael Jordan could not have pulled off a sweeter three-point play.

Alex did very well at political functions, and I was proud of him. When people said he was not as fluent as his uncle, I told him that during my first campaign, I, too, was nervous and stammered at times. The race was much closer than most people expected. Had Alex not been outspent by over five to one, approximately $200,000 to $40,000, I think he would have won.

After Senator Evan Bayh announced he would not seek reelection in November of 2010, throwing the nomination process into the hands of the state Democratic Central Committee, Mayor McDermott announced his intention to seek the nomination. He called me up and asked if we could be friends. I said sure, that I always had a hand out in friendship for those who are sincere. He asked for my support for his Senate bid and promised to help me should I decide to run for governor. My radio show on WJOB in Hammond aired right after the mayor's, and host Jim Dedelow asked if I would appear together with him. I agreed. Not surprisingly, Dedelow asked whether I supported McDermott for senator. Yes, I replied. McDermott added that I knew important party leaders around the state and had made phone calls on his behalf. Dedelow then asked McDermott if he would support me for governor. Yes, indeed, was the reply.

There had been speculation that Evan Bayh wanted to run for president in 2016 and that being governor would be a better springboard than remaining in the Senate. I made it plain that I would not run against Bayh should he be a candidate for governor in 2012. He was a mentor and dear friend. Besides, he would be unbeatable. On the other hand, had he made the decision to run for governor, I would have been honored if he desired that I be his running mate. I saw it as a possibility. We have had a long association and mutual respect, going back to 1985, when he first ran for secretary of state, and later when I headed the Worker's Compensation Board while he was governor. He was familiar with my record as Lake County sheriff. I have been through many storms and did not sweep problems under the rug, but worked to correct them. Not only do I think he believes me to be qualified, but having a Hispanic lieutenant governor would help him in a future presidential campaign in many parts of the country, including the populous states of California, Texas, Florida, New York, and Illinois. In the end he discouraged all speculation about his running for governor.

## LEAVING OFFICE

As I was preparing to leave the sheriff's office, I wrote my successor, John Buncich, wishing him the best and offering my help. I told him I would not be a candidate for sheriff in four years because I was ready to start a new chapter in my life. After that, I purposely stayed away from politics or endorsing specific candidates. In office my antenna always had to be attuned to politics, and it was comforting to be able to step back, spend more time with my family, resume my legal practice, volunteer my time to community organizations, especially those helping veterans, and take time to assess my future.

# Core Values

In every conceivable manner, the family
is link to our past, bridge to our future.

ALEX HALEY, author of *Roots*

Leaders honor their core values, but they
are flexible in how to execute them.

COLIN POWELL, former secretary of state

CONCLUSION

# Core Values

*America has always produced leaders who are optimistic about the future, whether it be entrepreneurs, political leaders, or civil rights agents of change such as Martin Luther King Jr. and César Chávez. Each wave of immigrants to our shores, given a fair chance, has contributed to the American Dream. Hispanics are now taking an enhanced place to help carry that dream to unprecedented heights.*

## PROJECT HOPE

In 2006 I helped organize a group called HOPE. The acronym stands for the Hispanic Organization Promoting Excellence. The primary mission is to promote excellence in the areas of education, employment, and image. I wrote to members of the Hispanic community, such as judges, lawyers, prosecutors, business executives, educators, union leaders, and other professionals, asking them to help do something to reduce the high school dropout rate and increase the number of Hispanics seeking higher education. By some estimates over half the Hispanic students in Lake County were dropping out of high school. With few job prospects, dropouts were susceptible to recruitment by gangs and drug dealers.

The group formed a Hispanic Youth Leadership Academy, and for the past three years we have enrolled 200 students in a summer program promoting leadership skills, ethics, and practical information on filling out college applications and applying for financial aid. As a result, virtually all of the students from our leadership academy enrolled in college.

In 2007 I convinced Dr. Joe Arredondo to assume a leadership position in Project HOPE's Leadership Academy. He has done an outstanding job.

To promote cultural awareness HOPE sponsored a Latino Festival at the Lake County Fair on Saturday, August 8, 2009. We brought in Roberto Clemente's son and Tierra, a Grammy-winning Latino rock band from California, and held a Latino Idol contest. Los Cordoba, a talented local musical group, performed. It was a great success, and HOPE has continued the annual tradition.

## ROLE MODELS JILL LONG, ROBERT RUCKER, AND JUAN ANDRADE JR.

Northwest Indiana has produced its share of civic-minded leaders. Jill Long studied at Indiana University and received her doctorate in business. She was elected to the Valparaiso City Council in 1983 while an assistant professor at Valparaiso University. She and her husband, Don, live on a farm near Argos, Indiana. In 1986 she lost her effort to unseat Senator Dan Quayle, but after Fourth District congressman Dan Coats became senator following Quayle's elevation to the vice presidency, Long won a special congressional election to fill that vacancy. Despite it being considered a Republican district, she twice won reelection before losing to Mark Souder in 1994. For the next six years she served in President Bill Clinton's administration as undersecretary of agriculture for rural development. In 2008 she became the first woman to become a major party candidate for governor in Indiana. Her tenacity and intelligence are an inspiration to all who know her.

After returning to the city of Gary from the Vietnam War, Robert Rucker was very angry at racial and societal conditions in America. My wife Betty's father, Ponciano Olayta, became his martial arts instructor and also his spiritual mentor. When her family moved from Seventh and Polk to Miller, Bob Rucker bought their old house on Gary's north side in part because he wanted to have the aura of living where Mr. Olayta had resided. After graduating from IU and Valparaiso Law School, he became a top-notch Lake County deputy prosecutor, winning every single case he tried.

While I was working for prosecutor Jack Crawford, Rucker campaigned for county court judge against Steven Bielak. A third candidate, Jim Frank, planned to run but then dropped out and threw his support to Bielak. Before the election a newspaper ad appeared announcing that Frank was throwing his support to Bielak and including photos of the two remaining candidates to make certain voters realized that Rucker was African American. Bielak won, and the suspicion was that his organization had paid for the ad. Jack Crawford was just livid. As a result, a statute was enacted requiring that advertisements specify who paid for and authorized them.

In 1991 when a vacancy occurred on the Indiana Court of Appeals, I encouraged Rucker to apply. He was working for legendary East Chicago attorney Henry Walker at the time and reluctant to do so, given what had happened previously. Many friends encouraged him as well, especially Gary activist attorney Hilbert Bradley. I told Rucker I'd do what I could on his behalf. He filed an application for consideration to be on the Court of Appeals, and Governor Evan Bayh appointed him. Eight years later, Governor O'Bannon recommended his appointment to the Indiana Supreme Court, where he currently still serves.

Dr. Juan Andrade Jr. is one of only two Latinos to receive the Presidential Freedom Medal "for the performance of exemplary deeds to the nation." For more than twenty-five years he has headed up the nonpartisan United States Hispanic Leadership Institute based in Chicago. His organization has trained thousands of future leaders and been involved in registering over two million new voters. A good friend of mine, he has given me valuable counsel over the years. Dr. Andrade has invited me to speak at training sessions on leadership and voter registration. It was very rewarding to interact with young people and to encourage them to have the tenacity to succeed in an ethical manner.

Prior to the Senate vote to confirm Supreme Court nominee Sonia Sotomayor, Dr. Andrade warned that people would see a "Nay" vote against a very well qualified jurist "as a vote against our community." He was invited to Justice Sotomayor's swearing-in ceremony and arranged for me to attend a reception in her honor on October 15, 2009.

## RECEPTION FOR JUSTICE SOTOMAYOR

On October 15, 2009, at the invitation of Dr. Juan Andrade Jr., I was one of approximately three hundred people who attended a special reception at the National Education Association Foundation headquarters for incoming United States Supreme Court Justice Sonia Maria Sotomayor. It was sponsored by some two dozen Hispanic organizations that constituted themselves as "Friends of Justice Sotomayor." In a reception room the justice greeted groups of fifteen, who would pose in two rows for a commemorative photograph. She was very pleasant and down to earth in her responses to questions and comments. As my group was leaving, I shook her hand, congratulated her, and asked if she would autograph my business card. Smiling at me, she said, "Sweetheart, if I started to give autographs, I wouldn't be able to do anything else." Now when asked what I remember about meeting her, I tell folks that Justice Sotomayor called me "Sweetheart."

After the photo sessions Justice Sotomayor joined the guests in the main hall where drinks and hors d'oeuvres were served and a podium had been set up. After others spoke briefly, she talked about receiving the call from President Obama, informing her that he was submitting her name for confirmation by the Senate, and how proud it made her family. At some point a guest interrupted her prepared remarks by shouting out in Spanish, "Estamos orgullosos de ti [We're proud of you], Justice Sotomayor." She stopped, turned beet-red, and the room fell silent. With a quiver in her voice the justice replied in Spanish that she was proud of all of us for having helped her obtain the high honor of serving on the nation's highest court. The spontaneous outburst must have struck an emotional nerve. Switching back to English, she said that only in America could someone of her background achieve such an honor. It was a heartfelt moment, and then the audience erupted.

The next morning I flew to Dallas for a Hispanic summit organized by Jorge Ferraez, the publisher of the magazine *Latino Leaders*. Ferraez had me at the head table and introduced me to a crowd of approximately four hundred, encouraging them to support me if I ran for governor. Receiving a round of applause when I announced that I was born in Texas, I told the audience how important it was for Latinos to continue pursuing our dreams without barriers.

## POLITICAL HEROES

While our government has not lived up to its ideal, we've had brave individuals who have spoken out against unjust policies. César Chávez has always been a hero of mine, and a framed picture of him is prominently displayed in my office. My daughters, Veronica and Maria, found a tattoo artist who had a design of the United Farm Workers flag and its motto, "Sí, se puede." It means, "Yes, we can" – the same motto Barack Obama used successfully in the 2008 presidential race. They both got one as a way of honoring those in our family and others who worked as migrant laborers. Tattoos have always been symbols of life experiences or things cherished or worthy of being honored. My maternal grandfather, for instance, had a tattoo of Lady Columbia on his left forearm.

Chávez believed that by serving others, we find life. His was truly an inspired life. My friend Oscar Sanchez shares my admiration for Chávez. After Oscar retired from his District 7 United Steelworkers union position, I asked him to come be my administrative assistant. My dad had introduced us; they hailed from the same area of Texas and knew each other's relatives. Oscar was someone I could always turn to and trust like an older brother. After the chief of staff for civilian employees retired, I moved him into that position. From time to time I will run ideas by him to solicit his advice. While I was deciding whether to run for governor, he reminded me to set my sights high because what once seemed impossible is coming to pass. I think the election of Barack Obama demonstrates that.

Martin Luther King is an inspiration to us all. He was working for all the people, not just one race or class, to help create a more open, integrated, egalitarian society. Dedicated to nonviolence, Martin Luther King, like César Chávez, defied the odds and conducted himself with dignity and integrity. Recently my daughter Maria texted me this quote: "Evil triumphs when good men do nothing." I thought it might be from Martin Luther King but learned that the sentiments have been attributed to English statesman Edmund Burke. I'm usually the one who sends my daughters "words of wisdom" or uplifting messages such as "Pursue your dreams" and things of that nature. Despite all the hatred he endured, Martin Luther King was an optimist who worked for social change using nonviolent methods. I was delighted when the country declared Martin Luther King Day a national holiday to honor what an inspiring change-agent he was.

In short, I am fortunate to have lived during an age that produced such inspirational leaders as Martin Luther King and César Chávez, and in the political arena, the Kennedy brothers and Evan Bayh. All of them made great sacrifices to devote their lives to public service and noble causes. As Barack Obama wrote in his brilliant book *The Audacity of Hope,* "We long for that most elusive quality in our leaders – the quality of authenticity, of being who you say you are, of possessing a truthfulness that goes beyond words." He also wrote, "I think about what Benjamin Franklin wrote to his mother, explaining why he had devoted so much of his time to public service: 'I would rather have it said, He lived usefully, than, He died rich.'"

Ben Franklin also once said, "Whatever is begun in anger ends in shame." I try not to act out of retribution. Sometimes it is hard because it's an emotion we all have in the heat of battle. I try to live according to the spirit of Abraham Lincoln's words, "With malice toward none; with charity for all," uttered at the sixteenth president's second inaugural near the end of the Civil War. As a young congressman he had spoken out against the Mexican War. During the election of 1860 he was showered with abuse and called an ignorant, ugly monkey. Yet in the face of threats and unprecedented challenges he preserved the Union and abolished slavery.

Most Hispanics didn't have an issue or bitterness with either whites or African Americans. Well aware of the scourge of slavery and the long history of discrimination against women and minorities, Hispanics have been in the forefront of battles for civil rights and have revered leaders who have taken up the cause of equality and liberty and who have stood alongside women and minorities to fight for an end to discriminatory practices. It has taken generations for Americans to start treating minorities with dignity and respect and as equals with certain God-given inalienable rights. Although we have made significant progress, Martin Luther King's "Dream" has not yet been fulfilled. Before we reach the "Promised Land," all God's children need to have equal opportunity to enjoy life, liberty, and the pursuit of happiness.

President Franklin D. Roosevelt laid the basis for a just society by persuading Congress to enact his New Deal programs, such as social security. Lyndon Baines Johnson, seen by some as a usurper after John F. Kennedy's assassination in Dallas, Texas, championed civil rights legislation and helped launch Medicare and Medicaid for the elderly and poor. We have regressed since then. Today, a few health insurance corporate giants make billions while every thirteen minutes someone in America dies as a result of not having access to health care.

Jimmy Carter was president at a time when the nation's economy floundered, and he had to deal with a hostage crisis in Iran that was not resolved until after he lost the 1980 election to Ronald Reagan. Nonetheless, President Carter was an advocate for democracy and human rights, and since leaving office he has worked tirelessly for world peace and social justice. He, too, is an American hero for his advocacy of democracy and compassion for poor peoples of the world.

Despite being imprisoned for twenty-seven years on Robben Island, after his release in 1990 South African leader Nelson Mandela sought reconciliation rather than retribution. Winner of the Nobel Peace Prize and elected president of his country in 1994, Mandela worked tirelessly and nonviolently for people who had been victims of apartheid.

I greatly admire those who move out of their comfort zones on behalf of noble ideals. Former prime minister Benazir Bhutto, twice ousted from office on bogus charges of corruption, returned from exile in 2007 in hopes of leading Pakistan away from military rule. Tragically she was assassinated two months later after addressing her supporters at a rally. Thirty years ago the military had overthrown and executed her father, Zulfikar Ali Bhutto. In 1986 Benigno Aquino was murdered on orders from Philippine dictator Ferdinand Marcos when he attempted to return to his country to lead a pro-democracy movement. Rather than retreat from the political arena, his widow, Corazon Aquino, picked up his torch and three years later helped topple Marcos. She went on to serve as the democratically elected president of the Philippines for six years.

There will always be stiff winds swirling around officeholders, so leaders need to have a good sense of who they are and where they are going and remain confident without becoming arrogant. President Barack Obama deserves high marks for getting health care reform passed into law despite the crescendo of vocal critics and Republican obstructionism. He stayed focused during the year long fight while also dealing with such pressing matters as the war, the recession, and budget deficits. He had a sense of what was right for the country and how best to accomplish it. A few weeks before passage the bill appeared to be dead, and Republicans were claiming that Democrats were going to take a beating during midterm elections. Self-interest groups ran misleading ads and organized "Tea Party" rallies at which Obama was demonized as a socialist and even compared to Hitler. Thanks to his doggedness, millions of Americans are on the road to receiving health care. Had Ted Kennedy been alive, he'd surely have been cheering. The long-overdue reform is a tribute to Obama's soul and spirit as well as his leadership skills.

## IN THE MAINSTREAM

As I contemplate my future in public service, I have had people around the state of Indiana introduce me as Roy Dominguez rather than Rogelio "Roy" Dominguez as in the races for sheriff. I've always been known as Roy to friends and family – except when my mom was upset at me, then it was Rogelio. My campaign advisers developed a website, Indianaroy .com, and came up with an image of me in a cowboy hat and holding a lasso that was a takeoff on the movie character Indiana Jones.

Lake County residents take pride in learning to pronounce ethnic names, but in going around the state I found people sometimes stumbling over pronouncing Rogelio, and then they were becoming embarrassed and apologetic. First impressions in politics are so important, so if someone cannot pronounce my name, it can create a problem in presenting my candidacy. Rather than possibly make folks uncomfortable, I decided just to use Roy. Nobody should presume I'm not honoring my Hispanic heritage – Dominguez is very identifiable as Hispanic. It's similar to Karl Malden not using his given name Sekulovich, even though he was very proud of his Serbian heritage.

When people from across the state of Indiana are curious about my background, I find it humbling and endearing. I tell them that my ancestors lived on land that was first part of New Spain, then part of Mexico, then part of Texas, and now part of the United States. While my parents' generation were referred to as Mexicans, I am proud to be regarded as an American of Mexican heritage. What progress we have made in that regard. I understand ethnic pride and certainly am proud of my heritage and its customs, but what is most important is to respect everyone and not look down on others' traditions. When I think of my heritage, my first thought is of my forefathers and mothers and the sacrifices they made that enabled me to live a productive life.

Reading other public servants' autobiographies, I have been struck by certain similarities with and parallels to my own life. In *Marvella: A Personal Journey,* Evan Bayh's mother described her humble but proud Oklahoma roots. She survived more than her share of tribulations, including a terrible car accident shortly following her marriage to Birch Bayh, a plane crash in 1964 that almost killed Ted Kennedy, and a mastectomy in 1971, before succumbing to a reoccurrence of the breast cancer. I found her resilience in the face of these tribulations inspiring and her life filled with classic inspiration. Evan Bayh's 2003 autobiography, *From Father to Son,* is a tribute to both his remarkable parents.

Having read several books about the brothers Kennedy, including Max Kennedy's *Make Gentle the Life of This World: The Wisdom of Robert F. Kennedy* and Ray Boomhower's *Robert F. Kennedy and the 1968 Indiana Primary,* I am struck by the excitement they brought to politics and how competitive they were without sacrificing their principles. To succeed in such a rough profession one needs both toughness and the ability to connect with constituents. The example of the Kennedy brothers makes one appreciate the fragility of life and inspires me to make the most of my years in public service.

In *View from the State House: Recollections and Reflections, 1961–1965,* Indiana governor Matthew Welsh mentioned how he refrained from speaking negatively about opponents. Rather than engage in personal insults, he'd stick to the issues and refer to detractors in the abstract. What I admired most was that he was a real gentleman in a profession that can be quite combative. While it is not always possible to ignore those who are aggressively negative toward you, I seek to promote my values and programs, not personally disparage others. I pride myself in not holding grudges. As Abraham Lincoln believed, forgiving an enemy purges one's mind of unproductive thoughts. It's not so much that enemies deserve that bygones be bygones as that you yourself deserve it. Besides, as British wit Oscar Wilde observed, "Always forgive your enemies – nothing annoys them so much."

My goal has been to explain to people the inspiration of my passion for life and public service. It started, I believe, with my parents and grandparents imparting to me values to live by and to love this country and have faith in its people. They taught me to believe in America. I believe in the Lord's blessings, and I have tried to follow my parents' advice to "be a good man" and take care of your family.

I want to bring my life experiences, talents, and core values into action in some useful purpose, such as serving as a public servant. It may sound like pie in the sky, but I believe a leader can set a tone to help create a kinder, gentler society. The focus needs to be on helping individuals, especially young people, stay in school, find jobs, begin careers, and start their families. My generation was fortunate in coming of age when jobs were plentiful and opportunities were growing. Now many college graduates, young professionals, and laborers cannot find jobs. Despite its being a time of economic uncertainty and insecurity, people's safety nets are disappearing when it comes to health insurance and state programs pertaining to unemployment compensation and family services.

## EPILOGUE

The first week of January 2011, shortly after leaving office as Lake County sheriff, my brother Hector and I visited old haunts in the Rio Grande Valley of south Texas. Our first stop was for hamburgers at Whataburger, where Dad always took us on trips back during the 1960s. The orange-and-white-striped A-frame was a welcome site, though the Whataburgers are no longer a quarter like a half-century ago. Urban renewal claimed our old home during the mid-1960s, and a highway has supplanted the dirt road. A Walmart and a CVS Pharmacy are nearby, but in many respects the city of Mercedes hasn't changed all that much. Still standing are the English and Spanish theaters, where we spent many Saturdays. Mom would give us quarters for the movies. The Spanish theater only cost fifteen cents, a dime less than its English competitor. We'd often go there even though we couldn't understand all the dialogue. We'd pool our change and buy popcorn, drinks, and candy.

We visited Our Lady of Mercy Church in Mercedes, where I was baptized and received my first holy communion, and Our Lady of San Juan del Valle Cathedral in San Juan, Texas, where the family went on special occasions and at critical times when they needed, so to speak, to call upon God's blessings. It was very much a spiritual experience and reminded me of how fleeting life is and how much I was molded by the teachings and values my parents, grandparents, and those before them passed on to me. Among those core values were respect, consideration, and looking out for family. Translated into action, that meant making sure that your children got a good education and that nobody pushed them around. Hopefully I have passed these on to my two daughters and others whose lives I have touched.

Near the Dominguez family church and cemetery were two separate border patrol units looking for illegal immigrants crossing the nearby Rio Grande River. I had never seen guards there before. We decided not to venture into Mexico, something we had always done in the past, because of the reported violence and drug wars going on there. I first crossed the International Bridge into Mexico with my dad around 1961. We took a dirt road into the town of Las Flores, encountering wooden carts drawn by horses or oxen. Poor people were begging for food and money, and schoolchildren were dressed in white shirts and dark pants. There were wooden planks but no sidewalks. My father would generally get a haircut and buy supplies and treats for us kids. If Mom accompanied us, she'd buy medicines.

We grieved for family members who had passed away and visited others still residing in the Valley, starting with Uncle Pablo and Aunt Elva. Twelve years my senior, Pablo during my youth was a physical presence and family protector. He was feared by many, and rightly so. When Dad was away working in Indiana, he was like a big brother. Robust until eight years ago, Pablo suffered a stroke that left his left arm and leg partially limp and aggravated his back problems. He walks with a cane and endures other physical challenges with a positive outlook. As he says, "I'm glad to be alive." After praying at my Uncle David's memorial site, we chatted with his niece Mary Gomez, who gave me the last photo taken before he left for Korea, never to return alive. Hector asked our maternal Aunt Jacinta whether as youngsters she and her sisters had aspirations for a better life. Other than to find work and raise a family there were no such dreams, she replied, no thought even of completing high school. They had no TV, so recreational pleasures were simple, playing marbles, hopscotch, or other games. They didn't consider themselves poor and rarely went without. Currently undergoing chemotherapy for cancer, Aunt Jacinta cried when we left, the first such time we could remember, as if she feared she wouldn't see us again.

At the Valley Museum an exhibit traced the history of the area's development. Around ninety years ago new machinery and increased demand set off a farming boom that created a great need for Mexican agricultural workers willing to work hard. That's when my maternal grandparents emigrated. Grandfather Hinijio Mata always said, "I came across over the bridge, not swimming the river" – in other words, legally. The tropical climate and fertile ground yielded bananas, pecans, oranges, grapefruit, avocados, carrots, and other crops. My great-grandfather Juan Mata died peacefully at age ninety sitting in a chair in Rotan, Texas, where the family had found work, probably a day's journey from their home. There wasn't enough money to bring his body home, so he was buried there, something that still brings tears to his descendants' eyes. My enduring impression of those relatives who came before me is their dignity and, more than that, valor, how they faced tribulations without complaint and sacrificed for the sake of family.

On a final note, allow me to repeat a famous principle of life as stated by César Chávez on March 10, 1968, as he was ending his fast on behalf of nonviolence. He said, *"When we are really honest with ourselves we must admit that our lives are all that really belong to us. So, it is how we use our lives that determines what kind of men we are. It is my deepest belief that only by giving our lives do we find life."* As I step forward toward the future, it is with faith and hope, as stated by the late Senator Robert Kennedy, to "make gentle the life of this world."

JAMES B. LANE

# Afterword

I FIRST MET ROGELIO "ROY" DOMINGUEZ DURING THE 1980S while we were both active in the Latino Historical Society. Jesse Villalpando Sr., the organization's founder and driving force, treated us to a delicious, spicy breakfast at Casa Blanca, a Mexican restaurant in the Indiana Harbor section of East Chicago, following a Saturday morning meeting, at which time Roy proceeded to tell us about his remarkable family background.[1] An attorney, Roy drew up the society's by-laws, took care of various legal matters, including registering as a nonprofit organization, and was very supportive of the group's main goal, which was to collect materials pertaining to the history of Hispanics in the Calumet Region of northwest Indiana for preservation at Indiana University Northwest's Calumet Regional Archives, of which I was codirector. An alumnus of that institution, Dominguez set up an IU Northwest scholarship in his name and staunchly supported the student group ALMA (Alianza Latina del Medio-oeste de America). In 1996 Roy was the recipient of the prestigious President's Award from the IU Alumni Association.

Over the years I followed Roy Dominguez's political career with interest and, because he was someone I deeply respected, rejoiced when he won election for Lake County (Indiana) sheriff over the entrenched machine's candidate. In February of 2008, I ran into him at a function honoring former Gary mayor Richard Gordon Hatcher, along with Cleveland's Carl Stokes, one of the country's first African American chief executives, and one we both admire, and suggested he donate his personal papers to the archives. I told him they'd be of great interest to future historians.

A month later, Sheriff Dominguez invited me to lunch at the Country Lounge in Hobart, long a watering hole for Lake County politicians. He kept me in suspense for an hour as to the purpose of the meeting, and then informed me he was taking me up on the archives offer.[2]

In the spring of 2009, Sheriff Dominguez again treated me to lunch, this time for the purpose of discussing a book project. We debated the various merits of biography versus autobiography and agreed to collaborate on the latter. I suggested a series of interviews during which he could tell me his life story. For the next six months we got together at the Calumet Regional Archives on average several productive hours a week. What he had to say was compelling indeed. Afterwards, I'd transcribe the taped interview and pass the typescript on for his additions, corrections, and editing (only rarely were there deletions, generally names of adversaries he didn't want to embarrass). After integrating the material into a coherent, chronological, and ever-expanding manuscript, we collaborated on numerous revisions until the product took firm shape. Other than to suggest quotations for chapter introductions and to recommend moving some passages around for the sake of continuity, I basically convinced Roy to tell the story in his own words. Which is what he did, in an intimate, informative, and inspiring narrative.[3]

Scholars, I am confident, will find *Valor* a significant and original contribution to the social, ethnic, and political history of northwest Indiana. Hoosiers throughout the state will recognize in this saga elements familiar to their own family histories. Like so many immigrants, Roy's parents, Jesse and Inocensia, traveled to the heavily industrialized Calumet Region in order to earn a decent wage and provide their children with opportunities for a more fulfilling life than had been possible for them. Their core values served Roy well as he encountered hurdles growing up in the gang-plagued "Steel City" of Gary, on the way to becoming the first Hispanic Indiana state trooper, graduating with distinction from Indiana University Northwest, getting through Valparaiso Law School after a rough start, and maturing into a successful attorney and officeholder. Emulating his dad, he was a "good Joe" with the knack for putting folks at ease. Like his mom, he viewed politics as an honorable path to public service.

Hispanics were once a group largely neglected by historians and social scientists, but during the past half-century, starting in the consciousness-raising sixties, a rich literature has documented the lives of Hispanics in the Midwest, and in particular, northwest Indiana – not only scholarly output but also notable biographies and memoirs.[4] As overt forms of discrimination abated after World War II, it became possible for talented individuals to obtain leadership positions in business, commerce, law enforcement, and industry, to run successfully for union and political offices, and to achieve distinction in areas ranging from athletics and advertising to the arts and academics. *Valor* exemplifies the American promise for those persistent enough to beat the odds and muster the resilience needed to confront life's vicissitudes.

John Bodnar's epic *The Transplanted: A History of Immigrants in Urban America* (1987) developed the paradigm of immigrants and their offspring as active agents rather than merely victims. I had a similar epiphany after interviewing Gary steelworker Paulino Monterrubio. All I initially wanted to question him about were the ways he was discriminated against, which he was, and that's certainly part of the story. But he wanted to tell me about being a neighborhood warden during World War II, and he was eager to show me his citizenship papers, union card, and pictures of his family. Thankfully, I was a good listener, the first prerequisite for an oral historian. Paulino put up with the discrimination, but the reality of his life – the way he wanted to be remembered – was not just as somebody who was kicked around but as a man who had this, did this, and left a mark through his relatives and his kids.[5]

Just when Dominguez was ready to start a family and embark on a promising legal career as a deputy prosecutor, he was stricken with Guillain-Barré syndrome. How he coped with and eventually overcame this debilitating affliction is a compelling subtheme of *Valor*. The experience matured him, required patience and humility, and steeled him to meet future crises with wisdom, perspective, and grit. As chairman of the Worker's Compensation Board under Governor Evan Bayh, Dominguez made an impact statewide. Consumer groups, labor unions, and enlightened employers alike heralded the long-overdue overhaul of workers compensation regulations that he shepherded into being.

Roy truly stands on the shoulders of forefathers – and mothers – Texas landowners on one side, migrant workers on the other, who believed in family first and instilled confidence in a remarkable public servant whose compassion for people comes though vividly in these pages.[6] His preferred leadership style emphasizes achieving outcomes through consensus; but when decisiveness is called for, he does not back down from necessary fights. Strong as the steel forged in northwest Indiana's mills, he rebounded from physical and political setbacks that would have felled lesser men and comprehends that life is fleeting and unpredictable and that one should put his talents to the best possible use. He is a proven leader capable of meeting whatever challenges the future holds for him.

## NOTES

1. Jesse Villalpando worked at Inland Steel Company before becoming a schoolteacher in East Chicago. Mr. V, as students called him, was a dear friend and IU Northwest graduate who reinforced our belief in the efficacy of documenting the history of Hispanics in northwest Indiana through the medium of autobiography. See James B. Lane, "Steelworker Interviews," in "Calumet Region Steelworkers' Tales," *Steel Shavings* 19 (1990): 61–63.

2. See James B. Lane, "Out to Pasture but Still Kickin': A Retirement Journal, 2007–2008," *Steel Shavings* 40 (2009): 100, 177.

3. The tapes are deposited in the Roy Dominguez Collection housed at Indiana University Northwest's Calumet Regional Archives (CRA). Roy's good friends Oscar Sanchez, Julia Jent, John Kopack, John and Linda Key, George Van Til, brother Hector, and wife Betty provided suggestions that improved the final product.

4. See, for example, James B. Lane and Edward J. Escobar, eds., *Forging a Community: The Latino Experience in Northwest Indiana, 1919–1975* (Chicago: Cattails Press, 1987); "Weasal: The Autobiography of Louis Vasquez," *Steel Shavings* 24 (1995); Señoras of Yesteryear, *Mexican American Harbor Lights* (privately published, 1992); Ramón and Trisha Arredondo, *Maria's Journey* (Indianapolis: Indiana Historical Society Press, 2010). Mexican Americans populate Indiana's major cities as well as numerous small towns and rural areas. See Samuel Shapiro, "Hispanics," in *Peopling Indiana: The Ethnic Experience,* ed. Robert M. Taylor Jr. and Connie A. McBirney (Indianapolis: Indiana Historical Society Press, 1996); Ann V. Millard and Jorge Chapa, *Apple Pie and Enchiladas: Latino Newcomers in the Rural Midwest* (Austin: University of Texas Press, 2004).

5. See James B. Lane, *"City of the Century": A History of Gary, Indiana* (Bloomington: Indiana University Press, 1978), 75–76; Sam Barnett, "Steel Shavings," AREA *Chicago* (Fall/Winter 2009), 9. Thanks to Studs Terkel, Michael Frisch, Donald Ritchie, Alessandro Portelli, and other oral history pioneers who broadened the parameters of our profession by their "from the bottom up" approach.

6. Our first working title was "Continuing the American Dream on the Shoulders of the Greatest Generation." In the end Roy thought it too derivative and awkward. Then he considered "Spirits from the Fields," which evokes Roy's spirituality as well as acknowledging the importance of family influences in molding his personality. In the end Roy chose "Valor" because it signifies worth or character as well as bravery.

Born in south Texas, ROGELIO "ROY" DOMINGUEZ grew up in Gary, Indiana, and graduated from Indiana University Northwest and Valparaiso Law School. He served as a deputy prosecutor and then was appointed chairman of the Worker's Compensation Board by Governor Evan Bayh. After establishing a successful law practice, Dominguez was elected sheriff of Lake County, Indiana, in 2002 and reelected in 2006.

JAMES B. LANE is Professor Emeritus of History at Indiana University Northwest, codirector of the Calumet Regional Archives, editor of *Steel Shavings* magazine, and author of numerous books, including *"City of the Century": A History of Gary, Indiana,* published by Indiana University Press.